The Challenge of Change in EU Business Associations

Also by Justin Greenwood

The Effectiveness of EU Business Associations (ed.)
Interest Representation in the European Union
Inside the EU Business Associations
Representing Interests in the European Union
European Casebook or Business Alliances (ed.)
Organized Business and the New Global Order (ed. with Henry Jacek)
Collective Action in the European Union (ed. with Mark Aspinwall)
Organized Interests and the European Community (ed. with Jurgen Grote and
    Karsten Ronit)

The Challenge of Change in EU Business Associations

Edited by

Justin Greenwood

in association with

First published 2003 by
PALGRAVE MACMILLAN
Houndmills, Basingstoke, Hampshire RG21 6XS and
175 Fifth Avenue, New York, N.Y. 10010
Companies and representatives throughout the world

PALGRAVE MACMILLAN is the global academic imprint of the Palgrave
Macmillan division of St. Martin's Press, LLC and of Palgrave Macmillan Ltd.
Macmillan® is a registered trademark in the United States, United Kingdom
and other countries. Palgrave is a registered trademark in the European
Union and other countries.

ISBN 1–4039–0653–X

This book is printed on paper suitable for recycling and made from fully
managed and sustained forest sources.

A catalogue record for this book is available from the British Library.

Library of Congress Cataloging in Publication Data
The challenge of change in EU business associations / edited by Justin Greenwood.
        p.   cm.
    "A selection of keynote contributions to a conference on 'The challenge of
change in EU business associations' held in Brussels from May 7 to
10 2002"—Introd.
    Includes bibliographical references and index.
    ISBN 1–4039–0653–X (cloth)
    1. Trade associations—European Union countries—Congresses.
    2. Pressure groups—European Union countries—Congresses.
    I. Greenwood, Justin.

    HD2429.E87C43 2003
    338'.006'04—dc21
                                                                2003043608

10   9   8   7   6   5   4   3   2   1
12   11   10   09   08   07   06   05   04   03

Printed and bound in Great Britain by
Antony Rowe Ltd, Chippenham and Eastbourne

Contents

List of Tables and Figures   vii
List of Abbreviations   viii
Notes on the Contributors   xi
Acknowledgements   xiii
Foreword by Philippe Busquin   xv

Part I   Overviews

1   Introduction   3
    Justin Greenwood and Alfons Westgeest
2   Horizontal Business Associations at EU Level   33
    Werner Teufelsbauer

Part II   EU Institutions

3   How the Architecture of the EU Political System
    Influences EU Business Associations   45
    Edgar Grande
4   The White Paper on Governance: Challenges and
    Opportunities for EU Business Associations   60
    Jerome Vignon
5   The Challenge of Managing Relations with the European
    Parliament: How Well Do EU Business Interest Associations Do?   64
    John Russell and Paul Adamson
6   EU Competition Law and Trade Associations   74
    Alan Reid

Part III   Sectoral Characteristics

7   Primary, Concentrated and Regulated Sectors: Steel   93
    David Rea
8   Textiles   103
    Michiel Scheffer
9   The Construction Industry   115
    Ulrich Paetzold
10 Operating in Contested Environments: The Experience of
    the Chlorine Industry   123
    Barrie Gilliatt

Part IV   Internal Environment

11   David against Goliath: Are Big Lobbying Organisations
     More Efficient than Smaller Ones?   139
     Daniel Guéguen
12   Juggling Resources and Autonomy: Issues and
     Opportunities for 'Specialised Associations'   150
     Alfons Westgeest and Bruno Alves
13   The Role of the Secretary General   161
     Zygmunt Tyszkiewicz
14   Establishing an EU Business Association under Belgian Law   171
     Dirk Lontings

Part V   Trust

15   In the End the Only Thing that Matters – Is Trust   191
     Ian Locks
16   Trust: A Sceptical View   197
     Wyn Grant

Part VI   Geographical Perspectives

17   The Challenge of Geography: Recruiting and Retaining
     Members from the South in EU Associations   207
     Irini Pari
18   The Organisation of Business Interests in Central and
     East European Countries for EU Representation   213
     Nieves Pérez-Solórzano Borragán

Part VII   Public Interest Groups

19   The Challenge of Managing Relations with the European
     Parliament: Insights from a Public Interest Group   229
     Jim Murray

Part VIII   Outlook

20   Outlook   235
     Alfons Westgeest and Justin Greenwood

Appendix: The International Association – New Belgian
Legislation of 2 May 2002   246
Luc Stolle and Alfons Westgeest

Bibliography   250
Index   258

List of Tables and Figures

Tables

7.1	Global steel consumption of finished steel products	94
11.1	Number of lobbying associations in Brussels	140
11.2	The largest European lobbying associations	141
18.1	Lobbying preferences among the business community in Central European countries	216
18.2	Assessment of government negotiating positions	217

Figures

7.1	Steel production and exports	94
7.2	The International Iron and Steel Institute	95
7.3	The European Confederation of Iron and Steel Industries	96
7.4	Inter-regional steel trade 2001	98
7.5	Two weeks in the life of the steel industry	99
7.6	Global steel capacity	101
8.1	Policy Mix and Euratex Role	107
8.2	The virtuous associative helicon	110
11.1	Pyramid of lobbying associations in ratio to number of employees	141
11.2	Example of the representation of the chemical industry in Brussels	143
11.3	Links between factors of effective lobbying	148
12.1	Options for specialised associations	157
12.2	Association models and dependence of resources	158
18.1	Central and Eastern European Offices of Representation, 2002	215

List of Abbreviations

AEA	Agricultural Engineers Association
AMC	Association Management Companies
AMCHAM-EU	The EU Committee of the American Chamber of Commerce
AMUE	Association for the Monetary Union of Europe
APEC	Asia Pacific Economic Cooperation
ARM	Alternative Regulatory Models
ASAE	American Society of Association Executives
BARCON	Barcelona Convention for the Protection of the Mediterranean Sea
BEUC	The European Consumers' Organisation
BIA	Bulgarian Industrial Association
BIAs	Business Interest Associations
BITC	Bureau International de Technique de Chlore
CAPE	Chambers' Accession Programme for Eastern Europe
CCC	Chlorine Chemistry Council
CCIS	Chamber of Commerce and Industry of Slovenia
CEA	European Insurance Committee
CEECs	Central and Eastern European Countries
CEEP	European Centre of Enterprises with Public Participation and of Enterprises of General Economic Interest
Cefic	European Chemical Industry
CEMBUREAU	European Cement Industry Association
CEO	Chief Executive Officer
CEOE	Confederación Española de las Organizaciones de Empresas
CEOR	Central and Eastern European Offices of Representation
CI	Chlorine Institute
COGECA	General Committee of Agricultural Cooperation of the EU
COPA	Committee of Agricultural Organisations in the EU
COREPER	Committee of Permanent Representatives

DDT	dichlorodiphenyltrichloroethane
DG	Directorate General
EIA	Extended Impact Assessments
ECC	European Community Contractors
ECF	European Construction Forum
ECVM	European Council of Vinyl Manufacturers
EEC	European Economic Community
EEIG	European Economic Interest Grouping
EFFC	European Federation of Foundation Contractors
EFPIA	European Federation of Pharmaceutical Industry Associations
EIC	European International Contractors
EICTA	European Information, Communications and Consumer Electronics Technology Industry Associations
ERT	European Round Table of Industrialists
ESF	European Services Forum
ETUC	European Trade Union Confederation
EU	European Union
EUDIM	European United Distributors of Installation Materials
EURATEX	European Textile and Apparel Organisation
EUROCHAMBRES	Association of European Chambers of Commerce and Industry
EUROFER	European Confederation of Iron and Steel Industries
EYAM	Ernst and Young Association Management
FAIB	Federation of International Associations Established in Belgium
FIEC	European Construction Industry Federation
GATS	General Agreement on Trades and Services
GATT	General Agreement on Tariffs and Trade
GDP	Gross Domestic Product
HBA	Horizontal Business Associations
HCCI	Hungarian Chamber of Commerce and Industry
HELCOM	Helsinki Commission for the Protection of the Baltic Sea
IFM	Institut Français de la Mode
IISI	International Iron and Steel Institute
INPA	International Non-Profit Association
ILO	International Labour Organisation
INPA	International Not For Profit Association
IT	Information Technology

KNUG	Royal Dutch Society of Geographers
MLG	Multilevel Governance
NAFTA	North American Free Trade Association
NGOs	Non Governmental Organisations
NIROC	Network of Interest Representation Offices from Candidate Countries
OBI	Organization of Business Interests
OECD	Organisation for Economic Cooperation and Development
OSPARCOM	Oslo Paris Convention for the Protection of the North Sea
PCBs	polychlorinated biphenyls
PCC	Polish Chamber or Commerce
PHARE	Poland and Hungary Assistance Reconstruction Economic
SBRA	Slovenian Business and Research Association
SMEs	Small and Medium Sized Enterprises
TENs	Trans European Networks
TNCs	Transnational Corporations
UASG	UNICE Advisory and Support Group
UEAMPE	European Association of Craft, Small and Medium Sized Enterprises
UN	United Nations
UNEP	United Nations Environment Programme
UNICE	Union of Industrial and Employers' Confederations of Europe
US	United States
USA	United States of America
VAT	Value Added Tax
WCC	World Chlorine Council
WKÖ	Wirtschaftskammer Österreich
WTO	World Trade Organisation

Notes on the Contributors

Paul Adamson is Chairman of Weber Shandwick Adamson, Brussels.

Bruno Alves is a Senior Consultant with Ernst & Young Association Management. He is General Secretary for the European Audiovisual Production Federation (CEPI) and is an advisor for other European and global associations in different industry sectors.

Barrie Gilliatt is Executive Director of the EU chlorine industry association, Euro Chlor.

Edgar Grande is Professor of Politics at the Technical University of Munich.

Wyn Grant is Professor of Politics at the University of Warwick and first published on the subject of EU business associations in the early 1970s.

Justin Greenwood is Jean Monnet Professor of European Public Policy at the Robert Gordon University, Aberdeen, and a Visiting Professor at the College of Europe in Bruges. He is the author of a number of titles on EU public affairs, including *Inside the EU Business Associations* (Palgrave Macmillan, 2002) and *Interest Representation in the European Union* (Palgrave Macmillan, 2003).

Daniel Guéguen is the Managing Director of the Brussels based CLAN Public Affairs. He founded the first European school of lobbying, has written several books of reference on European topics, including *A Practical Guide to the EU Labyrinth*. He has served as chief executive officer of COPA–COGECA, the head organisation of the farmers' associations and agricultural cooperatives of the European Union, and one of the largest lobbying groups in Europe.

Ian Locks is Chief Executive of the Periodical Publishers Association, part of the alliance of the £22bn UK publishing industries, and recently Chairman of the UK Trade Association Forum.

Dirk Lontings is a member of the Brussels Bar and the managing partner of Lontings & Partners.

Jim Murray is Director of BEUC, the European Consumers' Organisation.

Ulrich Paetzold is Director General of FIEC, the European Construction Industry Federation, and German barrister-solicitor (Wiesbaden Bar).

Irini Pari is head of the Brussels office of the Federation of Greek Industries (FIG), and has been a member of the EU Economic and Social Committee since 1998.

Nieves Pérez-Solórzano Borragán is Lecturer in Politics at the University of East Anglia.

David Rea is Director of UK Steel.

Alan Reid is Lecturer in European Law at the Robert Gordon University, Aberdeen.

John Russell is Chief Executive of Weber Shandwick Adamson, Brussels.

Michiel Scheffer is CEO of Noeton Knowledge Management BV and advises companies and associations in European affairs. He is especially involved in the textile industry and in textile regions.

Luc Stolle is an Advocate with the law firm Peeters Avocats.

Werner Teufelsbauer is Professor of Economics, recently at the Wirtschaftskammer Österrreich.

Zygmunt Tyszkiewicz is currently President of the Swiss-based Lanckoronski Foundation which finances educational and cultural projects connected with Poland, and from 1985 to 1998 was Secretary General of UNICE, the main European business association based in Brussels. Before that he spent 28 years with Shell, working in Latin America, Africa and Europe.

Jerome Vignon was Head of the Governance Team at the Secretariat of the European Commission until September 2001, and is currently Director for social protection and inclusion in DG Employment.

Alfons Westgeest is a partner of Ernst & Young Association Management in Brussels, leading an international team of over 20 professionals who represent and manage a dozen EU and international business associations and interest groups. He serves on the Board of both the American and the European Society of Association Executives.

Acknowledgements

The editor would like to thank all the staff of Ernst & Young Association Management (EYAM) who worked on the conference and this post-conference product, and in particular to Bruno Alves and Alfons Westgeest. Thanks, also, go to Nicole Schulze, the conference administrator from the Robert Gordon University who worked with the EYAM team on site in Brussels. Finally, the editor would like to thank the European Commission for providing the funding for the conference (under Framework Programme V, High Level Scientific Conferences), and the event sponsors. These were: Weber Shandwick Adamson; Wirtschaftskammer Österreich; the European Information, Communications and Consumer Electronics Technology Industry Associations; IRIS b2b technologies; and the American and European Societies of Association Executives. I am also grateful to the media partners for the event, who were: *European Voice*; Euroconfidentiel; the EU Committee of the American Chamber of Commerce; the European Information Service; and EurActiv.com. Finally, thanks go to all the contributors to this volume. In respect of Chapter 3, the author, Grande, places on record that the work benefited from research financed by the Deutsche Forschungsgemeinschaft (DFG) for a project on transnational co-operation in European science and technology policy at the Technische Universität München. Last, but not least, thanks are due to Elina Steinerte, who prepared the book's index.

Foreword

At a time when Europe is debating its future constitution and its institutions are trying to reinvent the way in which they operate and connect with citizens, this book provides a welcome contribution on the opportunities and challenges that the business community faces in organising itself at a European level.

It has its origins in a conference held in Brussels in May 2002 and sponsored as a 'High Level Scientific Conference' (HLSC) under the EU's Fifth Research Framework Programme. The HLSC scheme sought to bring together the leading thinkers in a subject field concerned and to ensure knowledge transfer to the next generation of researchers. This conference brought together leading practitioners who work in EU business associations with policy-makers from EU institutions and academic researchers on the subject. It enabled researchers to subject their ideas to validation from practice, and offered practitioners the opportunity to access research about key issues affecting the way in which their organisations function and to put these in a wider perspective. It also offered to practitioners, within the setting of an interested research audience, the opportunity to see the perspectives of those in the EU institutions with whom they engage, and to learn something of the perspectives of their peers.

This volume lists the key presentations, expanded and adapted so as to make them accessible to those who could not be at the event. Professor Greenwood has brought together contributors who include the Head of the team responsible for the EU White Paper on Governance, the longest-serving Secretary-General of UNICE, and a host of seasoned observers and analysts from EU and national contexts drawn from practice and research.

The individual chapters address topics rarely aired in public before, such as EU competition law and trade associations, the impact of the Governance White Paper on associations, the role of the Secretary-General, the legal framework for associations, recruitment and retention of members from the south of Europe and enlargement countries, perspectives from public interest groups and contested environments, and the role and value of trust in associations.

The effectiveness of EU business associations is a subject close to the heart of the Commission, because it values highly the quality of its relationship with civil society. Organisations need to be capable of communicating effectively in both directions between their members and EU institutions. Organisations need be effective enough to provide collective opinion from the constituencies they represent, as well as high-quality information for policy-making and monitoring purposes. Just as important, organisations can provide us with fresh thinking which can help the process of making Europe, in the words of the Lisbon process, the most dynamic and competitive knowledge-based economy by the year 2010. In sum, EU associations can help drive the process of European integration forward. This collection goes some way towards identifying the context in which associations can effectively undertake these tasks, and it is recommended to practitioners and researchers alike.

PHILIPPE BUSQUIN

Brussels   *European Commissioner for Research*

Part I

Overviews

1

Introduction: Conference Issues and Themes

Justin Greenwood and Alfons Westgeest

We are pleased to present a selection of keynote contributions to a conference on 'The Challenge of Change in EU Business Associations' held in Brussels from 7–10 May 2002.

The conference was the second event in a wider, two-part series themed as 'The Effectiveness of EU Business Associations'. This series was designated an official 'EuroConference' under the 'High Level Scientific Conference' section of Research Framework Programme V of the European Union. It arose from a partnership application by us under competitive conditions in 1999, which provided the principal source of funding for the events, both held in the names of The Robert Gordon University and Ernst & Young Association Management. Under the funding programme, the European Commission seeks a process of knowledge transfer to a new[1] generation of researchers. To this objective, we added the task of knowledge transfer between analysts of EU business associations, primarily based in universities, and those who work in, for and with EU business associations, whether as staff, contract managers, members, consultants or the EU institutions. This 'academic–practitioner dialogue' has never been undertaken on such a scale before, and in this sense the series was quite unique, involving over 300 delegates. We wanted academics to have access to the 'coal face' experiences and information that practitioners could provide, and to subject their interpretations and analyses to the acid test of practice. Similarly, we wanted practitioners to have access to some of the overviews and interpretations that academia could provide. We recognised at the outset that establishing a dialogue between 'practitioners' and 'academics' would be a challenging task, and encouraged each of our speakers and authors to present and write in a way that would be accessible to each of these audiences. In this book we have sought also to meet this challenge, and have drawn together authors who include those drawn from the highest level of EU business associations, the EU institutions, and academic analysts, many of whom have been key contributors to the subject matter over a substantial period of time.

In the spirit of the event, we were delighted to welcome as event sponsors the names of Weber Shandwick Adamson; Wirtschaftskammer Österreich; the European Information, Communications and Consumer Electronics Technology Industry Associations; IRIS b2b technologies; and the American and European Societies of Association Executives. We are also grateful to the media partners for the event, who were: European Voice; Euroconfidentiel; the EU Committee of the American Chamber of Commerce; the European Information Service; and EurActiv.com. The event attracted around 50 speakers of the highest calibre and 160 registrations during the week, with the outline presentations and abstracts available on the conference web site, http://www.ey.be/euroconference.

The issues

The first event in the series investigated the conditions under which EU business associations vary in their abilities to move beyond the 'lowest common denominator' of those of its members. The second event extended this focus by including examination of factors affecting the ability of associations meet the challenges of change. These factors include:

- The new climate of loss of trust in public institutions and large companies, and the changing orientation of EU politics from a 'wealth creation frame' (the single market and its aftermath) to a 'Citizens' Europe' frame. These include the recent debates on 'governance' and 'better regulation', and shifts in the all important policy relationship with the European Commission they herald which are both opportunities and threats for associations. Other factors included within this are the role of the European Parliament, that of public interest organisations, and 'corporate social responsibility' in which there are now expectations that business has a 'triple bottom line', that of social and environmental performance, to accompany financial issues.
- The end of the period of substantial growth of EU business interest representation, and a consolidation of the place of large firms as public affairs activists, together with the reorganisation of the EU

business interest association landscape which large firms brought with them to Brussels. In turn, these factors raise a whole series of issues about the internal organisation of business interest associations, and about a change in perception of the leading business interest representative organisations. There are also 'organic' changes at work within EU business associations that might be expected from the size of constituency. These include issues such as mergers as sectors are redefined by technologies (telecoms, consumer electronics and IT are an obvious example), different formats for 'virtual' associations (such as the web), and the availability of formats such as outsourced association management (Chapter 12).

- Internal changes to the composition of business interests, including the continuing changing basis of European wealth creation from a manufacturing to a service economy, new technology activities, and the changing basis of sectoral definition. One presentation at the conference, from the Director General of the European Information, Communications and Consumer Electronics Technology Industry Associations (EICTA), forecast that associations in high change oriented sectors would last for two to three years before re-inventing themselves. EICTA, itself the result of a merger, recently merged with the European Association of Consumer Electronics Manufacturers' Association (EACEM).
- The new climate of information accessibility and transparency, in which the ease of accessing information directly reduces the reliance by members upon their associations to obtain it for them.
- Enlargement and the range of issues currently being considered under the umbrella of the Convention on the Future of Europe.

Business interest associations can be an anchor and a familiar routine in times of uncertainty. Their routinised, formalised structures can also make them ill equipped to deal with change and unconventional contexts. Our own estimates indicate that there is a total of 950 formally constituted business interest associations organised at the EU level, based on a 'head count' in the various directory sources[2], our contacts, and by counting those advertising in public domain sources such as the *European Voice*. As this introductory chapter makes clear, there are a number of factors common to all EU business interest associations drawn from the shared environment in which they operate. On the whole, these are factors that limit the impact that such associations can have. They include the limited remit which most EU associations have in comparison with their national counterparts. While national associations undertake a range of functions and membership services, EU associations are almost exclusively based around political representation. Their members – national associations, and large firms – do not seek business services such as investment and export advice, training and access to low cost insurance policies – but rather established EU associations for the purpose of their political representation in EU policy making. Consequently, EU business associations are almost entirely dependent upon their members' subscriptions for income, rather than having independent income streams. This means that most EU business associations have relatively low levels of resources (in Chapter 11, Guéguen estimates that the average secretariat staff is between four and five), and lack autonomy from their members. The temptation is, therefore, that they will end up by articulating their short term demands rather than having the ability to lead their members' perceptions as to what their interests are on given issues. The job of business interest associations is to represent interests, rather than opinions that may be based on shaky foundations. These factors were given extensive consideration in the predecessor collection to this volume, *The Effectiveness of EU Business Associations* (Greenwood, 2002a), and in recent work by one of us (Greenwood, 2002b). The issue of autonomy triggered a debate at the conference, with a somewhat different emphasis presented by some General Secretaries, whose position is well summarised by Tyszkiewicz in Chapter 13. In that chapter, he stresses the importance of association leaders reflecting the views of their members. We suspect that the differences are more apparent than real, and that we can agree upon the normative formulation he arrives at, namely that 'while leading, they constantly glance over their shoulders to see if their members are following' (p. 164).

This collection covers somewhat different ground from the first. The first group of contributions (Chapters 3–6) in this volume examine common influences originating from the impact which EU institutions exert upon EU business interest associations. Some of these are change factors, such as new ways in which the Commission is engaging with outside interests, and which carry important implications for business interest associations (see, for instance, Chapter 4 on governance). Others are factors which are not formal policy initiatives, but which convey significant opportunities and threats for associations (see, for instance, Chapter 6 on Competition Policy; subsidy related issues are also included in Chapter 11).

There is a large degree of variation among the constituency of business interest associations, and the second group of chapters (7–10) examine the ways in which characteristics of particular sectors influences variation in the performance of business interest associations. Where there are shared common interests and similar structural characteristics of their members, so business interest associations can be cohesive and responsive organisations, developing mechanisms to deflect external threats. One chapter files a report on an association that is as close as one could imagine to the 'model business association' (Chapter 10), arising principally from the characteristics of the sector concerned and the issues surrounding it. Nonetheless, the 'effectiveness' of an association is both a product of the characteristics of its constituency and the issues they engage, and of the internal factors which are within the remit of individual associations to change. Thus, a third group of chapters (11–14) focus analysis, for the first time in a public domain book collection, upon the internal environment of associations. These touch upon some issues which cannot be found in the literature on business interest associations, such as the role of the General Secretary and their relationship with the President (Chapter 13), and different types of legal structures for associations. A fourth pair of chapters (15–16) examine, apply and debate an increasingly fashionable concept borrowed from the economics literature, that of trust, in an attempt to understand both its application and the extent to which it holds a key to the performance of associations. A final set of chapters (17–18) look at perspectives which hardly feature in the literature, geographical issues from the south and east of Europe which have increasing relevance in the context of enlargement, and at a perspective from public interest groups (Chapter 19).

EU institutions: the common external environment, and trust

In one sense, the perspective embracing the first group of chapters – the impact of EU institutions upon associations – is already well reported (see, for instance, Greenwood 2002a and 2002b). However, this group of chapters contain some unique gems. They include some new perspectives from the former Head of the Governance Team in the European Commission, Jerome Vignon, of the issues for EU associations surrounding EU governance. They also include a perspective which can hardly be found in the public literature, that of the position and issues surrounding EU Competition Law and business interest associations, which Alan Reid has ably taken on from a presentation at the conference by Georg-Klaus de Bronett, Head of the Cartels unit in DG Competition. Other perspectives in this section also add value, such as Edgar Grande's articulation of a critical issue which explains why EU business associations will always have limitations, that of the institutional architecture of the EU and its decision making system. And two consultants at the leading edge of Brussels practice who have partly built their reputations on managing relations with the European Parliament, John Russell and Paul Adamson, assess how well EU business associations perform this task, and provide some sharp insights about the relationship for both associations and analysts.

An opening presentation at the conference, from David Wright, a Director with DG Internal Market, gave a perspective from the Commission of the ways in which the relationship between the Commission and business associations could bring value to both parties (Wright, 2002). The basis for this was that of reciprocal understanding of perspectives, respect for the mutual roles undertaken and of the perspectives of other stakeholders, and trust – including confidentiality – and a mutual willingness to dialogue. From his perspective, the key property of an association was not the degree to which it was representative of its constituency, but rather its credibility, assessed by the extent to which it brings added value to the EU policy process.

Policy input

These 'added value' properties centre upon the ability of an association to make itself useful to the Commission by providing policy relevant input, but also by doing so in a particular style. The first of these, policy relevant input, involves:

- Forward vision with new ideas, on the basis that early advice geared at shaping thinking can influence the outcomes.
- Reliable data, particularly economic impact data, based around facts (and a sound legal basis) rather than opinion, and clearly worked examples. Cost/benefit appraisal is particularly welcome in which the assumptions underlying the calculations is transparent.
- Bringing forward infringement cases to the Commission, for example, delayed implementation or non-compliance with EU legislation.

The style that needs to accompany input should include:

- Acknowledgement of the benefits of a particular measure as well as the costs, and an indication of flexibility as to which measures can be accommodated.
- Acceptance that there are other stakeholders (such as the public interest) whose concerns may be very different, and that the

Commission has to balance a wide range of interests in its policy making, and not just those of one sectoral interest.

- Crisp, short papers, with priorities identified, and options outlined, which take a broad European perspective.
- Avoidance of aggressive stances against officials and EU institutions, and denigrating the EU in the Press. The speaker reminded the audience that European politics is about compromise, and of the importance of common courtesy.
- Willingness to participate in meetings/hearings, and so forth.

David Wright gave some useful examples of unhelpful practice. These were largely the mirror image of the above, and included:

- 'Last minute panic merchants,' such as lobbying after a common position had been decided, or a paper with thirty pages or more on the morning of a Council meeting seeking a last minute change of direction. Long and rambling papers have little impact on busy people who do not have the time to read them.
- Aggressiveness, which inevitably leads to rebuttal and entrenched difficulties.
- Manipulating the Press.
- Massaged data, presenting a one sided picture.
- Lack of effort to respond to Commission consultations.

In return, outside interests could reasonably expect from the Commission:

- A readiness to meet/discuss, with access to the highest levels, including Commissioners where appropriate and where justified by the importance of the issue.
- Openness and transparency, including a proper consultation process, and communication strategies (including notification of timetables, and a willingness to respond to correspondence on time).
- Clear explanation of policy positions adopted, including, whenever possible, a developed cost/benefit analysis, and full respect of proportionality/subsidiarity principles.

These sensible list of points are largely self-explanatory, and entirely consistent with advice given by other senior Commission officials (White, 1997). For the purposes of our analysis, three points are worth drawing out and focusing on in greater detail. The first of these concerns the coupled point of Commission transparency, together with the pledge to provide explanations for policy positions adopted. The second concerns the emphasis placed upon credibility rather than representativity, and the third issue is that of trust. These are considered in turn shortly, structuring debate for the rest of this section of the chapter.

John Russell and Paul Adamson also focus on policy input in their examination of the relationship between business associations and the European Parliament. In a useful contrast between the Commission and the Parliament, they argue that

> Such relationships with the Commission remain necessary, but in isolation they are no longer sufficient for success. The nature of the Parliament and its working patterns mean that business associations cannot simply emulate their modus operandi for the Commission: whereas the Commission is ostensibly apolitical and technocratic, the Parliament is by nature political with a strong tendency toward popularism (pp. 64–5).

Among the useful advice they include for EU business associations is to recognise that:

- Political groups may split along national or regional lines on particular issues. Unanimity in the EP is strongest where it considers its territory is challenged by other institutions or where it is seeking to extend its mandate.
- MEP loyalty ultimately rests with national or regional party machines in order to maintain a high position on the party list (which helps explain why attendance at plenary and committee meetings is patchy). This is also an impression held by Jim Murray in Chapter 19, who sees MEPs elected by the list system as less sensitive to public opinion.
- Customisation works, in that differing political perspectives of MEPs, the party or the relevant EP Committee should be central to the selection of arguments to put forward, and to customise slants accordingly.
- It is often possible to find a faction within a political group or a national delegation willing to throw up an appropriate amendment, and astute observation and analysis aimed at spotting these will pay dividends.
- Committee members will only focus on an issue in the weeks prior to a vote in committee or plenary, respectively. Other than commu-

nication to raise the profile for a subject, detailed submissions should be left to those periods.

- The secretariat of the Parliament supporting the committee is also an important source of advice on the prevailing attitudes of members and the functioning of the committee.
- The staff within the main political group secretariat write the background briefs for committee members.

In confirmation of the role for associations outlined by Russell and Adamson, John Purvis MEP emphasised in his presentation to the conference the extent to which the EU needs input from EU Business Interest Associations on a technical front. He emphasised employment issues as the strongest suit of EU business interest associations, although in general confirmed the more difficult role for business associations with the Parliament compared to its more natural constituency of public interest groups. Other speakers stressed the unpredictability of the European Parliament, particularly in the circumstances of coalition breakdown.

Transparency

'Transparency' has become a clarion demand of public democratic institutions over the past decade, often from elite constituencies or private interests using public interest rhetoric but seeking to capitalise upon their ability to access information. The Society of European Affairs Practitioners (SEAP), for instance, has long made transparency of decision making in the Council of Ministers, in particular, one of its major planks. EurActiv.com, whose raison d'être is access to information, has also been a long-term campaigner on the issue. The EU Committee of the American Chamber of Commerce (AMCHAM-EU) used the 'window' of the EU governance debate to extend the transparency issue by calling for justification of the adoption of particular policy approaches taken by the EU institutions (EU Committee, 2000). David Wright's conference presentation indicates that the request appears to have touched the right buttons, in that the concept has been partly embraced by the Commission's 'Better Regulation' package announced in October 2002 (European Commission, 2002a). The latest position is outlined in Chapter 4, where Jerome Vignon, writing six months after the conference, indicates that feedback is to be provided to consulted parties on if, and how, their input has been taken into account. In addition to this, however, is that any important initiative involving a legal and compulsory basis will carry with it an ex-ante 'impact assessment.' Whilst this has long been sought by a variety of business associations, including both AMCHAM-EU and the Union of Industrial and Employers' Confederations of Europe (UNICE), the way in which the Commission has defined this will be of considerable interest. That is, the Commission will try to evaluate not only the impact on immediate stakeholders, but also what Vignon describes as its 'side effects,' that is upon those who may not articulate an interest on the proposed measure in question.

As Vignon makes clear, this is a double-edged sword for business interest associations. On the one hand, it may provide the opportunity for some associations to improve the value they provide to their stakeholders by enhancing their ability to anticipate and thus involve their members and to respond to issues. Whilst the measure appears to satisfy the long sought demand for impact assessments, it extends the scope of these to embrace those who may have completely different interests to those of business. It is clear from reading his chapter, and from the wider governance debate and its 'Citizen's Europe' antecedents, that in doing so the Commission has cast itself in the role of the 'guardian of the weak', and that it has in mind both SMEs and public interests. His chapter includes an explicit reference about fresh attempts to reach beyond the usual dialogue partners. Ironically, as is outlined later in this chapter, the scope of 'the weak' could also be extended to embrace substantial parts of the organised business interest constituency beyond SMEs. However, the all important policy 'frame' is that of a 'Citizen's Europe'. Just as the drive to establish a new framework for wealth creation through the European single market created a business friendly environment in the 1980s and the first part of 1990s, so the new Citizen frame has driven EU policy making since attempts to ratify the Treaty on European Union. It is clear from reading Jim Murray's impressions in Chapter 19 that the development of new forms of regulation is of substantial interest to public interest groups. However, there is also a significant qualification in his reflection that 'we also insist on the primacy of the public authorities...we do not believe in a Europe run by stakeholders or by European associations, not even consumer associations' (p. 231). This is partly based upon his recent (December 2001) experience of signing an agreement on the use of 'trustmarks' with UNICE, a certification scheme to boost consumers' confidence in e-commerce. Reflecting that the scheme was the minimum that would have been accepted, he has elsewhere raised concerns about the demands such agreements make on the time and energy of senior staff (BEUC, 2002, p. 3).

Increased transparency and openness of EU policy making, as Vignon remarks, will provide additional challenges for EU business associations, and particularly those which have been able to monopolise dialogue with a particular Commission service. Thus, 'transparency' is not a universal good for particular constituencies of public affairs actors, or a concept to be used as a selective and convenient weapon against public democratic institutions. The wider climate of the governance debate has already had an impact upon policy-making officials in the Commission, in that whereas previously there may have been private bilateral dialogue, now there is a preference to place documents on the internet and to welcome all input. Beyond this, requirements for greater transparency may carry with them the dangers that officials required to disclose information will be evasive, or supply misinformation, or over-supply information with the result of overload and confusion (O'Neill, 2002). Calls for greater transparency in the name of the public interest have, therefore, to be made with greater care than has been evident from the wider business community thus far.

A final issue for EU business associations surrounding 'transparency' is the way in which the increasing access to information it yields, together with the common currency of the web, changes the nature of the relationship between EU associations and their members. Access to information has traditionally been part of the membership rationale for national associations, rather than large companies who rely more upon their own resources to obtain it. For national associations, the ease of acquiring information might conceivably upset the membership calculus. A compensating factor might conceivably be information overload, in that members need their associations to cut a path through the jungle for them. Both of these issues are raised directly by Jim Murray in Chapter 19. There is as yet no evidence of declining membership of EU associations among any type of membership constituency. Elsewhere, it has been argued that membership of EU business associations is normal political behaviour for national associations (Greenwood, 2002b). This is because many national associations established EU associations for the purpose of finding political representation at the EU level, and that little is required by them in the form of material membership incentives (Greenwood, 2002b). Nonetheless, there is evidence that some associations are seeking to compensate for the loss of dependency by developing other information functions which give it a natural monopoly. Euro Chlor is one example of this, reported elsewhere in this chapter, whilst at the conference the Secretary General of the European Insurance

Committee (CEA) emphasised the strategic importance to his associ-ation and its policy positions, and the wider industry it represents, of research relationships forged with researchers in universities.

Credibility and representativity

Vignon outlines a new obligation upon the Commission as part of its governance agenda to take into account the track records of participants in previous consultations. There is also a new emphasis upon represen-tativity, particularly for the direct involvement of associations in the regulatory process through 'co-regulation'. (Chapter 4). Vignon takes the view that by enhancing the ability of associations to anticipate issues it will, ultimately, enable those associations with a broad mem-bership to produce a higher level of collective positions than has previ-ously been possible. In the new Commission politics, representative organisations, it seems, have enhanced prospects. This is an issue put into sharper focus by Russell and Adamson, who argue that the White Paper on Governance means that 'in exchange for increased trans-parency on the part of associations, the institutions would commit to increased consultation with them in the context of a formal partner-ship' (p. 72). Russell and Adamson highlight the principal strengths of associations; they

- possess a considerable wealth of expertise
- represent common interests rather than individual ones
- have pan-European coverage.

They argue that 'In most cases, European associations have been able to make the most of these fundamental advantages which has allowed them in some cases to establish robust legitimacy and become quasi-institutional players' (p. 63).

These factors provide a quite different perspective to that of David Wright, who emphasised the importance of credibility over represen-tativity. This is an interesting contribution to a long-standing debate, in that his comments clearly lean towards associations representing a small number of large firms directly, rather than large membership confederations. Around 16 per cent of all EU business associations are solely direct company membership organisations, a proportion that has now remained at a stable plateau after an intense period of for-mation during the 1990s. These associations almost exclusively repre-sent large firms, and their formation reflects the politicisation of large firms towards EU activities. As large firms came to Brussels, so associations emerged or transformed to include them in membership, acknowledging both the reality of their presence alongside traditional federative structures and the resources they offered. Some were created because of the issues faced by broadly based membership federations when building common positions, so that exclusive communities of large firms could act with greater fleetness of foot. These associations had entirely different types of strengths. The direct (large) firm representative organisation was quick to come to a reasonably strong common position, but lacked the authority of speaking for a wide constituency, and could sometimes be overcontrolled by a small number – sometimes, a very small number – of members. Federations, while slower to reach common positions and to find a quality of collective viewpoint, draw their strength from their depth and breadth of constituency, which insulates them from control by any one particular constituency. In Chapter 13, Tyszkiewicz argues that

> Those who deride consensus views developed in multinational bodies as 'lowest common denominators' would do better to consider them as 'miracles' that so many different nationalities succeeded in agreeing common positions. Progress in the EU depends always on consensus and can be achieved in no other way.

> Of course the CEOs of big corporations are more glamorous and express views more rapidly than associations, but their opinions cannot be taken to represent the wishes of the majority (p. 163).

Tyszkiewicz's latter comment hints at an issue that is becoming an open debate in Brussels. When large firms first came as EU public affairs actors they had a major impact on the landscape of EU business interest associations, and representative organisations of them, such as the European Round Table of Industrialists and the EU Committee of the American Chamber of Commerce, quickly established reputations as the credible, big hitters of the business community. Whilst the name of these organisations still carry respect, it is now an open question as to whether they are quite the lead organisations that they once were. Some of this may be related to age (all organisations are said to become conservative and bureaucratised with age), some of these may be due to issues surrounding the organisations themselves (the ERT, for instance, has recently displayed a high degree of membership turnover), while other factors are external environment issues. One aspect of this is the emphasis upon the representativity of organisations and upon transparency in the governance debate, and in measures designed to implement it. Another is the increased public mistrust of 'big business'. Some of this is 'post Enron', but some pre-dates this. The most visible manifestation of this is evident from the ways in which 'new public activists' have targeted large firms for protests, but its wider currency is also evident from surveys. One recent survey of a Europe-wide population, for instance, found public trust in Amnesty International, Greenpeace and the World Wild Fund for Nature running at just over two-thirds, whereas trust in most large, named companies hovered around the one-third level, and in some cases down to as low as 12 per cent (Edelman/Strategy One, 2002). Whilst EU business interest associations are not in the forefront of responding to this agenda (specialist organisations such as Corporate Social Responsibility Europe are), the wider issue is now on their agenda as a change agent.

Trust

Trust is the third concept from David Wright's list highlighted in this opening chapter. In an analytic sense, it is also an increasingly fashion-able concept, and one that is borrowed from the Economics literature. In mainstream public policy debate, its linkages include those to that of transparency, in that calls for greater transparency from public demo-cratic institutions are partly based on the (somewhat debatable[3]) premise that this would be a mechanism of assuring trust in them. In terms of economic management and the context of business interest associations, the origins and articulation of the concept are traced by Grant (Chapter 16), and applied to the practice of business interest associations by Locks (Chapter 15). In essence, the concept refers to the extent to which mutual relationships can be developed and managed by each party for shared benefit. In business, some of the principal costs arise from the need to use binding mechanisms to assure transactions, such as contracting, whereas trust between the transacting parties may reduce the need for costly compliance mechanisms. In some national and local economies, the presence of trust has been held to be a contributory fac-tor to significant economic performance through reducing transaction costs (Williamson, 1975, 1985; Putnam, 1993). Business interest associ-ations themselves partly function to manage the transaction costs of their members (Schneiberg and Hollingsworth, 1991), and both the formal activities they undertake, and the informal relationships built within them, can bring added value in this way. Three chapters written by practitioners explicitly refer to the value of this. In Chapter 17 Pari argues that

Participating in (informal) groups, coming together in a systematic way, exchanging opinions and views, does create in the longer term a certain cohesion where some basic ideas and principles are shared (p. 211).

In Chapter 10, Gilliatt similarly explains in the case of Euro Chlor that

Creating social cohesiveness was one technique that we used to improve collaboration between our members. Because of the special-isation of the industry, many people stayed in the same jobs for long periods and it was possible to build strong relationships by ensuring that they met regularly. In the early days, we had an average of 250 committee and working group meetings per year. We encouraged members to bring their partners to regular industry conferences. This meant that people got to know each other well. The net result was that greater trust and understanding existed, thus permitting more rapid decision-making on issues of mutual concern (p. 127).

Linking the concept of trust with that of openness and transparency, Gilliatt goes on to argue that

Enhancing transparency and openness is a key element in winning trust and confidence and Euro Chlor works continuously to provide access to information about its activities and positions on issues of concern (p. 131).

Ian Locks, the Chairman of the UK Trade Association Forum and a CEO of a UK association which has grown from employing nine people to forty under his leadership, chooses to begin Chapter 15 on Trust with the statement that

four things matter for business associations: trust, trust, trust... and trust. With these in good shape, the association is guaranteed a perception among its stakeholders that it is a successful and valued intermediary (p. 191).

The four trusts which Locks outlines involve:

- trust between members with potentially competing interests,
- trust between associations when acting as alliance partners in demonstrating a broad constituency of support for a measure

- trust between alliances and political institutions, touching on the same issues outlined by David Wright. In addition to this, long term partnership arrangements, including corporatist type 'co-regulation' arrangements, are both the result of, and generators of, trust
- and trust by the members in the association executive.

As a business association CEO, Locks reflects that

> My proposition is that it is the associations that trust their executive to get on and run the show within the remit they are given that move the business on and do the best job for their constituency (p. 193).

Locks also goes on to make the point that too high a level of trust in the CEO can lead to members of an association disengaging from the association and leaving it all to the secretariat. The pessimistic side of this issue was spelt out as long ago as 1915 by Robert Michels, whose 'iron law of oligarchy' foresaw an inevitable process whereby organisational control would pass over time from lay 'principals' (such as members, or shareholders) to the permanent agents (such as Chief Executive Officers) (Michels, 1958). This perspective remains a hotly disputed one, particularly in circumstances where there is a low degree of structural autonomy in associations. This very scenario is one outlined by Werner Teufelsbauer in Chapter 2, where there are a small number of large members who are in a position to over-dominate the association.

Alan Reid's chapter focuses on the scenario whereby there is too high a degree of trust between members to the extent that they offend EU competition policy (Chapter 6). He makes the point that business interest associations tend to pose difficulties for the competition authorities where the sector they represent is oligopolistic, and there is a low level of product differentiation in that sector. Thus, commodity products which are difficult to differentiate on factors other than price may incentivise cartel-like behaviour. National and EU business interest associations which have been the subject of EU case law include those in the sectors of asphalt, cement, inland waterways, water industry, fur trade, building trades, salmon farming, crane operators, fruit auctions, steel, and tractor producers. Here, the guideline is that the rules concerned must be proportionate to the aims of the association. If the business interest association has been involved in a collusive agreement, the Commission is entitled to fine either the undertakings which are members of that association or the association itself. If the Commission is minded to fine the association, the Commission is entitled, when assessing the level of fine to be applied to the association, the turnover of the members of the association. In order to fine the association, the Commission must prove that the association's rules have the power to bind the members. The highest fines of all have been reserved to punish secretive behaviour, up to a maximum of 10 per cent of the turnover of the year preceding the decision (de Bronett, 2002). Reid mines the nuances of case law to provide guidance as to the parameters within which associations may act; de Bronnet's guidance was, however, simple: protect yourselves by transparency, and do everything open and publicly. A number of speakers referred to competition policy issues throughout the conference, including some General Secretaries who identified how their statutes were being revised to bring them into line with competition policy. Increasingly, EU competition policy appears to have restricted the traditional roles which association have played in the national context, such as managing overcapacity.

One highly interesting change factor to which Reid draws attention is a possible softening of the principle of direct and individual concern. He outlines the rather limited set of circumstances in which an association is able to bring an action under EU law, and the restrictions upon them so doing. Reid cites a case in the Court of First Instance in May 2002 and its aftermath that may lead to an enhanced ability for a collective entity representing a cause (rather than only an individual being directly affected by an issue), such as an association, to bring a case before the Court in its own name. If this highly plausible scenario comes to pass, it could revolutionise the style of EU public affairs through resort to legal process, with damaging implications for the use of trust as a governing mechanism for relationships.

A dose of realism as to the practical possibilities to put the concept of 'trust' to workable use is injected by Grant, who argues that 'there is also a danger of it [*trust*] becoming a "warm word" which offers a blanket panacea for the challenges that business associations face' (p. 197).

Whilst the concept is difficult to operationalise in practice, the types of measures outlined above by associations themselves indicates the value which they place upon it. Whilst 'trust' may not be a panacea, any measure which reduces opportunistic behaviour on the part of members is likely to increase the cohesion and effectiveness of the association.

The common institutional architecture

David Wright's advice list, reproduced earlier in this section of the chapter, is a sensible one for any association engaging EU institutions. Grande, however, draws attention to a quite different set of factors which limit the impact that business interest associations have in the EU environment, and which therefore places action directed at 'effectiveness' within certain confines of achievement. Business interest associations are extremely sensitive to the political environment in which they operate. Typically, political systems which are fragmented (such as the EU) afford ease of access, but a low degree of influence because of the dispersion of decision-making powers. Where business interest associations are embedded in unfavourable structures of fragmented political decision making, so the prospects for them to bring value to their members are unfavourable. On the other hand, political systems where power is concentrated make access difficult to achieve, but, once obtained, influence can be very high (Risse Kappen, 1995). Where business interest associations gain access to concentrated political decision-making structures, so they can be highly influential, quasi-autonomous intermediaries between government and civil society undertaking public interest governance functions.

Grande's point is that the fragmented architecture of the EU political system and its dispersal of powers between different institutions and policy actors dilutes the influence which any type of interest can have. The EU political system is insulated from domination precisely because of the shift of decision-making arenas between the Commission, Parliament and Council, in that new rules of the game apply as policy shifts venues. More than this, Grande shows how this architecture enhances the hand of the European Commission *vis-à-vis* outside interests. Building on earlier work by Scharpf (1988), he shows how joint decision-making systems typically temper the demands of groups in that they have to take into consideration the political and institutional constraints of range of actors involved, such as the need to formulate proposals in ways in which other institutions and actors will find acceptable. Thus, public actors integrated into multi-level systems of joint decision-making are in a much more favourable position to refuse unwanted or unrealisable claims made by companies and associations than are autonomous decision-making bodies. In a cumbersome negotiation process the Commission rearranges the composition of the negotiation groups time and again, and very skilfully uses the concessions made by one side to gain concessions from the other.

The common EU institutional environment and power-sharing system certainly helps account for the fragmentation in the landscape of EU business interest associations. There is no 'EU state', and consequently no 'patron' able to 'license' associations as governance partners. An even greater lack of institutional capacities in regional organisations such as APEC, NAFTA and MERCOSUR also disables associations. Associations do not play the role of corporatist style intermediaries in EU politics, organising their members for compliance with agreements reached with political authority, and delivering public interest governance, which can be found within other political systems.[4] Associational coherence is achieved more by specialism than through investiture with state authority, with the emphasis upon, in Grande's terms, the 'logic of membership' over the 'logic of influence'. These factors lead Teufelsbauer to conclude that the interest–political authority relationship resembles more Anglo-Saxon pluralism than Germanic corporatism (Chapter 2). Guéguen, similarly, draws attention to the high degree of fragmentation in the landscape of EU associations. Puns apart, one of the best examples of this was provided in a presentation at the conference about the glass industry, whereby five differentiated associations representing speciality interests in glass work together under the umbrella of a sector-wide association, with four of these sharing a common, small secretariat (van Houte, 2002). Plenty more examples can be found, with associations representing the interests of specialisms such as manufacturers of natural sausage casings, autoclaved aerated concrete, and bathroom valves. At the other extreme are associations of the European Chemical Industry Association (Cefic), where well over a hundred staff work. Variations between sectors form the next set of chapters.

Sectoral characteristics, causes of variation, and the internal environment

Whilst many of the factors outlined above are common influences upon the constituency of EU business interest associations, there are considerable patterns of variation between associations in their effectiveness. Much of this variation arises from the different characteristics of the sectors concerned, but some of it also arises from the internal environment of associations. At the conference, Brian Ager, General Secretary of the European Federation of Pharmaceutical Industry Associations (EFPIA), gave the view that some 50 per cent of associational time is spent in reaching internal consensus.

The first group of chapters explore some of the ways in which different characteristics of associations influence the effectiveness of associations, defined as the ability of an association to unify its members' interests and to reach common positions. In sum, where there are shared common interests and similar structural characteristics of their members, so business interest associations can be cohesive organisations. These particularly involve similarities in:

- the characteristics of members, including the size of firms and ownership structures, and the structure of competition
- a relatively high degree of consolidation, coupled with the challenges of overcapacity and low profit margins
- high transaction costs, and high value and asset specificity
- a common external threat (Bennett, 1997; Greenwood, 2002a).

The illustration of these factors drove the selection of presentations for the conference agenda, and are evident in the sectoral chapters within this collection. At the conference, for instance, Jacques Briquemont explained how members of the European Broadcasting Union were able to work together because there is marginal competition between (a limited number of) member state broadcasters across borders (Briquemont, 2002). The limited structure of competition also helps explain the relative strength of the European Confederation of Iron and Steel Industries, EUROFER, described by David Rea in Chapter 7. Here, the European Commission had required EUROFER to be involved with market arrangements in the 1980s. Steel associations have historically been locked into government systems because of the importance of steel to the Cold War arms race. This partly explains the importance of steel to the economies of the former Soviet bloc countries. Steel trade remains ruled by trade blocks, such as NAFTA (North American Free Trade Association), MERCOSUR (Southern Cone Common Market), ASEAN (the Association of South East Asian Nations), and the EU. World overcapacity in steel is estimated to be equivalent to the annual EU output. These are favourable circumstances for associations to operate in, with a common shared problem (overcapacity) coupled with a 'common enemy' (other trade blocs), and an historic institutional patron (the European Coal and Steel Community). Indeed, traditionally associations often emerge in precisely these kinds of conditions. A change agent for the steel industry has been the end of the Coal and Steel Community, and EUROFER has downsized as this has disappeared and as European steel production has slimmed. A similar story is told in Chapter 8, where the European Apparel and Textile Organisation (EURATEX) has also had to grapple with the end of a protectionist tariff regime, the Multifibre agreement, at the global level, and downsizing as a result of overcapacity. Whilst the textile industry is dominated by

SMEs, its organisation is assisted by its concentration in certain regions, and a strong tradition of national lobbying organisations present in Brussels.

An organisation whose cohesiveness appears to be driven by a 'common enemy' is Euro Chlor (Chapter 10). The industry's opponents described chlorine as the man-made devil's element, and chlorine was seen as a threat to the entire human race. The use of slogans by Greenpeace such as 'Chlorine free by '93' meant that European industry leaders were faced with a task to change representative organisations from those which were more introspective to those which were more proactive, open and transparent. Barrie Gilliatt comments that

> The environmental provisions of the various European treaties are unique. In no other jurisdiction is so much prominence attached to environmental matters. It is clearly an area in which Europe leads – and wishes to be seen to lead – the community of nations. Taken together with its comparative prosperity and its history of social justice, all the three elements of sustainable development – economic security, social well-being and environmental conservation – are present... Trade associations that understand Europe's mission to green the world as a whole, and can work on the international scene, will be those that will have the greatest impact (p. 135).

Euro Chlor became a proactive organisation by seeking to go beyond the natural cohesiveness brought by the common threat to the industry. Among the notable actions it has undertaken are

- to acknowledge the legitimacy of public concern about the impact of chlorine production upon the environment, and to engage with it, on the basis that enhancing transparency and openness is a key element in winning trust and confidence
- to position itself as part of the solution instead of part of the problem. Its present position on PCBs (polychlorinated biphenyls) envisages a quicker phase out than is the current policy position of the European Union
- to become the lead supplier of technical information about chlorine to public authorities, replacing national governments as the official supplier of data to transnational organisations. A high level of scientific expertise is present among its secretariat of 14 full-time employees
- to develop a comprehensive set of safety standards and voluntary agreements applicable industry-wide

- appointing a lead company in each country to co-ordinate with the national association
- including SMEs in the management committee, thus demonstrating that it embraced the structure of the industry among its membership
- developing an Extranet for 1700 industry managers in 35 countries
- fostering intra member trust by encouraging members to build strong and lasting relationships through regular meetings, and building in social time to these, encouraging members to bring along their partners. The association found that the greater trust and understanding that resulted enabled more rapid decision-making on issues of mutual concern.

In Chapter 9, Ulrich Paetzold reflects on some of the practicalities that make it easier to agree on common positions. These include the simple, yet devastatingly important, points that time constraints make it easier to agree on common positions, as well as a warning not to underestimate the importance of linguistic difficulties in coming to common position. Whilst the construction industry contains only some of the predictors for cohesiveness in a transnational association (statistically there is, for instance, little cross-border activity in construction, an SME lead sector, and whereby a small number multinational companies that also adopt a local profile), he points to the role of the association in making good these natural deficiencies. These include the association building the networks it needs with other organisations, such as the role of FIEC (the European Construction Industry Federation) in the creation of the European Construction Forum, bringing together the range of interests in the construction sector. The types of factors outlined in this case, and in that of Euro Chlor, emphasise that there is more than simply sectoral and market characteristics in determining associational effectiveness. Rather, a whole range of internal environment factors also play a key role.

The internal environment

The conference agenda provided the opportunity to focus upon internal environment issues which cannot be found in the wider literature. These included

- the role of the General Secretary
- the legal framework of establishment
- options for small and specialised associations.

The role of the General Secretary

Zygmunt Tyszkiewicz, whose term as UNICE General Secretary from 1985 to 1998 makes him by some distance the longest serving such postholder in the organisation, was uniquely qualified to comment on the role at the conference. His presentation appears as Chapter 13 in this collection, and forms a valuable redress to his own observation that there is no written guide for postholders, many of whom come to it without previous experience. However, caricatures in some accounts of the Secretary General of yesteryear as a retired military figure with no experience of business or associations (see, for instance, Boleat, 1996) have little foundation in the reality of EU business associations. Such postholders tend to arrive in associations with recent experience of either business practice or associations. A further caricature, that of the position of the Secretary General as a 'pre-retirement' post or a 'consolation prize' for an applicant who has narrowly lost out in a quest for another corporate position and who now needs to be moved out of the way of the successful applicant (*ibid.*), also bears little resemblance to the present constituency of EU business interest association Secretary Generals.

As Tyszkiewicz outlines, the post of Secretary General of an EU business association calls for a rare combination of skills. The required combination of board level experience in international business and in international associations is a rare one. Experience of the former carries credibility with external stakeholders (such as EU institutions) and company members, while associational experience carries greater credibility among members who are themselves associations, staff, and with other associations. As has been outlined, EU association resource levels are highly restricted, and thus the levels of remuneration involved are unlikely to be especially attractive for those from a business practice background, particularly coupled with the high levels of taxation in Belgium. On balance, an associational background is more common than a business practice background for most post applicants. For those who do come from a business, rather than an associational, background, the first task is to get used to the idea of becoming a network manager of members, rather than a hierarchical manager directing others as is common in business practice. He reflects that

> Handling a multinational organisation where membership is voluntary and over which the Secretary General has no hierarchical authority is a daunting challenge...Secretaries General do not exercise power. They organise the power of others (pp. 162–4).

Because his experience is that associations have a natural tendency to split into factions, a major role of the Secretary General is to manage the network of members to prevent this from happening. One of the ways he achieved this was to invest time working with the permanent delegates managing the Brussels offices of national employer associations, rather than going over their heads to the less well informed national association Secretary Generals, who rely upon their Brussels delegates for information, and who often have a limited knowledge of EU affairs. This spirit of working at street level forms the basis for another of 'Tyszkiewicz's tips', that of making it a first priority to win the support and confidence of the staff. Whilst this can be true of managing in most organisations, a special issue for associations is his point that some staff are abused by members, and it is therefore particularly important that such staff feel supported. Another key relationship highlighted by Tyszkiewicz is that between the Secretary General and the President. He reflects that

> Sound relations between the EU association's President and its Secretary General are crucial for success. Presidents can be tricky. Left to themselves they can sometimes act like unguided missiles. Differences may well arise but these must always be discussed and resolved strictly in private. It is up to the Secretary General to take the initiative and to create a harmonious partnership with the President, though this may sometimes require hard talk. Secretaries General should make full use of the President's political stature and influence to propagate the association's views. They should organise frequent meetings for the President with top officials, politicians and opinion formers. If offered a prestigious platform, Secretaries General should first offer it to their President and never appear to be stealing the President's limelight (p. 164).

The motivation of the Secretary General, he emphasises, has to be dawn from factors other than pay, and among these he identifies factors such as European integration, the politics of business, and 'the challenge of achieving the impossible' (p. 162).

In similar vein, he emphasises the 'miracle' of achieving common positions between members with often highly diverging interests, as a retort to the cheaply made point about associations being slow to reach common positions and reaching no more than lowest common denominators. Associations which are designed to draw their strength from their role as encompassing and representative organisations should not therefore be the subject of criticism when they undertake their democratic tasks. In any event, Tyszkiewicz challenges those who see associations as slow to locate specific examples, rather than to draw caricatures, and at the conference provided contrary examples of where direct firm associations had been unable to act on an issue because of its sensitivity to a large firm member. Instead, the association had quietly asked UNICE to take up a position on the issue. At the conference Brian Ager told delegates about the use of Priority Action Teams in EFPIA, a part federated and part direct membership association, for specific issues as a means of achieving speed, which a company Chief Executive Officer would be asked to Chair.

Among the qualities Tyszkiewicz includes for postholders within his job description are:

- skills as a linguist, communicator, leader, diplomat and administrator
- equanimity, robust health, boundless energy and stamina
- feelings of delight, not exasperation, when faced with European diversity and idiosyncrasies
- the confidence to speak to Prime Ministers and the humility to lick the stamps and post the letters.

Small and specialised-associations and the legal framework of establishment

Westgeest and Alves (Chapter 12) notice an increasing demand for remuneration data. The seller's basis of the Brussels employee market, the presence of Brussels-based Executive Search agencies specialising in associations[5] and the very special requirements outlined by Tyszkiewicz above, suggest that those who have such a profile can command a premium. Where the cost of staff is prohibitively high for an association, where associational or specialist expertise is required, or where a neutral arbiter is required, so association management can be an option, particularly for small or specialised associations. As the authors of Chapter 12 suggest, association management can lead to a more active participation by all members, and a higher perception of membership value. Outsourced association management can also provide a solution to the physical cost of a Brussels presence, which is currently around €250 per square metre for premium office space, an increase of 20 per cent since 1998 (Lontings and Neven, 2002).

Lontings outlines the issues involved in establishing an EU business association under Belgian law, and carefully assesses each of the alternative options available (Chapter 14). This is now a 'live' change factor for all EU associations, in that there is a new piece of legislation updating and modifying predecessor legislation under which most associations are registered. This new law is expected to become operational during the course of 2003, and will require action by most associations over the next five years. Hence, the chapter will be attractive to those seeking to get to grips with new legislation of 2002 and the issues involved, and to associations wishing to weigh up all the various options open to them. The vast majority of EU business associations are presently incorporated under the terms of a 1919 Belgian law which was specifically designed to make Brussels the centre of international non-profit activity. This law was incorporated into other legislation and updated by a new instrument of May 2002 which, while partly designed to consolidate the number of options available, has some important variations from its 1919 derivative which may make it a less attractive format. The freshness of the legislation means that a number of 'grey areas' remain to be tested, of which one is a continuing issue about the boundary of economic activities which are membership incentives. A quicker route to incorporation has been to register under the terms of a 1921 Belgian law on domestic non-profit associations, which has also been subject to a number of significant modifications under the new 2002 legislation. Another solution has been to act as an organisation registered in another country but to obtain recognition to operate in Belgium, although this carries with it fewer legal rights and thus abilities to conduct certain activities. One partial solution among a number of options has been to use a 1986 European Convention on the recognition of the legal personality of international NGOs. The new law updates and eases the position for this type of legal personality through some enabling Articles which carry with them some new requirements, although again there remain some grey areas requiring clarification. Of interest, however, is that the requirements of European Economic Interest Grouping (EEIG) legislation has made this an unattractive option for most associations (Chapter 14).

Comparative perspectives

The conference website includes presentations on comparative topics such as the role of associations in other political systems, and societies of association executives in Europe and the US. From among the comparative perspectives presented at the conference are included two geographical assessments for this collection, focusing upon the organisation of interests for EU representation and participation in the south of Europe, and among Central and East European countries. The penultimate chapter in this collection draws comparison between public interest groups and business interest groups with a particular focus upon relations with the European Parliament, seeking to identify what business interests can learn from the experiences of the European Consumers' Organisation, BEUC.

In Chapter 17, Irini Pari outlines the position in respect of Greece. Only two organisations have a lobbying office based in Brussels; many EU business associations have no Greek member; and those which do find that their participation is low. These factors can be explained by a lack of resources when coupled with the distance from Brussels, the lack of Greek multinationals and an absence of collective action tradition, and the relationship between Greek entrepreneurs upon their government. This latter, dependency relationship extends into one of reliance for EU representation, and is generalised by Pari as applicable to Portugal. Beyond this, she identifies a number of factors applicable to much of the south of Europe which conditions EU collective action. These include lower incomes, a large number of SMEs, less research and development, higher deficit and inflation levels, a social model based on family solidarity rather than state systems, similar industrial relations, and 'a certain common idiosyncrasy, temperament' (p. 210). These factors also lead to some common agenda seeking in EU politics, such as economic and social cohesion, research and innovation, and regional development. However, she observes little co-ordination between interests from across the Mediterranean Sea region.

In Chapter 18, Nieves Pérez-Solórzano Borragán turns the spotlight onto central and eastern European countries (CEECs), identifying 27 interest representation offices operating in Brussels across business and regional representations. The financial basis to some of these is illustrated by the plight of the Eastern Poland office, established initially with PHARE financial support lasting for a two-year period. Once this funding ran out, so the office had to close due to its inability to locate its own, alternative funding basis. A more stable development agent has been the work of EUROCHAMBRES, which has for some time been unusual among EU business interest associations in providing advice, training and technical assistance support to its members. Whilst few EU business associations undertake these functions because of appointment by their members to concentrate on political representation,

EUROCHAMBRES has gone down this route because of its weakness as a political representative. Its larger members find political representation elsewhere, leaving EUROCHAMBRES to be a channel of political representation for only its smallest members without other alternatives. To its larger members, EUROCHAMBRES is more a network than a political representative. In consequence, the organisation has found another niche for itself in membership services for its smaller members, which inevitably embrace those from CEECs. Since 1991, it has developed, in collaboration with the European Commission, a number of training and technical assistance programmes aimed at strengthening the position of chambers of commerce from CEECs and their associated organisations. Nieves herself remarks that the EUROCHAMBRES situation is unique, in that she finds little evidence that the Brussels offices of representation have established effective patterns of interaction with either interest associations or political institutions which translate into effective influence on the policy-making process. In the main, these offices are engaged in the mutual transfer of information and know-how. Whilst a substantial number of EU business associations do have members from the candidate countries, even those from these countries which have been incorporated into full (rather than associate) membership are rarely, if ever, to be found in the front line of participation. At the domestic level, Nieves finds, unsurprisingly, very undeveloped structures of civil society in these fledgling democracies, and very weak patterns of state–civil society interaction.

In Chapter 19, Jim Murray, Director General of BEUC, reflects on NGO relations with the European Parliament. Almost all areas of importance to BEUC are co-decision power fields, justifying his description of co-decision as one of the major political events of the past forty years. Whilst the 'citizen frame' currency in EU policy making is a favourable one, there are also some signs that 'NGO influence' has reached its apex. NGO demands over issues such as a 'civil dialogue' to accompany a 'social dialogue' show no progress, and the 1998 crisis of funding of NGOs by the Commission following a ruling from the European Court of Justice has had a long-term impact upon the stability of many NGOs. The Commission's new agenda of representativeness is a difficult one for NGOs to follow, in that they are organisations which have emerged as outlets *for* a particular cause, rather than delegate representative organisations *of* one. Some recent work by Warleigh has also found very limited links between NGOs organised at the European level and their grass roots constituencies, and very little interest among them in performing wider political socialisation roles in 'bringing the EU to their members' (Warleigh, 2001). These factors undermine the Commission's historic reliance upon working with interest groups as partners for the development of European integration.

Nonetheless, the agendas unleashed by 'Better Regulation', the White Paper on Governance, and the Convention on the Future of Europe, have together unleashed significant change factors for the ways in which interest associations of all types work. In Chapter 4, Jerome Vignon makes clear that the intention behind the governance agenda is to decrease the number of groups in an attempt to ratio-nalise diversity and fragmentation, and as a means of trying to encourage broadly based associations. As John Russell and Paul Adamson succinctly summarise in Chapter 5, in exchange for an increased transparency on the part of associations, the institutions would commit to increased consultation with them in the context of a formal partnership. Whilst there are limits to the extent to which a corporatist style partnership can develop at the EU level (Chapter 3), the endowment of associations with public governance functions would help to increase their appeal to their members, and provide them with autonomy as intermediaries in the way described earlier in this chapter. With enhanced strength, associations may be able to turn away from narrow specialisms as an alternative device to find coher-ence (Chapter 11), and find a greater breadth in their interest con-stituency. Perhaps, after all, the days of associations organising manufacturers of bathroom valves, autoclaved aerated concrete, and natural sausage casings, are numbered. An obvious way forward for such associations to respond to the new agenda is to seek new part-ners, and, following the path outlined by the European Information, Communications and Consumer Electronics Technology Industry Associations, to find strength in unity rather than diversity. For this association, such is the pace of change that no more than two to three years in one format is envisaged before the next change driver forces re-invention. In the modern world, nothing is quite as stable as the requirement to change.

Notes

1 Defined in Commission rules as those of under 36 years of age.
2 These include the European Public Affairs Directory (Landmarks, 2003) and the Directory of 12,500 Trade and Professional Associations in the European Union (Euroconfidentiel, 2002).
3 For a critique of the link between transparency and trust, see Onora O'Neill's 2002 Reith Lecture 4 on transparency (http://www.bbc.co.uk/radio4/reith2002/).

4   See Ben Ross Schneider's presentation on the conference web site (www.ey.be/euroconference) of the roles played by associations in different regional settings around the globe.

5   A presentation at the conference from Sigrid Marz of Russell Reynolds Associates can be found on the conference web site, www.ey.be/euroconference.

2

Horizontal Business Associations at EU Level

Werner Teufelsbauer

Brussels is home to more than a thousand business associations. Most of these associations are 'special interest' and/or 'special purpose associations'. Currently, only five organisations are considered to be 'horizontal', that is, representing general business interests. A closer look shows that none of these horizontal business associations (HBA) represents the interests of all European businesses. On the contrary, they tend to focus on different clienteles. These associations are, therefore, less in competition for clients than for the attention of EU bodies. Most HBAs at the EU level are 'umbrella organisations' of national associations, with individual big companies exercising a direct influence on some HBAs by one means or another. Compared to some vertical associations and even to some Brussels individual company offices, HBAs have a rather small staff, although the numbers given have to be interpreted with some care: some companies or national HBAs assign, at their expense, experts from their staff to their European HBA (secondments). Considering their role as umbrella organisations and their limited staff, the autonomy of European HBAs *vis-à-vis* their national HBAs is often very limited. National member associations have their say, and since they differ very much in terms of financial strength and expertise, some have more influence in their European HBA than others. The differences in strength do not only depend on the size and weight of the national economy, but also to a large extent on the specific organisational strengths of the specific national HBA. Some European HBA seem to be generally weaker than others because of the weakness of the general organisation of most of their national HBA members. The strength of interest representation by European HBAs, therefore, seems to be rather unbalanced, and this could give rise to some concern. The group of HBAs include:

- CEEP (European Centre of Public Enterprises) is the European Association for public ownership companies and companies with public interest activities (utilities). Founded in 1961 CEEP is recognised as a 'Social Partner' by the European Commission. Besides individual member companies, the 'European Broadcasting Union' is also a member. 'Associated Members' are admitted (presently from Hungary, Norway, Romania and Turkey). Member companies have their dominant activities in transport, telecom, postal services, broadcasting, electric power, gas and water. CEEP has approximately 270 member companies employing 6 million people. CEEP has a staff of approximately 10 employees.
- EUROCHAMBRES is the umbrella organisation of European National Chambers of Trade and Industry. Its members are 40 national chamber organisations (EU and non-EU), which represent more than 1500 regional and local chambers with a membership of some 15 million companies. Therefore, EUROCHAMBRES can be considered as the European umbrella organisation of national umbrella organisations of chambers of trade and industry.

  Chambers of trade and industry differ tremendously from country to country in terms of representativeness, focus, legal status and financial and political strength. Some are public law, mandatory membership associations covering almost all businesses (such as Austria), some are very small voluntary membership associations with a rather small membership mostly from big and medium-sized companies. Practically all chambers provide a broad selection of services to their member companies. Public Law Chambers in particular are important providers of professional training. Some of them are in charge of running harbours, airports, stock exchanges, and so on. Some chambers are also important political actors at a national level, the Austrian Chamber organisation also acts as the central employers association negotiating collective agreements with trade unions. To summarise, EUROCHAMBRES membership is very heterogeneous with a dominant common interest in the services and training area and less interest and power in the field of general economic policy. It has a staff of 22 employees. EUROCHAMBRES is not considered as a 'Social Partner' by the European Commission.
- UEAPME (European Association of Craft, Small and Medium Sized Enterprises): European employers association for SMEs and for handicraft in particular. There are about 70 national member organisations (including associated member organisations from non-EU-countries) representing 7 million companies (30 million employees) out of

a total of 20 million SMEs in the EU. Again, membership is very heterogeneous, perhaps even more than in the case of EUROCHAM-BRES. In several countries there are competing SME-associations with very different ideologies (socialist, Christian, and so forth), which can all be UEAPME members. In some countries SMEs (in particular hand-icraft) are organised in public law, mandatory membership organisa-tions (such as Austria, Germany), in other countries voluntary membership is the dominant organisational principle. In the latter case, membership can sometimes be low, and national associations often have a relatively weak financial and political position. UEAPME is not recognised as a 'Social Partner' in its own right by the European Commission. There is, however, an agreement of cooperation with UNICE, which provides access to European Social Partner consult-ations and negotiations.

- UNICE (Union of Industrial and Employer's Confederations of Europe): founded in 1958, UNICE comprises 34 member associations from 27 European countries plus some associations with observatory status. As a designated 'employers organisation' it has a 'Social Partner Status' from the European Commission. This is why it is often considered to represent all European private business. But since public law associations are excluded from membership, countries like Austria, where a public law association is the official social partner, are not represented in UNICE by the national social partner. Therefore, UNICE appears to represent more the interests of big business rather than those of SMEs. Secondments from large compa-nies to supplement UNICE's staff, and occasional direct financial contributions from a group of European companies, support such a conclusion.

European HBAs were created mainly as links to EU-bodies. In this role, they pursue the lobbying activities typical for all business associations, be it horizontal or vertical. Beyond lobbying, European HBAs sometimes have contracts with EU-bodies for specific projects of mutual interest. The EU funding of such projects usually covers some overhead costs of the respective HBAs, hence establishing a certain dependence of EU asso-ciations on EU institutions. These may restrict the nature of projects which can be carried out by HBAs, and their ability to freely express critical comments about them. There is a third level of interaction between EU institutions and HBAs which is a more recent achievement and deserves closer attention. This is the level of 'formalised dialogues' (for example, 'Social Dialogue', 'Macroeconomic Dialogue'), where the EU invites selected HBAs (such as the 'Social Partner' HBAs) to enter into a formalised continuous discussion on policy issues. In the case of social dialogue, the European Commission has to automatically accept legislative proposals submitted jointly by all Social Partners as a legislative initiative to be transmitted to the EU-Council. This is a first step, where subsidiarity as a principle of EU-governance is not only applied in its regional but also in its 'functional' dimension.

In formal negotiations for legislative purposes, the question of representativeness is of the utmost importance. Since there is no direct membership for companies in European HBAs (with the exception of CEEP), the issue of representativeness should be considered from two different angles. At EU level, one should examine the extent to which the relevant national associations are members of the respective European HBA. On the national level, one should check the national associations and the extent to which they are able to express the opinion of the companies established in the country. The latter question cannot be answered as easily as one would think. Indeed, existing formal membership does not automatically mean effective membership in terms of being heard in the association. This can be particularly true in cases where associations have a few (sometimes very) big companies as direct members, and small companies are involved only indirectly via membership of their (sometimes weak) association. Some national employees' associations are organised in such a way. In these cases, up to 90 per cent of the funding comes from the small group of big direct members (sometimes not more than 20), who nevertheless account for only one third or less of the added value and employment in their respective industry. Member associations are usually poor and in some cases even get subsidies from their umbrella organisation (which is why they join). Therefore, they have little power and little chance of being heard or even considered. For big business they are the electorate needed to obtain a level of representativeness which – in addition to financial power – impresses policy makers both at the national and the EU-level.

In some countries, public law associations with mandatory membership and application of the 'one person – one vote' principle were established decades ago. These associations, by definition, have 100 per cent representativeness and usually a sound financial basis, and also mean that small companies are on an equal footing with larger ones. In the European HBAs, these national public law associations are in membership together with associations of the private law type. The obvious exception to this is UNICE, which excludes public law associations on the grounds that they are regarded as insufficiently independent from the machinery of governments. This is certainly true for some countries. On the other hand the general application of the exclusion rule excludes fully independent public law associations as WKÖ (Austrian Federal Economic Chamber) which acts as the central Austrian employers association.

In conclusion, European HBAs have a very heterogeneous membership both in terms of organisational strength and fields of activity. Heterogeneity seems to be stronger in HBAs than in vertical (sectoral) associations. Large businesses seem to be more efficiently organised than small businesses. At least at first glance big businesses are more successful in achieving higher representativeness than small businesses. Traditionally, EU bodies have better established relations with big business HBAs (for example, the provision of Social Partner status) than with small business HBAs, although small business by far outnumbers big business not only quantitatively, but also in terms of added value and employment. This may not have constituted a major problem in the early years of the European Economic Community because small businesses were local businesses at the time, and the EEC did not interfere with local businesses very much. This has changed fundamentally since the beginning of the Single Market project and European Monetary Union. Today small businesses are affected as much as big businesses by EU-decisions and EU-procedures.

It seems that the European Commission became uncomfortable with the problem of unbalanced representation of business interests in Brussels. The Commission attempted to set up 'business panels' and survey-systems, thus bypassing HBAs. This, of course, can never substitute consultations with HBAs, because there is always the danger that members of the consultative groups are picked in a way that the groups' opinion will tend to be affirmative rather than critical.

As a consequence, there is no alternative except to make European HBAs in general, and small business HBAs in particular, more representative and stronger. Why has small business not been able to achieve this goal on its own yet? Was it just inefficiency or were there other reasons?

A theoretical consideration: the inherent weakness of big groups of small members to self-organise

As already indicated, European HBAs have little autonomy and must rely heavily on their national member organisations. The strength of European HBAs therefore depends very much on the strength of their national member organisations. At the national level there is, one way or the other, direct membership of companies. Companies have both specific interests, characteristic of the line of business they are active in (vertical group), and encompassing interests typical for larger groups, such as utilities, and so on (horizontal groups). Usually horizontal groups are bigger than vertical ones. Some horizontal groups (such as small business) are much bigger than others.

Companies are in the business of buying, transforming and selling goods in markets at prices covering their cost ('private goods'). But there is also a demand for goods, which cannot be bought and sold on the market at cost covering prices, as, for example, favourable legislation ('public goods'), because 'free riding' is possible. Therefore, public goods are not available on the market place. If public goods are to be produced, they have to be financed by contributions given by the interested parties constituting an interest group (association). In this context, Mancur Olson (1965) has shown very clearly that depending on their size and the relative share of the individual member, different groups have a different ability to set up an association capable of supplying the desired public good. Big groups composed of relatively small members have a lower capability or even an inability to self-organise as opposed to small groups made up of relatively large members.

If Olson is right, then small businesses encompassing interest groups have a low probability of establishing powerful HBAs irrespective of managerial efficiency considerations. There seems to be overwhelming empirical evidence that Olson is indeed right, although there are also important examples of powerful small business HBAs, the existence of which seems to contradict Olson's hypothesis. A closer look into these examples shows that they prove rather than falsify the hypothesis.

Public law and public assistance as a basis for powerful small business HBAs

There is a group of EU countries where the problem of self-organisation of big groups has been solved for businesses (in Austria this has also been because for labour, farmers and other professional groups) by the provision of a public law statute with mandatory membership and membership fees. These associations do not usually only provide public goods. They are also significant providers of merit goods (such as training, foreign trade promotion, and so on), giving substantial relief to government in this area. Some have certain privileges *vis-à-vis* the government, such as the right to be consulted in the legislative process at an early stage. Some of these public law organisations are considered to be rather close to government, yet some of them have a very strong democratic structure with a high participation rate of members which makes the associations fully independent of government and able to be a strong co-operative partner. This is true, for example, for Austria. The relatively high participation rate of mandatory members in Austria may be due to the fact that the respective public law association (WKÖ – Austrian Federal Economic Chamber) has a hierarchical structure. The chamber is the mandatory umbrella organisation for public law vertical associations where member companies can more easily identify themselves with the organisation. Membership at the peak level is taken care of by elected delegates from the vertical associations although formally there is also direct membership of companies at the peak HBA.

Where there are no public law HBAs and where, nevertheless, strong HBAs with voluntary membership do exist, public assistance in one way or another can be observed. A simple and rather primitive method of public assistance is subsidies for general or specific purposes (such as foreign trade promotion, training, and so on). Sometimes there are formal contracts between governments and associations stipulating the provision of specific public and/or merit goods.

There are more sophisticated and indirect ways for public assistance. In several countries and under certain conditions, governments, by decree, make collective agreements generally applicable. In many cases, such collective agreements include the regulation that all companies, to whom the agreement is applicable to, have to pay mandatory fees into a 'parity fund' dedicated for the funding of merit goods like training. The fund is usually managed by the negotiating associations both from businesses and labour. In most cases, the same associations are the dominant providers of the respective merit goods and the revenue (at least partly coming from the 'parity fund') also helps to cover overheads due to the public goods line of business. This model of public assistance (the privilege to get general applicability for a collective agreement from government) implies that not only member companies but also non-member companies have to pay for services rendered by the association. Hence, would it not be more rational for a company to become a member right away, assuming direct membership fees are low, and more substantial payments (to the 'parity fund') have to be made in any case?

In many cases, associations have a dominant market position in certain areas like training for licensed professions. At the same time, it is rather difficult to obtain a government licence without formal training and examinations. The dominant training association then frequently follows a price discrimination strategy, favouring members. Since prices are usually rather high, it may pay to become a member. From a strict competition law point of view, this procedure is highly questionable. Nevertheless, some governments seem to tolerate this model.

More competition law objections can be made where members of associations are connected in a vertical supply chain, and agree on privileged or exclusive business relations for member companies on the basis of 'quality control arrangements' (van Waarden, 1994). Van Waarden mentions a contract in the Dutch bituminous roofers business. According to the contract, producers were only allowed to supply officially established and recognised roofers, who satisfied certain training criteria. The agreement was tolerated by the Dutch authorities, but later rejected by the EU.

To summarise, there are many models of public assistance to business associations to overcome the problems of self-organisation and self-financing. Countries with a high level of public assistance have much stronger associations (both vertical and HBAs, because HBAs in many cases are supported or even constituted by vertical associations) than countries with a low level of public assistance.

Conclusions for the EU-Level

Major changes at national level for associations cannot be expected because national patterns reflect deeply rooted traditions and ideologies. It has also to be taken into consideration that with EU enlargement there will be new member states where business associations (in particular HBAs) are rather weak and there is little respect for subsidiarity at the national level. In addition, there is practically no way in which such a situation at national level could be substantially addressed by EU policy.

It is also unclear which attitude EU institutions will have towards horizontal business associations in the future. In the past, business associations were considered rather in the Anglo-Saxon tradition, as rent-seeking institutions which internalise goods and externalise cost. They have access to vital information, but they make the information available only in a selective and, therefore, biased way. To get a balanced picture, one has to keep them at arms' length and to play off one against the other. In this model non-competing HBAs are less favoured than competing small and/or vertical associations.

If the orientation were to change in the direction of a more Germanic model of governance, strong European HBAs could become favoured cooperative partners in a system where to a certain extent the responsibilities of governance are shared according to the principle of subsidiarity. The EU Social Dialogue certainly constitutes a step in this direction.

But European HBAs are not fully ready yet. There is a low degree of autonomy and there are imbalances in the organisational power.

Taking into account the very limited scope for changes on the national HBA level, efforts should be made at the European HBA level to obtain a more balanced situation and more open-mindedness for cooperation. A practical contribution to this end could be the provision of some public assistance for European HBAs in terms of funding (open purpose or contracts) in order to enable the respective HBAs to have a sufficiently large and competent staff. It is true for all European HBAs; more staff would automatically allow them *de facto* to gain more autonomy *vis-à-vis* their national members. In order to facilitate co-operation, it would be worthwhile considering the establishment of a stable platform for continuous open and mutual discussions between EU institutions and European HBAs on the basis of joint analytical instruments (Traxler, 2001). This should supplement the more formalised Social Dialogue procedure.

Part II

EU Institutions

3

How the Architecture of the EU Political System Influences Business Associations

Edgar Grande

European integration has been distinct from other forms of regional integration (Asia Pacific Economic Cooperation/APEC; North American Free Trade Association/NAFTA) not only because of the far-reaching transfer of legal competencies, functions and activities from the national to the supranational level. This process has also been accompanied by the establishment of a comprehensive framework of political institutions at the supranational level. The result is not just a larger space for (almost) unrestricted economic transactions, but a completely new system of political governance, which has been shaped by a unique institutional architecture.

The role of institutions in the policy process has been emphasised by various concepts of institutionalism in political science, sociology and economics in recent years (March and Olson, 1989; Hall and Taylor, 1996). These institutionalist approaches are based on the assumption that institutions are not mere shells for (individual or collective) political action. Rather, they shape rules and norms of political action, allocate resources and authoritative power, structure opportunities for political action and the like. Various authors have shown that it is certainly possible to apply these institutionalist concepts to the study of European institutions and European integration (Bulmer, 1994; Kerremans, 1996; Pierson, 1996; Pollack, 1996); and, meanwhile, a large number of empirical studies on the European policy process have analysed the institutional aspects of European policy-making in some detail (Leibfried and Pierson, 1995; Hooghe, 1996; Kohler-Koch and Eising, 1999; Héritier, 1999; Scharpf, 1999; Grande and Jachtenfuchs, 2000).

It is the purpose of this article to analyse the role of institutions for the organisation and operation of business associations in the EU. The article is based on the assumption that the emergence of a multi-level system of governance has changed the possibilities of interest groups to organise, mobilise and to integrate members; and it has also affected their possibilities to influence public policy-making (Coleman and Montpetit, 2000). In most policy areas, policy-making meanwhile includes several (national and/or sub-national) ministries and government departments within each of the fifteen member states, the Council of Ministers, various Directorates General of the European Commission and their Cabinets, numerous committees, sub-committees, task forces and working groups, the national (and regional) parliaments, as well as the European Parliament – to mention only the most important public actors.

In the following, I will argue that this new institutional setting gives interest groups both advantages and disadvantages. Starting from a description of the institutional peculiarities of multi-level governance in the EU, I will then analyse the impact of this peculiar institutional setting on both the formation and articulation of business interests, and of the possibilities of interest groups to participate in the European policy process. The article shows that the institutional architecture of the EU significantly restricts the capacities of interest groups to organise and to co-operate in the European decision-making process. In the last decade, companies and business associations have responded to these difficulties in various ways, however, the solutions found so far have been rather ambiguous. They have created an 'effectiveness–legitimacy-dilemma' in the representation of business interests, which has not been resolved so far.

Institutional aspects of multi-level governance in the EU

Research on the institutional framework of EU policy-making and on the European policy process in the last decade has discovered a number of institutional peculiarities which have given rise to a new approach in European studies called 'multi-level governance'.[1] The basic assumption of this approach is that the European polity is highly differentiated and integrated both vertically and horizontally. Political power is distributed over various territorial levels and over various functional decision-making arenas. The EU polity thus reaches far beyond its formal jurisdictions, it is constituted by a large number of legally (at least partly) independent but functionally interdependent actors, institutions and decision-making arenas. Multi-level governance then focuses 'on the intermeshing of overlapping networks operating simultaneously in multiple functional arenas and at multiple geographic scales' (Ansell, 2000, p. 322).

Of course, institutional differentiation can also be found in hierarchical organisations. What distinguishes the EU from other institutional frameworks of decision-making is not the fact that it is internally differentiated, that is, that it is a multi-level system at all, but the fact that it represents a distinctive type of multi-level system. This European type of multi-level system can be characterised by three attributes: (1) the non-hierarchical institutional design, (2) the non-majoritarian mode of decision-making, and (3) the dynamic relationship between the various decision-making levels.

(1) The first – and without any doubt the most important – institutional characteristic of the EU is the non-hierarchical arrangement of its various territorial levels and functional arenas of decision-making. The supranational institutions are not hierarchically superimposed upon the member states; and the member states and their regions are not subordinated to the supranational powers. Rather, the relations between the different levels and arenas are characterised by a high degree of institutional and functional interdependence.[2] The main reasons for the institutional and functional interdependence between the EU, the member states and their regions is the intense institutional interlocking between supranational and national (sometimes, as in the case of federal systems like Germany, even sub-national) institutions. In European politics, national and supranational actors and institutions form integrated systems of joint decision-making (Scharpf, 1988). As a consequence, national actors are omnipresent in the bargaining and decision-making processes at the European level, and national institutions and regional actors have become indispensable for the implementation of decisions taken at the supranational level. Hence, it is not the differentiation but the non-hierarchical integration of decision-making levels and arenas which distinguishes the EU from other types of political decision-making.

(2) For obvious reasons, decision-making in such a non-hierarchical but integrated institutional arrangement cannot be based on hierarchical command or on majority voting in the first place. In both cases, the legitimacy of decisions would be (too) weak and the costs for their implementation would be (too) high. Therefore, the EU has to rely mainly on negotiations among the relevant actors and on a consensual mode of decision-making. Agreement in all important matters has to be reached by consensus. As Beate Kohler-Koch has put it, 'the EC is, by nature a non-majoritarian

system. It is a negotiating system which embraces Community institutions as well as economic and social actors and defines the role of "the state", i.e. member state governments and the Commission, not as an apex of a decision-making hierarchy, but as a mediator to come to terms with competing interests and an activator pushing for designing common policies' (Kohler-Koch, 1999, p. 30). The introduction of qualified majority voting has only modified and supplemented the dominant consensual decision-making style, it has not yet replaced it in matters of high importance. And, given the strong social, cultural and economic heterogeneity of the EU (even before its Eastern enlargement), there are severe limitations to an extension of majority voting in the EU (Abromeit, 1998; Grande, 2000b; Schmitter, 2000).

As a consequence, the European multi-level system of governance is, most of all, a negotiating system in which decisions are not produced by hierarchical power or by majority vote but by the negotiating capacities and skills of the actors involved. Policies are the joint product of the interactions of various decision-making levels and arenas with different functions, interests and resources, and of the consensus of a large number of different actors, organisations and institutions.

(3) Finally, the European multi-level system of governance is a dynamic system. Its dynamics primarily result from the fact that the competencies and functions of the different levels have not been fixed precisely yet – and there are good reasons to assume that they cannot be fixed precisely at all. This at least would be the lesson to be learned from federal systems in which system dynamics originating from the co-existence and interaction of different levels of governance have been observed before (Nicolaidis, 2001). Compared to federal systems, however, the system dynamics of the European system of multi-level governance so far are distinct in one important respect. Whereas in federal systems the interactions of different levels of governance are 'disciplined' by constitutional norms, in the case of the EU, these constitutional boundaries are much weaker. Despite the large stock of treaties and jurisprudence, the process of European integration is in many respects still an open project without precedent and without a final goal. As a consequence, the relations and interactions between the different levels of governance are much more variable and flexible than in a federal system; and institutional conflicts – that is, conflicts about the appropriate distribution of competencies – are permanent and intense.

These institutional characteristics of the European type of multi-level system have a number of consequences for the governance of the EU. Among them are:

- a considerable amount of institutional competition for competencies, tasks and resources between the different levels, mainly because of overlapping jurisdictions and shared powers;
- an extremely high demand for policy coordination both between the various institutions with formal competencies and between the wide range of societal actors relevant in a policy area in order to organise and mobilise support for policy proposals;
- a partial redistribution of power within organisations involved at the advantage of those actors who act at the interfaces between levels and arenas of decision-making;
- a significant increase in the number of strategic options for the actors involved, for example, by offering more opportunities for the organisation and mobilisation of 'advocacy coalitions' (Sabatier, 1998); by offering additional channels for political participation (Richardson, 1996; Greenwood and Aspinwall, 1998); and by offering new strategic games as, for example, the shifting of problems between the different levels ('cuckoo game'; Wassenberg, 1982);
- the growing importance of interaction effects between the different levels and arenas of decision-making. These interaction effects can be both negative (such as administrative competition, policy deadlock) and positive (for example, policy diffusion, policy learning);
- new problems of democratic legitimacy because of the lack of openness and transparency of negotiating systems and of the structural gaps in the democratic control of decision-making processes resulting from the differentiation of decision-making power (Greven and Pauly, 2000);
- serious problems to organise, aggregate and represent social interests and political preferences.

The main question to be addressed in this article is whether and how the institutional architecture of multi-level governance affects the role and the power of business associations in the EU. In the following, this question will be answered in two steps. In the first step, I will examine the impact of a multi-level system on the associations' ability to organise, to aggregate interests, to build up organisational capacities and to integrate members. In the second step, then, I will analyse their possibilities to participate in European policy-making, to influence its results, and to increase organisational power. Philippe C. Schmitter and Wolfgang Streeck (1999) have argued that these two functions require different skills and resources and that they are following different logics. Whereas the organisation and integration of members follows a 'logic of membership', the participation in public policy-making follows a 'logic of influence'.

Multi-level governance and the logic of membership of European interest groups

In the last decade, the formation of European interest groups has been one of the major fields of European policy studies (Greenwood *et al.*, 1992; Mazey and Richardson, 1993; van Schendelen, 1993; Pedler and van Schendelen, 1994; Gorges, 1996; Greenwood, 1997, 2002a, 2002b; Wallace and Young, 1997; Greenwood and Aspinwall, 1998; Pedler, 2001; Peschke, 2001). As suggested by neo-functionalist concepts (Haas, 1958), the establishment of a European level of decision-making and the transfer of competencies and resources have triggered the formation of interest groups at the European level ('Euro groups'). For years, the European Commission has actively supported this process, for example by granting privileged access to these new 'Euro groups'. The acceleration and intensification of the process of European integration since the mid-1980s then has stimulated the formation of European interest groups significantly. The most recent study on the subject done by Greenwood estimates that meanwhile there are about 1400 EU-level interest groups, of which about 950 are business associations (Greenwood, 2002b, p. 3f.). Empirical analyses of these groups (Greenwood, 1997, 2002a, 2002b) have shown, that compared to most national interest groups they possess peculiar organisational properties, regarding, among others, (1) their membership, (2) their resources, (3) their internal structures and (4) their organisational domains.

Membership

The first and most important peculiarity of interest formation at the European level relates to the membership of 'Euro groups'. Most of the European interest groups do not organise individuals (or individual companies); rather, they organise organisations. There are no European trade unions with direct membership; and most of the business associations are federations as well. Recent estimates suggest that about 58 per cent of European business associations are associations of national associations, and only 16 per cent of 'Euro groups' are based on direct company membership only (Greenwood, 2002b, p. 10). Of course, this is due to the fact that the process of European integration hitherto has mainly included highly organised industrially advanced societies. Therefore, interest formation at the European level has been based first of all on existing national organisations. From the perspective of interest groups, this has been both an advantage and a disadvantage. On the one hand, it has relieved the emerging 'Euro groups' from the difficult task of recruiting members in the member states of the EU with their different national cultures, organisational practices and systems of interest inter-mediation. Instead, it has required the transfer of organisational power from the national to the European level and this has turned out to be very difficult. In the 1990s, some of these Euro groups have changed their membership rules and accepted individual membership too. Meanwhile, there is a considerable number of business associations with mixed membership (Greenwood, 2002b, p. 10; Kohler-Koch, 2000, p. 142). Nevertheless, most associations are still mainly organisations of organisations and this has consequences for their resources, their organisational structure, and their domain.

Resources

Hitherto, national organisations have been very reluctant to transfer resources to their European peak organisations. Depending on the status of these 'Euro groups' (formal vs. informal) some of them are not even financed by regular membership fees; instead, they have to rely on voluntary donations from their member organisations or on support by the European Commission.[3] In any case, their budgets are small and, as a consequence, their organisational capacities are very limited. For example, the annual budget of half of the European business organisations is smaller than €100,000. There is a considerable number of 'Euro groups' which lack a permanent staff of their own. In these cases, the groups' office is made available (and financed) by one of the member organisations. Even when the groups are able to finance a permanent staff out of regular membership fees, this staff usually is very small, consisting of a few persons only. About three-quarters of the European business group employ a staff of no more than five persons (Greenwood, 1997, pp. 102–3).

Internal structure

Regarding the internal decision-making structure of these interest groups, in particular their relation to the member organisations, the most striking feature is the almost complete lack of autonomy of the peak organisation. The strategic and tactical 'degrees of freedom' (Scharpf, 1978) of the groups' permanent staff and of their official representatives are very small, if existent at all. Some of these organisations do not even have the mandate to prepare policy statements on their own initiative and, needless to say, they do not have a mandate to enter into formal negotiations with European institutions (such as the Commission) or with trade unions. The formulation of the organisations' goals and their activities are tightly controlled by the member organisations (Greenwood, 2002b, p. 106). It is true that some of the peak organisations – in particular those which participate in the 'Social Dialogue', introduced by the Maastricht Treaty – have reorganised their internal structure in the course of the 1990s. Both UNICE and ETUC changed their rules for the delegation of a bargaining mandate and for the internal acceptance of negotiation results in order to strengthen the power of the peak organisation. Despite these changes, however, the national member organisations have secured most of their influence (Hartenberger, 2000, pp. 216–40).

Domain

With respect to the organisational domains, we can observe that the scope of their membership and of their respective activities is highly specialised. This is partly due to the fact that most of the European interest groups have been formed on the basis of existing national organisations. Because of the diversity of these national organisations, the diversity and fragmentation at the European level has been multiplied. As a consequence of this specific logic of interest formation in the European multi-level architecture, the aggregation of interests at the European level is only weak, or, to put it more precisely, interests are aggregated either too high or too low. The aggregation of interests does not follow a functional logic, as in national systems, rather, it follows a territorial logic. This results in a system of interest representation in which European umbrella organisations of national peak organisations with their highly generalised interests on the one hand coexist with highly specialised European peak organisations of national groups on the other.

In sum, the European system of multi-level governance has produced a distinctive type of interest group system. Complementary to the institutional differentiation of the public policy process, a system of multi-level organisations has been emerging with a large number of new interest groups organised at the European level. It is true that there is 'considerable variation in performance between associations in different business domains' (Greenwood, 2002b, p. 79) and some groups have been able to achieve an authoritative position both in relation to their members and to European institutions. However, most of these European business associations can be considered as being rather weak, in particular compared to their national member organisations. Partly as a consequence of this weakness, the 1990s have witnessed a fragmentation and transformation of interest representation in the European policy process. In addition to the existing 'Euro groups', alternative – but not necessarily novel – methods of interest representation have gained importance which are supposed to be faster, more flexible, less costly and more effective. Most important in this respect have been four strategies of interest representation, which have all in common that they bypass the existing European interest groups:

- *Re-nationalisation* of interest representation: First, national interest groups and associations have started to act directly at the European level thus ignoring their European umbrella organisations – and avoiding the (high) costs of consensus building with associations from other countries. A large number of national business associations meanwhile have offices of their own in Brussels and they are in direct contact with supranational institutions. Almost three-quarters of UNICE members have offices in Brussels as well. Much of their work is highly coordinated with UNICE. However, 'these contacts can also be a dual-edged sword. The offices are also independent entities, and while the balance of their contributions to UNICE is supportive, it would be naive to think that they do not undertake their own lobbying activities when the positions of their patrons differ from those of UNICE over matters of some importance to them' (Greenwood, 2002b, p. 119). The results of a survey done by Bennett (1997) on the lobbying activities of British business associations show that for 16.5 per cent of the associations direct lobbying activities in Brussels is the most important route to gain influence on the European policy process.

- *Informalisation* of interest representation: A second alternative is the formation of small informal clubs, round tables, or ad hoc coalitions. In the last two decades or so, there has been a number of these informal groupings organising in particular business interests (Pijnenburg, 1998). The most prominent examples are the European Round Table of Industrialists (ERT), formed in 1983 (van Apeldoorn, 2002); the EU Committee of the American Chamber of Commerce, established in 1985 (Cowles, 1995, 1996); the European Information Technology

Industry Round Table (EITIRT), set up in 1981 (Cram, 1995); or the Transatlantic Business Dialog (TABD), established in 1995 (Coen and Grant, 2001). The most important factor influencing the creation of these groups 'was the perceived inability of traditional business associations to effectively, proactively represent the interests of industry in Brussels policy-making' (Cowles, 2002, p. 75). The work of these informal groupings of business is based on consensus as well; however, since they are highly selective in their membership and targeted on very specific goals only, they manage to reduce the costs of consensus-building among their members. An additional advantage is that they require (almost) no transfer of resources and organisational power and nevertheless allow to articulate interests at the European level effectively.

- *Privatisation* of interest representation: In the course of the 1990s, individual companies – large multinational firms in particular – have addressed their lobbying efforts directly to the European institutions, thus avoiding the costs of consensus-building within business associations. They have established offices at Brussels and have gained access to the European policy process. As a consequence, large firms have become major political actors in the EU (Coen, 1997, 1998).[4]

- *Commercialisation* of interest representation: Finally, the number and importance of professional lobbyists, that is, of 'public affairs representatives', 'law firms' and 'consultants' in Brussels has been increasing considerably. Most of these consultancies were founded in the late 1980s and early 1990s, in the aftermath of the Single European Act and in anticipation of the approaching single European market (Lahusen, 2002). Professional consultancies service predominantly individual companies. They allow firms to invest in highly specialised advice for very specific purposes without the costs of permanent offices or of cumbersome consensus-building.

The consequence of this differentiation of interest representation is an extreme pluralisation of organisations and a remarkable richness of forms of interest representation at the European level. Despite this diversity of interests and organisations, however, the process of interest formation and articulation at the European level does not correspond with the ideal world of pluralist theory. It is true that the institutional properties of European governance restrict the possibilities of all interest groups to organise at the European level and to represent the interests of their members. But these limitations do not affect all types of interests in the same way. There are some interests, which can make better use of the various alternative ways of interest representations, thus avoiding the ineffectiveness of traditional associations. This holds less for business interests in general, rather it holds for large firms in particular, which have established a variety of venues and methods to influence the European policy process. However, this is not to say that business interests, in particular the interests of large European corporations, would be privileged in the European policy process. The following analysis of the logic of influence in the European policy process will show that the institutional architecture of the European policy process also restricts the influence of business interests in European policy-making.

Multi-Level governance and the logic of influence of European interest groups

The emergence of a multi-level system of governance in Europe has not only changed the possibilities of interest groups to organise, to mobilise and to integrate members; it has also changed their possibilities of influencing public policy-making. As a consequence of this institutional transformation, the 'target structure' (Almond, 1958, p. 278) for interest groups has changed fundamentally. The new institutional setting gives interest groups both advantages and disadvantages. Quite obviously, a multi-level system of decision-making increases the number of 'important points of access' (Almond, 1958, p. 278) to the decision-making process considerably. However, the mere plurality of actors and the complexity of the decision-making process can be serious obstacles for private interest groups as well. In such an institutional setting, it is virtually impossible for any single interest or national association to secure exclusive access to the relevant officials, let alone to secure exclusive influence.

In addition, we can observe changes in the logic of influence of the European policy process which can significantly alter the power distribution between public and private actors, mostly to the disadvantage of interest groups.[5] In general, there are at least three possibilities how the bargaining position between public and private actors (such as business associations, companies, lobbyists) may change in joint negotiation systems.

The first and most obvious possibility is that interest groups make joint decision-making more complicated if they are able to enforce binding commitments from public actors. In this case, they reduce the autonomy of public actors, thus making the 'win-set' for solutions in negotiations smaller. Policy-making in the EU provides plenty of empirical evidence that powerful national interest groups are effectively able to bind the respective national officials in European negotiations to their special interests. In such a constellation, joint European negotiations are extremely cumbersome, and sometimes (national) firms or associations are even able to prevent any agreement in joint European decision-making. Alternatively, interest groups may exploit public actors' needs to compromise by intervening strategically in joint decision-making processes to their own advantage. In all these cases, joint decision-making strengthens the power of at least some firm or some association in one way or another.

A second possibility was identified by Scharpf, Reissert and Schnabel (1976, pp. 18–20) in their study of German federalism. They observed that joint public decision-making does not benefit interest groups; rather it tempers their demands because groups must take into consideration the political and institutional constraints of the public actors involved. Extreme preferences that are outside the 'win-set' of joint negotiations have no chance of being recognised. Hence, instead of favoring interest groups, joint decision-making domesticates them, although it does not affect the distribution of power between public and private actors.

With respect to effective problem-solving in European policy-making, the third possibility is the most interesting. In this case, joint decision-making may change the distribution of power between public and private actors in favor of the former. This possibility presupposes that public actors can purposefully use the various 'internal' ties and commitments produced by joint decision-making to strengthen their bargaining position *vis-à-vis* 'external', that is, private, actors. In theories of international negotiations, this logic of 'self-commitment' (Schelling, 1960, p. 27) is well known and in research on the European policy process this has been called the 'paradox of weakness' (Grande, 1996). As a consequence, public actors can compensate their loss of autonomy because of their integration into a system of joint decision-making by gains in autonomy *vis-à-vis* elements of their social environment, such as business associations.

In the EU policy process, there are a number of possible ways in which public actors can make use of the strategic opportunities of their bargaining position in joint decision-making. First of all, public actors integrated into multi-level systems of joint decision-making are in a much more favourable position to refuse unwanted or unrealisable claims made by companies and associations than autonomous decision-making bodies. In European IT policy, for example, the reservations and requests made by the member states and by several Directorates General involved have not only been obstacles to an effective European policy; these commitments and obligations have also been used deliberately by the Commission to turn down demands from companies.

In addition to this power to 'say no', public actors can use their internal commitments and obligations to strengthen their bargaining power in negotiations with business associations and companies, and to improve the results of negotiations to their advantage. Commission officials are often able to improve their bargaining position by referring to the fact that the consent of other public bodies (especially the Council and other Directorates General of the Commission) is required. In the case of the IT policy, for example, despite the distinguished – and in many cases overestimated – role of the big IT companies and their associations in the European IT programmes, the Commission has been able to 'gently...influence the direction in which IT policy has developed in the EU' (Cram, 1994, p. 204).

In the most favourable case, public actors like the Commission officials can use their integration in joint decision-making systems to improve their bargaining position *vis-à-vis* both sides, that is, the interest groups and the other public actors involved. The development of the first European research programme in telecommunications illustrates this point well. This programme was highly controversial among all the major actors: the national PTT administrations, the public network operators and, to some extent, the large telecommunications equipment manufacturers. In this constellation, the European Commission used its role as a 'multilateral broker' (Mandell, 1988, p. 408) in bilateral and joint negotiations with industry and national administrations to gain consent from both sides. In a cumbersome negotiation process, the Commission rearranged the composition of the negotiation groups time and again, and it very skillfully used the concessions made by one side to gain concessions from the other.

Consequences and implications: the effectiveness–legitimacy dilemma

The process of European integration has not only established a new level of supranational policy-making, where we can observe the same actors and the same 'games' already familiar from domestic politics. As a consequence of the new institutional framework of multi-level decision-making, new types of actors have emerged, and both the logic of membership within the European interest groups and the logic of influence between public and private actors show some important differences.

First of all, a multi-level system of decision-making adds some new difficulties of organisation and power distribution to the well-known problems of collective action. As a result, most of the European business associations are weak and their capacities to enter into negotiations with public bodies, to arrive at binding agreements, and to take over implementation functions are very limited. Therefore, it is very unlikely that the EU will gain the benefit of corporatist arrangements at the supranational level and that policy networks of the various types may unfold their governance or self-governance potential there.

However, this is not to say that the institutional architecture of European policy-making only creates difficulties for business associations; it offers opportunities as well. An institutional analysis of the European policy process and of the logic of interest group formation suggests that group influence in a 'networked polity' is less the result of direct organisational power than the product of a group's indirect, positional power in a multi-level system of governance. The main sources of this indirect power of actors are: their capacity to transfer resources (for example, information) between the different levels and arenas of decision-making; to mobilise (public and private actors) in support of proposals; to promote a common understanding of problems and problem-solutions; to orchestrate negotiations and the like.

In recent years, some organisations of business have well been able to occupy the positions at the interfaces of decision-making levels and arenas and to make use of the indirect powers inherent in multi-level systems. The best examples for this new type of 'interface actors' are the various European business round tables and forums. The main sources of power of these associations are not organisational capacities but communicative competencies, for example their capacity to provide reliable information, to initiate political discourses, to mobilise political support for Commission proposals, and so forth. In these cases, the influence of business in European politics has been less the result of its direct lobbying efforts or of its structural power than a result of its (discursive) power to frame political debates consistent with its own interests. The debate on the 'competitiveness' of European industry has been one of the most striking examples of this power of ideas and public debates (Mazey and Richardson, 1997).

In this respect, the various alternative strategies of interest representation can well be interpreted as effective responses to the challenges and difficulties of organising and representing interests in multi-level systems of governance. This result is highly ambiguous, however. As a consequence of these organisational responses and innovations, the representation of business interests in Europe seems to be confronted with a protracted organisational dilemma. The choice is between traditional forms of interests organisation, which are, on the one hand, representative for their respective domains, but rather ineffective and, on the other hand, new forms of interest organisation, which can be quite effective, but not representative.

Notes

1 For a recent summary of the concept of multi-level governance and of its most relevant aspects see Grande (2000a) and Hooghe/ Marks (2001).
2 This is not to say that hierarchy is completely absent in the European polity. Most important in this respect are the decision-making powers of the European Court of Justice, which are immediately effective and independent both from the member states and from the other supranational institutions (Dehousse, 1998).
3 Over one-fifth of the groups survey by Greenwood claimed that they received EU funding and five per cent stated that this was their main source of funding (Greenwood, 1997, p. 10).
4 Bennett's study of British business associations shows the surprising result that there are even cases in which national associations use individual member companies to lobby for them at Brussels (Bennett, 1997).
5 For a more detailed analysis of this aspect see Grande (1996).

4

The White Paper on Governance: Challenges and Opportunities for EU Business Associations

Jerome Vignon

Revisiting European governance was the first amongst four main priorities endorsed by the Prodi Commission when it took office at the end of 1999. This move immediately raised concern on what exactly was meant by 'governance' within the Commission. Was it a general overhauling of policies, politics and polity in the European Union? Or was it rather about internal codes of conduct or administrative reform of the Commission? How could governance apply in the context of European political institutions, compared with 'good governance' in the case of countries supported by the International Monetary Fund (IMF) and the World Bank, or with 'corporate governance'?

After some hesitation, created by the fact that a few weeks beforehand the Commission had adopted a programme of work on 'improving European governance' (September, 2000), the European Council decided In Nice (December, 2000) to launch a comprehensive debate on the 'Future of Europe', in order to prepare a major constitutional reform of the EU-Institutions. It appeared that the Commission, with the launching of the Governance White Paper, had two major objectives:

- To engage itself and the other European institutions (that is, Parliament and Council of Ministers) in a process of improving the relevance and accountability of the decision making process in Brussels
- To demonstrate that such improvements could take place without changing the Treaties, and that even if they should be consistent with Treaty changes, to be considered by the forthcoming Convention on the Future of Europe.

The governance White Paper was adopted by the Commission on 25 July 2001. It was based on five major principles of good European governance. The first three dealt with what scholars usually name the principles of 'input legitimacy': openness, participation and account-ability; the last two belonged to the category of 'output legitimacy': effi-ciency and coherence. All five provided a renewed inspiration for reinvigorating the so-called 'community method'. The Commission argued that this method had not only achieved remarkable results dur-ing the preceding thirty years, but was even more relevant in the per-spective of increased diversity and complexity amongst member states, caused by enlargement. It also saw the governance debate as a means to address criticisms of the EU governance system.

One of those criticisms, directly related to the 'democratic deficit' of the EU, was the lack of clarity and efficiency in the relations between the Commission and the civil society, that is, the whole range of independent actors involved in European action, including of course business actors. Acknowledging, for the first time, the importance of the civil society, both at national and European level, was certainly one of the most striking elements in the Governance White Paper. From its earliest days, the Commission had drawn from professional knowledge, embedded within the representation of socio-economic interest groups, as an important input for the formu-lation of policy initiatives and instruments in the various fields related to the establishment of a common market. But two questions had to be solved: clarification of bids for information from stake-holders with a precise interest in the concerned matter for legislation; and the risk of overdominance of specific policy fields by certain types of stakeholders.

To overcome those growing imbalances in the informal process consultation, the Commission proposed, and has now decided, to commit itself unilaterally to implementing five basic standards for any significant political initiative at the initial phase of its drafting, prior to adoption as a proposal to be submitted to Council and Parliament:

- Clarity about the content of the consultation itself: what is the requested opinion about, and in which context of policy develop-ment?
- Transparency as to which specific target groups will be consulted, taking into account the relevance of very different stakeholders and their unequal ability to voice their concern

- Adequate time frames for the consultation, which should allow not less than eight weeks for interested parties to respond
- Feedback to consulted parties individually or generally on if, and how, their opinion has been taken into account.

Following sustained input by both business associations and representatives of EU associations of local and regional authorities, the codification of consultation was completed by the decision to also base any important initiative carrying a legal and compulsory basis with an ex-ante 'impact assessment'. The scope of these assessments is to be decided by the Commission itself, according to the concerns expressed by the civil society in the consultative phase, in the very early stage of the decision-making process. The communication about impact assessment, adopted within the so-called 'spring package' on governance, makes it clear that the Commission will try to evaluate not only the direct impacts which have motivated its proposal, but it should also try to investigate 'side effects'. Significantly, these include analysis about the impact upon those who are not the main stakeholders of the proposed or intended legislation.

Those new instruments are still to be tested and judged in the light of first experiences with them. Nevertheless, they already provide EU business interest associations with reasonable possibilities to improve the value they provide to their own stakeholders. From now on, a well organised EU business association, even with limited staff in Brussels, will be better placed to anticipate well in advance on which topics the Commission will engage in an impact assessment study. It might therefore focus more precisely its opinion ahead of the commencement of consultation on the proposed legislation, enabling its members to express views in a timely and adequate fashion. Further, the conduct of this consultation should be facilitated by a more focused approach from the Commission, thus encouraging EU business associations with a broad membership to produce effective opinion.

But, on the other hand, the increased transparency and openness of the consultation are a new challenge for EU business associations, especially for those trying to make their case on very narrow targets in the Commission's services. The standards on 'target groups of consultation', for example, specifies that the Commission, in determining the relevant parties for consultation, should take into account the following elements:

- the track records of participants in previous consultations
- large and small organisation or companies.

It also sets out that, when a structured consultative body is established, the Commission should take steps in order to ensure that its composition reflects properly the sector it represents.

Undoubtedly, increased accountability from the Commission in implementing its right of initiative will turn into a need for greater representativity from the consulted parties. These include EU business associations, even if representativity at this stage is not an explicit requirement from the Commission. Representativity and corresponding criteria will be required, when better regulation will lead to a direct involvement of those associations in the regulatory process itself, within the so-called 'co-regulation issue'. This concept is defined in the governance White Paper (European Commission, 2001), and in the latest communication on 'Better Regulation' (European Commission, 2002a) (http://europa.eu.int/comm/enterprise/library/enterprise/europe/issue9/articles/en/enterprise09_en.htm). EU business associations should be ready and prepared to work within the framework of such criteria. The first opportunity for this will come when the Economic and Social Committee, according to its new responsibilities deriving from the Nice Treaty, will report on this important subject.

5

The Challenge of Managing Relations with the European Parliament: How Well Do EU Business Interest Associations Do?

John Russell and Paul Adamson

Public affairs is a specialised form of communication, being that communication directed toward legislation and regulatory decision makers. Over the last decade, the number and range of organisations participating in the European Union public affairs 'marketplace' has increased markedly. During the mid-1990s, there developed a specialised press and a large international press corps in Brussels. Also, a range of daily and weekly print and web-based journals and papers are available, colloquially known as the 'village press', specifically targeted to follow and comment on the evolving European Union (EU) agenda. Think tanks related to EU affairs have multiplied.

There has been a cluttering of the Brussels environment with many more players vying to have their views heard and their interests accommodated. Significantly, the last few years have seen the emergence of NGOs and a vibrant civil society eager to press the EU to reorient its policies in line with their perspectives, which are often highly focused and single-issue based. These media and NGOs have raised the level of scrutiny and shifted the pattern from intrinsic to extrinsic decision-making.

In this environment, the European Parliament (EP) offers unique challenges for business associations. Many trade and professional associations have cultivated long-standing relationships with the pertinent sections of the European Commission, and have positioned themselves as useful interlocutors, with a history of consultation and participating officially or ex officio at relevant hearings and technical committees. Such relationships with the Commission remain necessary, but in isolation they are no longer sufficient for success. The nature of the Parliament and its working patterns mean that business associations cannot simply emulate their modus operandi for the Commission: whereas the Commission is ostensibly apolitical and technocratic, the Parliament is by nature political with a strong tendency toward popularism.

Hence, there is not a single challenge, but rather a wide range of challenges that European business associations have to consider when dealing with the European Parliament. These can be divided generally into two groups:

1. The challenges which are inherent to the complex setting of the Parliament or those that derive from the almost constant institutional reform since the Single European Act (SEA) in 1986;
2. Those challenges resulting from the complexities of European associations themselves. Internally associations are obliged to produce 'strong' and relevant common positions; and externally, when establishing a working relationship with the Parliament on a given issue.

European Parliament: complex and political

First, associations need to deal with the challenges inherent to the European Parliament. The Parliament is complex and requires effort and resourcing by any association, individual or company to comprehend and utilise, though it remains very much the most open of the European institutions. Cursory attention to the Parliament can lead to misunderstandings and failure.

The EP will sometimes act and speak in a single voice with the Commission, the Council or national Parliaments. However, it is a House of fifteen nationalities and seven political groupings, which are often a patchwork of national sub-groups. In many ways, the cultural, political and linguistic diversity of the Parliament is the broadest and hardest challenge to meet, as it requires an analytical approach factoring in personalities and tactics encompassing institutional, national and political group dimensions.

The diversity of the European Parliament manifests itself during day-to-day work by less disciplined political groups than is the norm for most national parliaments. Political groups may split along national or regional lines on particular issues. The Parliament can nonetheless show solid unanimity where it considers its prerogatives are being impinged by the other institutions or where it wishes to extend its institutional mandate.

The selection process for Members of the European Parliament (MEPs) impacts the ethos and loyalties of Members and should be appreciated by associations and factored into their issue management plans. No MEP is elected to represent a specific constituency. While some Member States have regional lists, most are drawn from national party lists. Sitting MEPs require no financial support from interest groups for re-election expenses. Loyalty ultimately rests with the national or, in some cases, regional party machines to maintain a high position on the party list. Subsequently, attendance of members at committees and plenary sittings of the Parliament is patchy.

The Parliament is not only a complex organisation, it is the institution which has seen its legislative powers grow almost uninterruptedly since the SEA's introduction of the co-operation procedure, then the Maastricht Treaty's creation of the co-decision procedure in 1992 and its extension at Amsterdam and further at Nice. The principal vehicles for Parliamentary work are its 17 committees. The powers of these committees varys depending on the their mandates. Where committees deal with issues specified by the Treaty as co-decision, the Parliament has co-legislative power with the Council. For issues where the Parliamentary writ requires only Consultation by the Council and Commission, the importance of an association's relationship with that Parliamentary committee is less.

From its beginnings as a supervisory or consultative body, the Parliament has grown into the role of full co-legislator in most policies that bear a direct impact on economic life. It has undergone constant change, and so obliged European business associations to adapt in turn and keep abreast of every institutional development affecting their commercial interests.

Many European associations have reacted by strengthening their presence in Brussels, modifying their structure to create specialised working groups on specific issues, and adapting their communication instruments to the EP audience. In many ways, European associations have had to develop parallel organisational processes to the EU institutions, often facing similar problems and sometimes replicating solutions adopted at an institutional level. It is interesting to note, for example, that many associations underwent the debate on unanimity versus majority voting with regards their decision-making procedures.

Challenges from the nature of European associations

European associations have had not only to adapt constantly to institutional change and the growing power of the European Parliament, they have had to cope at the same time with that second group of challenges: the difficulties inherent to association management. That said, European associations benefit from a number of advantages in their relations with the Parliament also linked to the very nature of associations: the fact that they represent common interests rather than individual ones; that they have pan-European coverage; and that they possess a considerable wealth of expertise. These are all features common to European associations, which, if positioned sensitively, make them almost natural counterparts to the EU institutions and the European Parliament.

With their strengths and weaknesses for European associations, the challenge is two-fold: working effectively internally to reach strong common positions, then communicating them appropriately and effectively to the Members of the European Parliament.

While decision-making in and between the EU institutions is a matter of political consensus building, the fundamental requirement for a European association is for its members, generally market competitors, to agree common positions without diluting their content to a position that is an emasculated 'lowest common denominator'. Nonetheless, when working with the European Parliament, there are a number of advantages that European associations can exploit. These are:

- *Credibility*: European associations are generally more credible than individual companies in the eyes of MEPs because rather than putting forward individual interests, their position is generally that of a whole industry sector. Moreover, the fact that European associations often bring together national associations further enhances their credibility.
- *Pan-European coverage*: The European Parliament, like other institutions, has an interest in prioritising consultation with associations which have already undertaken background work to identify the common interest of a sector. This saves the institutions from consulting with many individual companies, and likewise representatives of specific national interests. The Pan-European coverage is often an essential advantage that allows associations to play a central role in consultations with the EP.
- *Expertise*: European associations often bring together the expertise available in the Member States. MEPs will depend, to a certain extent, on the information brought to them by technical experts. The expertise of associations is usually of a very high standard given the considerable work undertaken internally to assess the economic impact of a specific measure and agree on a position that allows them to present a united front.

In most cases, European associations have been able to make the most of these fundamental advantages which has allowed them in some cases to establish robust legitimacy and become quasi-institutional players. Overall, the main weakness of European associations is that their positions often have to be diluted to fit the interests of all. This permanent challenge has been met with mixed success depending on the issue and on the association.

The success of a European association in its working relations with the European Parliament can be broadly measured by its legitimacy, which can take time to establish. It is often the result of long-term work with the European Parliament – from MEPs to their parliamentary assistants, political advisors or the Parliament's administrators. In addition to sectoral expertise, building a relationship with the EP also requires solid 'European' expertise to ensure the technical position is effectively communicated to the politicians. There are a number of simple rules European associations should bear in mind in order to convince MEPs of their arguments and ultimately establish strong legitimacy:

- *Adapt the message to the audience*: When dealing with the European Parliament, considerable effort must be made to adapt the position or the message to specific audiences. This applies not only to the different nationalities in the Parliament, or the EP administration, but even more so to the different parties, as well as the different EP committees. For instance, a British conservative MEP of the Transport Committee should not be addressed in the same way as a German socialist of the Environment committee. Depending on the MEP, the party or the relevant EP Committee, an association needs to put forward some arguments rather than others or cast a different light on its priorities and concerns.

    Submissions for legislative initiatives should be short, non-technical and they should offer specific language for amendments where appropriate.

- *Avoid individual lobbying*: Individual companies that are tempted to undertake their own uncoordinated lobbying represent a real danger for associations dealing with the EP. Nothing can damage an association's relationship with the Parliament more than the suggestion that its position is contested by some of its members. The credibility and the legitimacy of the association risk being directly affected and trust is broken internally. At best, for non-controversial issues it weakens the association's position, for contentious legislative initiatives these inconsistencies will be exploited by opponents within and outside the Parliament and are normally a recipe for ineffectiveness and failure. The subsequent impact on the association's reputation can be long term.

- *Act as 'European' experts*: It is useful for an issue management plan to include a clear understanding of the objectives and perspectives of the Parliament itself. The association should not only be seen to represent an interest or constituency, but also position itself as contributing to the evolution of better legislation. The importance of adopting an expert approach to the European Parliament cannot be overemphasised. Since the end of the Christian Democrat / Socialist coalition in the Parliament, there has been no real permanent majority. Majorities now often have to be identified for each specific issue, across parties and nationalities. Although this provides, in many ways, for a more open and democratic process, it also makes assessing the best way to approach the Parliament on a given issue more difficult.

Parliament's increasing role in the legislative process has developed MEPs with a much more expert and technical approach to issues, built to a great extent in their consultations with industry over the years, and lately with civil society. This helps to facilitate the work of European business associations, and associations have reflected this development by refining their lobbying techniques and learning to work with key players other than MEPs.

- *People and Timing*: This relative lack of cohesion within the Parliament provides both challenges and opportunities for business associations. A satisfactory communication with the rapporteur of the lead committee is in itself not a guarantee that the rapporteur's opinion on key points which concern an association, will carry the day in a committee vote. Conversely, all is not lost if there is an unsympathetic rapporteur. Also, there is another hurdle at the plenary vote where, from time to time, the committee opinion is overturned. Astute analysis and energising of existing networks can often throw up some faction within a political group or national delegation willing to table an appropriate amendment.

A sound knowledge of the procedures of the Parliament is useful to optimise the leverage of the association. Chairs, vice chairs and committee coordinators from the main political groups manage the allocation of dossiers to rapporteurs and influence the workflow, deciding on agendas and the allocation of time for particular items. The secretariat of the Parliament supporting the committee is also an important source of advice on the prevailing attitudes of members and the functioning of the committee.

Compared to many legislators, MEPs are relatively underresourced. The average number of staff for US Members of Congress is 16, while US Senators each have a staff in the range of 60. An active MEP who is the rapporteur on a complex initiative, is reliant on a more restricted level of support. He or she probably has one or two full-time assistants. The committee secretariat can give some assistance on procedural matters. For the larger political groups, support on content also comes from committee staff in the political group secretariat.

The staff within the main political group secretariat write the background briefs, especially if the rapporteur is drawn from another group. These briefs can influence the voting of members for members not fully versed in the detail of an issue. Assistants can also be highly influential due to their access to MEPs and their impact on determining attitudes to dossiers.

Timing for effecting communications with Parliament is an important element for success. Windows of opportunity open and close and it is necessary for business associations to adapt their issue management to these rhythms. Contacting the MEP rapporteur well before he or she is prepared to start writing a report may be useful for an introduction of intent or background briefing, but detailed, technical submissions are normally more relevant when the rapporteur begins the process of research and writing. A similar window for communication exists for the shadow rapporteur(s) from the main political groups. Members will only focus on an issue in the weeks prior to a vote in committee or plenary, respectively. Other than communication to raise the profile for a subject, detailed submissions should be left to those periods.

Amendments are the prime means to impact on the direction of policy development. The need for business groups to have sound intelligence early in the process cannot be overestimated. An appreciation of tactics is important. Even with an unsympathetic rapporteur or committee, it is important to seek sponsors to table amendments at the first reading. Parliamentary procedures preclude the tabling of new amendments at the second reading and conciliation, unless exceptional circumstances prevail.

The diligence and attendance records of MEPs to parliamentary work vary significantly. Votes can be lost or won by virtue of those members who attend on the day. Energising political groups or members can be an ingredient for success. A key motivation is to draw links to the impact on the nation, region, and even city, from which they originate. Jobs and investment, past and future, are useful means of leverage.

There are many competing interests pressing to have an influence on any emerging legislation. Associations should not only establish a strategy for their relationship with the Parliament as a whole, but define clear and achievable objectives for pertinent legislation. Many associations conduct SWOT (strengths, weaknesses, opportunities and threats) assessments that include identifying potential allies and foes. The subsequent 'issue management' plans then comprise a range of tactics, both inside and outside the Parliament, such as, one-to-one contact programmes, workshops, media and NGO outreach. Issue advertising is a recent but growing phenomenon.

Business associations need to acknowledge and confront the political character of the European Parliament in order to be effective. An issue is rarely treated in isolation, but rather linkages are made by individual MEPs, committees and political groups between issues. Associations should understand these linkages, the dynamics of political *'quid pro quo'*, or 'horse trading' in its crudest form.

In many instances, association positions need to translate into amendments. Definite wording for political amendments is often requested and should be provided. Understanding the inter-relationships between a web of competing amendments is necessary. Associations should consider giving their interlocutors some form of negotiating mandate, providing more flexibility and based on a clear understanding of the associations' 'bottom line' for concessions.

Legislative proposals passing through committees towards plenary votes should not be the only focus of associations. Relationships should be established and nurtured beyond submissions to specific pieces of legislation. MEPs are politicians and, as in all political environments, there is a symbiosis between politicians and their need for issues on which they can imprint their stamp. In the Parliament, questions by members to the Commission, and amendments at committee and plenary levels, are key mechanisms to raise the profile of a subject. MEPs' questions to the Commission can raise or highlight an issue, or press the Commission to justify the approach it is taking.

New patterns of governance

Overall, European associations are meeting the challenge of working with a Parliament whose legislative powers have developed considerably over the last decade. Business associations have adapted their structures and decision-making procedures and refined their approach to key EP decision-makers to reflect their increasing level of expertise and involvement in technical legislation.

The weaknesses of European business associations are still very much inherent to the nature of associations and essentially come down to the fact that speaking with a single voice and establishing legitimacy involves a long and often cumbersome process.

In its White Paper on European Governance, the Commission addresses in detail the issue of consultation with key stakeholders, the use of alternative regulatory models, such as voluntary agreements, and the possibility of striking partnership agreements and formalising relations between EU associations and the institutions. That is, in exchange for increased transparency on the part of associations, the institutions would commit to increased consultation with them in the context of a formal partnership.

These proposals are of direct relevance to EU business associations which in many cases already possess the legitimacy and the expertise that would make them 'natural candidates' for negotiating partnership agreements. With regard more specifically to the Parliament, business associations should systematically involve MEPs when alternative regulations, such as voluntary agreements, are being considered. As the Commission is looking at new and more flexible ways of regulating, and as relations between the Commission and EU business associations seem to be at a turning point, neglecting the Parliament in the process would be a gross and damaging mistake. European business associations therefore have a full role to play in shaping forthcoming initiatives which will improve governance for their direct commercial interest, but maybe first and foremost because they are an integral part of civil society.

Conclusion

To have an effective working relationship with the European Parliament, European business associations must meet two groups of challenges: those which are inherent to the complex setting of the evolving Parliament; and those challenges resulting from the complexities of European associations themselves. Associations should internally develop 'strong' and relevant common positions, and, externally, establish working relationships with the Parliament on specific issues.

The emphasis should be on flexibility, adapting messages to the flows, timings, processes and communication style of the Parliament.

Associations must keep in mind the necessity of being tactical: the Parliament is a marketplace of ideas where issues are never treated in isolation, and where an awareness of the wider policy context and the positions of counterparts, friends and foes are crucial.

Above all, the European Parliament should be regarded as a fertile ground for argumentation and achieving influence through long-term, beneficial relationships. Whilst framing issues in a broader EU context, business associations should strive to exploit established relationships with individual members and link issues to investment and jobs related to the Member State, and even the region, of the MEP concerned.

6

EU Competition Law and Trade Associations

Alan Reid

This chapter assesses the provisions of European Union competition law as they apply to trade associations. Trade associations, both national and European, are in a unique position *vis-à-vis* the European Union legal system. They act as representatives of their constituent members, lobbying the European legislature. They may act as enforcers of competition law, bringing infractions to the attention of the European Commission. They will be empowered to collate information about the sector of the market in which their members operate. This constitutional power, to gather and disseminate information concerning the industrial or commercial sector they are involved in, can be utilised for positive or negative purposes. The association may act as a repository for market information, which is indicative of collusive behaviour by a number of competing organisations. Conversely, the information repository may be used by the members of the association to facilitate anti-competitive abuses. The trade association may simply be a front for collusive activity. Trade associations must tread a fine line between adopting legitimate business practices and collaborating in collusive or abusive activity that is anti-competitive. The delimitation of the legality of trade association activity is one of degree. The factual situation appertaining to the market is vital in assessing the legality or otherwise of the activities of a trade association.

Purposes of European competition law

European competition law is predicated upon four major principles. The law is designed to:

- Prevent businesses forming cartels or groups where prices can be fixed, independently of non-members and consumers

- Prevent an undertaking taking over a less successful company if the take-over would give the business a monopoly or strengthen its dominant position
- Prevent a very powerful single company or small group of companies from abusing a position of dominance
- Fetter the power of the Member States to take action in the market-place, to the detriment of free competition.

In essence, European competition law pursues three objectives, *viz.*,

- economic efficiency
- the protection of consumers and smaller firms, and
- the creation and continuing operation of the internal market.

European Union objectives and competition law

Competition law is only one policy that has been instrumental in cre-ating and subsequently ensuring the smooth operation of the internal market. For example, the free movement of goods is a fundamental principle of the European Union. Articles 28–30 of the EC Treaty outline the main provisions that relate to free movement of goods. Articles 28 and 29 provide that quantitative restrictions and measures having equivalent effect to a quantitative restriction on imports and exports shall be prohibited. Essentially, goods produced in one Member State shall not be subjected to discriminatory treatment or indeed treatment that makes the importation or export of goods more difficult. If the European Union is to operate as a single market, then Member States should not erect barriers to trade that impede the free flow of goods across national borders. Public law barriers to trade that are erected by Member States must be eliminated, in the drive towards European inte-gration. Member States, if left to their own devices, will adopt protec-tionist policies that favour their domestic manufacturers.

Competition law can thus be seen as the private law counterpart to Articles 28 and 29 EC Treaty. The internal market would be seriously imperilled if member States either erected barriers to trade or if private enterprises were to re-erect national boundaries to free trade.

Substantive provisions of European competition law

Article 81 of the EC Treaty prohibits agreements between undertakings, decisions by associations of undertaking, and concerted practices which may affect trade between Member States and which have as their object or effect the prevention, restriction or distortion of competition within the common market.

The order of the prohibitions is significant. The most common and obvious violation of Article 81 is an agreement between undertakings. Competing undertakings, instead of acting independently and thus subject to the full rigours of a free market, voluntarily decide to co-operate with one another, in order to minimise their exposure to the vagaries of the market.

Clearly, companies that engage in such behaviour will employ their best endeavours to avoid detection by the Commission. Therefore, the prohibition applies to informal agreements as well as concerted practices where co-ordinated action has been undertaken to align prices. The collusive activity may be exempted, if the agreement satisfies the conditions for exemption, as outlined under Article 81(3).[1]

Competing companies will attempt to co-ordinate their responses in order to avoid the uncertainty inherent in an open market. However, the collusion of independent companies is not the only concern of competition law. An additional danger is that of umbrella organisations, such as trade associations, zealously attempting to safeguard the industry sector and member firms they represent, from competition.

Trade associations will pose difficulties for the competition authorities where the sector they represent is oligopolistic, there is a low level of product differentiation in that sector or the association (or group of associations) represents a number of actors in the sector, whether they be manufacturers, wholesalers or distributors.

The trade association paradox

The characteristic purposes of a trade association are to represent the views of the members to government and to feed back the views of government to the members, providing services to its members and handling the public relations of the industry sector. They may be involved in promotional campaigns for the entire industry, market research campaigns, public education programmes or standard-setting in terms of quality, technical requirements or customer relations.

Trade associations may wield great power over the members they represent. A great deal of the trade association's work will be entirely legitimate. However, their power of influence may create competitive tensions in the industry.

In the *Roofing Felt* Case,[2] the Belasco (Cooperative of Belgian Asphalt Producers) association represented Belgian companies involved in the asphalt industry. The co-operative agreement contained a number of innocuous, and indeed legitimate, objectives, *viz.*, the prohibition of bribes, collective advertising and measures designed to improve the efficiency of the manufacture and distribution of roofing felt. The agreement also included a number of ancillary objectives which were deemed to be anti-competitive. The agreement provided for minimum prices and list prices for all roofing felt sold in Belgium, the setting of quotas and the application of penalties in the event of violation of the terms of the agreement. The association's accountant enforced the quota system by levying penalties on members who exceeded their quotas. The system of collective advertising cultivated a perception of homogeneity between the members' products.

Similarly, in Case 272/85 *ANTIB* v. *Commission*,[3] Antib (Association of Independent Waterways Workers) was a French trade association whose members were firms or individuals involved in the carriage of goods by inland waterways. ANTIB entered into an agreement with a French trade federation of inland waterway freight forwarding agents. This agreement provided for a ten per cent levy to be charged on forwarded goods destined for the export market. The proceeds of the levy were passed to a French boatmen's co-operative. This fund was to be used for the commercial benefit of the entire trade and the running costs of the Fund. The agreement was anti-competitive since foreign carriers lost 10 per cent of their income; they were not compensated for this loss by getting new contracts. The new contracts would go to their French counterparts. The fund appeared *prima facie* to be an objective and non-discriminatory system designed to promote the industry, however, the main benefits were only passed to the domestic operators.

Rules of the trade association

The rules of the association do not need to be mandatory in order to invoke the prohibition of Article 81. Recommendations issued by the association will be defined as a 'decision by an association of undertakings' if the non-binding mandates 'constituted the faithful reflection of the applicant's resolve to co-ordinate the conduct of its members'.[4] Similarly, in the *Fenex* (Dutch Organisation for Logistics and Expeditions/Removals) Decision,[5] a Dutch freight association issued non-binding recommendations to its members. The Commission considered that the recommendation system was well established, the recommendations were updated annually and the circular that accompanied the publication of the recommendation was couched in exhortative language. Resolutions passed at meetings of the association may also fall within Article 81(1).

In Case 96/82 *IAZ International Belgium NV* v. *Commission*,[6] an association of undertakings involved in the water industry issued recommendations to its members to the effect that unauthorised appliances were not to be connected to the mains. Products could only gain authorisation through Belgian trade associations. This rule effectively foreclosed the Belgian market from competition, since the Belgian trade associations were minded to certify only national products.

In Case T–61/89 *Dansk Pelsdyravlerforening* (*Danish Fur Producers Association*) v. *Commission*,[7] the DFPA had over 5000 members. The members were subjected to a number of rules which restricted their freedom to contract. The members could not organise competing auctions or sell pelts independently in an emergency situation. The members had to sell pelts through the Association in the case of an emergency, such as an epidemic, in order to receive financial aid. Similarly, if a firm wanted to receive a subsidised loan, it had to agree to sell pelts only through the auction. The Commission considered that such rules had the effect of foreclosing the Danish market. The non-compete obligation, as regards auctions, prevented the member firms from competing with the Association. Similarly, the obligation to sell pelts only through the Association, in order to benefit from the insurance scheme, was not indispensable to that objective. Also, Danish producers accounted for 72 per cent of fur production in the EC and turnover was over €200 million, therefore the effect on trade would be appreciable.

The degree of influence over the national or regional market is essential for determining whether the trade association is acting illegally. If the trade association has the power to exclude potential members from the national or regional market, then it is likely that the activities of the association may be held to be anti-competitive.

In addition, both the written constitution of the association or the rules of the association *simpliciter* may violate Article 81.[8] The rules must also be proportionate to the aims of the association. If the rules go beyond what is strictly necessary in order for the association to fulfil its functions, then it is more likely that the rules will be adjudged anti-competitive.

Objectives of the association

In the EUDIM (European United Distributors of Installation Materials) Case,[9] EUDIM was an association of wholesalers of plumbing, heating and sanitary materials. The association's objectives were to promote European wholesaling through the exchange of know-how, information and purchasing data and combined purchasing and trading among members. The Commission found that the members of EUDIM had concluded a gentlemen's agreement. This agreement limited each member's rights to operate in another market other than their home market. The Commission found that there had been an exchange of confidential information relating to purchases on the sanitary market, but no exchange of information as regards selling prices. The exchange of information was held not to be anti-competitive since the information was general and non-confidential. In addition, the European sanitary market is covered by over 3000 wholesalers, thus the market is not oligopolistic. In fact, the market was highly fragmented and the information exchange would not have an appreciable effect on the sanitary wholesale market.

Case C-137/95 *SPO* v. *Commission*[10] the SPO (Association of Price Structuring Organisations in Building Undertakings) was set up by a number of Dutch building trade associations to 'promote and administer orderly competition, to prevent improper conduct in price tendering and to promote the formation of economically justified prices.' The Commission found that the Statutes and price-regulating rules of the SPO infringed Article 81(3) and could not be justified under 81(3). The second and third objectives of SPO could easily lead to anti-competitive action *per se*.

In the Case *Scottish Salmon Farmers' Marketing Board*,[11] the over-farming of salmon, particularly in Norway, had resulted in serious over-capacity in Europe, such that the price of salmon plummeted in the late 1980s and early 1990s. The Norwegians set a minimum price level for the price of their salmon. For such a system to work, it was vital that other salmon farmers respected the Norwegian minimum price set. Clearly, this agreement was an anti-competitive activity prohibited by Article 81.

Membership criteria

In Case T-206/99 *Metropole TV SA* v. *Commission*,[12] the European Broadcasting Union (EBU) was a non-profit-making association of radio and television organisations. Its objectives are to represent its members interests in the promotion of radio and television programme exchanges and other forms of co-operation. The Court of First Instance annulled the Commission's decision which rejected Metropole's allegations of anti-competitive activity by the EBU. The EBU operated a two-tier membership criteria, namely active membership and associate membership. Metropole was repeatedly rejected for membership of the EBU in either capacity. Other companies were admitted to the EBU and remained members of the EBU, even when they ceased to fulfil the membership criteria set by the Union. Thus, Metropole was excluded from the benefits of membership of the EBU in a discriminatory fashion.

Rules for conducting business

In Cases T–213/95 and T–18/96[13] the Court of First Instance upheld the Commission's decision that an agreement between crane operators and contractors for the rental of cranes in the Netherlands contravened Article 81 and did not qualify for exemption under 81(3). Both associations, the SCK (Crane Hire Certification Authority) and Federatie van Nederlandse Kraanverhuurbedrijven (FNK/Dutch Federation of Crane Hirers), were established to promote the interests of crane hirers. SCK established a certification system. Crane hirers who attained the requisite standards were permitted to join the association and in turn receive a certificate of quality. SCK members were directed to hire cranes from other SCK members only. FNK is an umbrella organisation for crane hirers in the Netherlands. FNK members, by virtue of its constitution, are commanded to hire cranes from other FNK members and should charge acceptable rates for the rental. In effect, non-SCK certified crane hirers were prevented from hiring cranes and the rate for hire was fixed by the association, even though the rate was only a recommended rate. The Court held that the cumulative effect of the two rules was to restrict new entrants from penetrating the crane hire market. The restrictions could not be justified under Article 81(3).

SCK is subject to the competition rules since SCK is a private law body, engaged in an economic activity. SCK charges a fee for the issuance of a certificate of compliance. SCK operated a closed system, since the association would not recognise certificates of compliance issued by similar associations. If the purpose of certification was to purportedly assure quality, then SCK should have accepted equivalent certification from other institutions. Additionally, the cost of obtaining membership of SCK for non-FNK firms was three times more expensive than for FNK members.

Rules for terminating membership

In the FRUBO (Dutch Fruit and Vegetable Importers Association) case,[14] the associations possessed the power to exclude importers or wholesalers from fruit auctions, if they violated the rules of the association. Thus, the terms of associations themselves may violate Article 81. The termination of membership prevented the importers from accessing fruit auctions and it was almost impossible for the excluded importers to import fruit other than through the auction. Thus, membership termination had serious consequences.

Exchanges of information

The most obvious example of anti-competitive activity that involves a trade association is an information exchange network. The collection of sensitive information and the subsequent dissemination and exchange of that information between competitors may produce anti-competitive effects. If sensitive price information is exchanged, it is likely that the Commission will be entitled to conclude that a concerted practice is in operation.[15]

In Case T-16/98, *Wirtschaftsvereinigung Stahl and Others* v. *Commission*[16] of 5th April 2001, the German steel industry trade association, and 16 of its members notified the Commission of an agreement on an information exchange system. The parties exchanged information concerning, the market shares held for each of the products by the producers on the German market and in the Community, data on deliveries by each producer, deliveries of steel on the national market by product according to qualities and by consumer industry and deliveries of certain qualities of steel by product in each of the member States. The Commission considered that the scheme violated Article 81. The Court of First Instance held that the Commission had erred as to the factual circumstances of the information exchange system. The information was not specific enough to empower the association and its members to calculate the market shares with any degree of accuracy. In such a situation, the decision had to be annulled. It ruled that

> It is apparent...that the Commission is of the opinion that the 'sensitive nature of the data is a fundamental factor in the assessment of the restrictive nature of an information exchange agreement, as is the fact that it reveals not only market position, but also the 'strategies of various individual competitors.[17]

In Cases T–34/92, 35/92 *Fiatagri UK, New Holland Ford and John Deere v. Commission*,[18] the Court held that an information exchange system between tractor manufacturers infringed Article 81 and could not be exempted under Article 81(3). The Agricultural Engineers Association (AEA) Limited operated an information exchange scheme in respect of tractors sold in the United Kingdom. Once a tractor has been sold, a vehicle registration form must be completed and sent to the UK Department of Transport. The form is highly detailed, containing information about the type and make of tractor, the serial number, dealer, location and identity of the purchaser. The AEA requested this information from the Department of Transport. Using this information, the AEA was able to produce a detailed database. This information enabled the participating members of the Association to identify parallel imports more easily. This transparency and openness would be welcomed in a healthily competitive open market with a large number of tractor manufacturers, however, in a tight oligopolistic market, dominated by a small number of manufacturers, this transparency can be destructive of competition. The price and customer destination of the tractors is freely available to all the competitors in the marketplace. Thus, the manufacturers are able to substitute the uncertainty of the market with parallelism *inter se*. The Court of First Instance found that

> general use, as between main suppliers of exchanges of precise information at short intervals, identifying registered vehicles and the place of their registration is, on a highly oligopolistic market . . . likely to impair considerably the competition which exists between traders since it has the effect of periodically revealing to all the competitors the market positions and strategies of the various individual competitors.[19]

> the more accurate and recent the information on quantities sold and market shares, the greater its impact on undertakings' future market behaviour.[20]

The options for an undertaking facing the threat of an information exchange are clear.

> Either the trader concerned does not become a member of the information exchange agreement and unlike its competitor, then forgoes the information exchanged and the market knowledge; or it becomes a member of the agreement and its business strategy is then immediately revealed to all its competitors by means of the information which they receive.[21]

The Commission is not against information exchange systems *per se*.[22] Statistical information is useful for improving a company's understanding of the market. If companies understand the market, then they are in a better position to compete effectively in that market. Historical information is unlikely to cause any competitive concerns, however, recent information about prices, deliveries and orders is likely to offend against Article 81, if the market is oligopolistic. Transparency is normally good for competition, however, in an oligopolistic market, such openness allows undertakings to co-ordinate their responses to market fluctuations to an unacceptable degree.

Most agreements that relate to individual companies will be anti-competitive since the information can be used by competitors to gauge their response to the activities of the rival. However, even information exchanges which are anonymous may violate Article 81 if the information exchange allows individual product import levels per Member State to be identified. The quality of the information, the specificity of the information, the currency of the information and the current state of the market are all factors that will be used to determine whether the agreement is lawful or anti-competitive. The more that a market resembles a close oligopoly, the less detailed the information exchange will need to be to induce or promote behavioural parallelism.

Classical anti-competitive collusive activity

In the *Cembureau* case,[23] the Commission found that there was an agreement between national cement trade associations and individual cement producers, to share the European market and to control the transhipment of cement between member States.[24]

In Cembureau, if a trade association has been involved in a collusive agreement, the Commission is entitled to fine either the undertakings which are members of that association or the association itself. If the Commission is minded to fine the association, the Commission is entitled to take into account, when assessing the level of fine to be applied, the turnover of the members of the association. In order to fine the association, the Commission must prove that the association's rules have the power to bind the members.[25]

Trade associations do not need to be involved in an independent commercial or economic activity, in order for Article 81 to apply. Article 81 applies to associations where its activities or the activities of its members are calculated to produce the results which Article 81 aims to suppress.[26]

If the Commission wishes to find an association liable, in conjunction with its members, the Commission is required to establish conduct on the part of the association, which is separate from that of its members.[27] In the present case, the Court held that the Commission had breached the requirements of procedural fairness in so far as the Commission's statement of objections did not set out the Commission's intention to fine nine associations of undertaking separately to their members.

State Aid

A trade association may take exception to the granting of State Aid by a Member State.[28] The State Aid will give competing undertakings in that Member State an unfair competitive advantage. A trade association may also consider that the State Aid was in actual event legitimate aid which has unlawfully been condemned by the Commission as illegal aid. In Case T-55/99 *Confederacion Española de Transporte de Mercancias* v. *Commission*,[29] the Spanish government adopted a scheme for subsidising the interest payment on loans granted for purchasing industrial vehicles or for leasing them with a view to purchase. The Commission had declared the system as illegal State aid. CETM brought an action to prevent the Commission from requiring the repayment of the illegal State Aid from its members. The Court held that the Commission was correct in holding that the aid was illegal aid. Conversely in the case T-613/97 *Union Française de l'Express (UFL)* v. *Commission*[30] the trade association UFL had complained that the French Post Office was providing logistical and commercial assistance to its subsidiary courier company. The Court of First Instance annulled the Commission Decision which found that the logistical and commercial assistance provided by La Poste to its subsidiary SFMI (French International Messaging Society) was State Aid.

Trade Associations as enforcers of competition law

Trade Associations may act as whistle blowers in the case of anti-competitive activity. Under Regulation 17/62, the Commission is the enforcement body of European competition law. The Commission will become aware of anti-competitive activities in one of three ways. The Commission may receive notifications from Member States, interested persons or it may undertake its own investigations.[31] In light of the increasing workload of the Commission both under competition law and its other obligations under the EC treaty, the Commission is becoming increasingly reliant upon interested persons and Member States to bring potential infractions of European competition law to its attention.[32] In Case T–308/94 *Cascades* v. *Commission*,[33] the British Printing Industries Federation (BPIF) lodged an informal complaint with the Commission, alleging the producers of cartonboard supplying the United Kingdom had introduced a series of simultaneous and uniform price increases.

See also Case T–95/99 *Satellimages TV5 SA* v. *Commission*,[34] where the trade association VPRT complained of Deutsche Telekom's methods of levying tariffs, since they appeared to discriminate between public and private satellite services.

The action for annulment and the action for failure to act

Under competition law, Article 3(2)(b) of Regulation 17/62 sets out that natural and legal persons are entitled to bring an action to terminate an infringement if they have a 'legitimate interest'. A trade association is entitled to bring an action for annulment of a Commission Decision under Article 230 of the EC Treaty. If a legal measure of the Commission affects the interests of the association itself or the interests of the members of the association, then the association will commence and action under Article 230. Under wider community law, the trade association will usually commence an action if it considers that the Commission has erred in law or in fact as to the competitive structure of the market. In Case 50/00 *Union de Pequeños Agricultores* (UPA) v. *Council*[35] 25th July 2002, UPA is a trade association which represents and acts in the interests of small Spanish agricultural businesses. The Association wished to annul Regulation 1638/98 which amended the original Regulation on the establishment of a common organisation of the markets in olive oil. Under Article 230 of the EC Treaty, a natural or legal person is entitled to bring an annulment action if the Regulation is, in fact, a disguised decision and the individual is directly and individually concerned, or indeed the measure is a legislative provision of general application which nevertheless has the effect of differentiating the person concerned from all other objectively identified class of person. The individual can only challenge the contested measure if the individual is differentiated from all other people affected by the measure. An association will only be able to challenge a measure in three circumstances:

- A legal provision expressly grants a series of procedural powers to trade associations

- The association represents the interests of undertakings which would, themselves, be entitled to bring proceedings[36]
- When the association is distinguished individually because its own interests as an association are affected, in particular because its negotiating position has been affected by the measure in question.[37]

Thus, the association will be entitled to take action on its own behalf or in order to protect the interests of its members.

In the instant case, the Court of Justice held that the association did not have *locus standi* to challenge the regulation since the association itself was not differentiated from any other undertaking affected by the measure. Similarly, none of the association's members were differentiated from other affected undertakings.

However, in the case T-177/01, *Jego Quere et CIA SA* v. *Commission*[38] of the 3rd May 2002, the Court of First Instance held that

> there is no compelling reason to read into the notion of individual concern, within the meaning of the fourth paragraph of Article 230, a requirement that an individual applicant seeking to challenge a general measure must be differentiated from all others affected by it in the same way as an addressee.[39]

> In those circumstances...the strict interpretation...of the notion of a person individually concerned...must be reconsidered.[40]

> In the light of the foregoing, and in order to ensure effective judicial protection for individuals, a natural or legal person is to be regarded as individually concerned by a Community measure of general application that concerns him directly if the measure in question affects his legal position, in a manner which is both definite and immediate, by restricting his rights or by imposing obligations on him. The number and position of other persons who are likewise affected by the measure, or who may be so, are of no relevance in that regard.[41]

This judgment improves the legal standing of non-privileged applicants under Article 230 by reinterpreting the definition of direct and individual concern as established under the case-law of the Court.

However, the Court of Justice judgment in *Union de Pequeños Agricultores* denied such a liberal interpretation of Article 230(4). In the hierarchy of norms of the Community legal system, Court of Justice decisions are to be preferred over decisions of the Court of First Instance.

The Advocate General in the *Union* case had proposed a relaxation of the test for individual and direct concern. Advocate General Jacobs had suggested a new interpretation of individual concern to the effect that an individual 'should be regarded as individually concerned...where, by reason of his particular circumstances, the measure has, or is liable to have, a substantial adverse effect on his interests.'

Unfortunately, the Court of Justice did not follow the Advocate General's Opinion. The Court was of the view that any change to the test for individual concern should be initiated by the Member States at an Inter-Governmental Conference.

It is likely that the liberal judgement of *Jego* may be appealed to the Court of Justice in the near future. However, the pressure to either reform the judicial interpretation of the test for individual concern or introduce a new fourth paragraph of Article 230 at an Inter-Governmental Conference is extremely strong. Trade associations already play a major role in the Action for Annulment procedure. Indications are that the future direction of Article 230 will be towards further liberalisation of the test for individual concern.

Under Article 232, a trade association may institute an action against an institution of the European Community for a failure to act. In contradistinction to Article 230, where the association will be representing the members of the association who are allegedly acting in an anti-competitive manner, under Article 232, the trade association will be representing undertakings which are negatively affected by the anti-competitive actions of other undertakings in the market. It must be noted, however, that the specific test for standing in relation to competition actions is more liberal than the general test applicable under Article 230.[42]

Conclusion

In summation, trade associations play a pivotal role in the European Union system of competition. The trade association may co-ordinate and facilitate the anti-competitive behaviour of its members. The constitution of the association itself may offend against competition law. The recommendations of the association, the collation of statistical information and dissemination of that information concerning the market may all produce anti-competitive effects on the market. A trade association is typically employed to promote the economic sector it represents. The trade association may adopt a short-term perspective to this objective. Protectionist policies may bring short-term relief from the full rigours of a competitive market, however in the long term, all European industry sectors must reform and rationalise in order to compete effectively on global markets.

Fundamental reform of the industry, which makes the sector competitive, is in the long-term interests of that sector. If a trade association is committed to such reform and competitive ideology, the association may act as a useful pre-warning system for the health of the industry it represents. It may identify anti-competitive behaviour on the market. The trade association may inform the Commission of anti-competitive action. The Commission may then decide to initiate enforcement action under Regulation 17/62, or in the case of State activity, initiate the enforcement action under Article 226. In light of the Commission's objective of decentralising the enforcement of competition law, the role of the trade association as an early warning mechanism for detecting anti-competitive activity becomes indispensable. The Commission will then be in a position to concentrate upon major infractions of competition law that are of Community significance. Additionally, the trade association may initiate an action for annulment under Article 230 of the EC Treaty. Presently, the trade association is only entitled to bring an action for annulment where a legal measure expressly grants the association a procedural power, the contested measure affects its specific interests or the contested measure affects the interests of the members of the association. The criteria for establishing direct and individual concern are likely to be relaxed in the future, thus further empowering trade associations in their review power. In a parallel development, the strengthening of the internal market has also resulted in a greater role for the European trade associations in improving the global competitiveness of European industry. Trade associations will continue to play a central role in competition law and policy in the twenty-first century. The question is whether the activities of the trade associations will be anti-competitive or pro-competitive.

Notes

1   Article 81(3) provides that collusive activity may be exempted if four criteria are satisfied, namely the collusive activity 'contributes to improving the production or distribution of goods or to promoting technical or economic progress, while allowing consumers a fair share of the resulting benefit, and which does not (a) impose on the undertakings concerned restrictions which are not indispensable to the attainment of these objectives; (b) afford such undertakings the possibility of eliminating competition in respect of a substantial part of the products in question'.

2   *Roofing Felt* 86/399, OJ L 232/15.

3   [1988] 4 CMLR 677.

4   Case 45/85 *Verband der Sachversicherer* v. *Commission* [1988] 4 CMLR 264.

5   96/438 (1996) OJ L181/28.

6   [1983] ECR 3369.

7   [1992] ECR II-1931.

8   *National Sulphuric Acid Association* 80/917 (1980) OJ L260/24.

9   EUDIM Re 1996 OJ C111/8.

10 [1996] ECR I-1611.

11 [1992] OJ L246/1.

12 [2001] ECR II-3177.

13 *Stichting Certificatie Kraanhuurbedrijf SCK* v. *Commission* [1997] CEC 1324.

14 Case 71/74 FRUBO [1975] ECR 563.

15 Cases 40–48, 50, 54–5, 111, 113–4/73 *Suiker Unie* v. *Commission* [1975] ECR 1663.

16 [2001] 5 CMLR 9.

17 *Ibid.*, at p. 39. See also the *UK Tractors Decision* 92/157/EEC of 17 February 1992 OJ 1992 L 68 at p.19, 'an agreement to exchange information which is both sensitive, recent and individualised in a concentrated market where there are important barriers to entry, is liable to restrict competition'.

18 [1994] ECR II-905.

19 As quoted by the Court of First Instance in the Case T-16/98, *Wirtschaftsvereinigung Stahl and Others* v. *Commission* of 5 April 2001 at para. 38.

20 *Ibid.*

21 *John Deere Limited* v. *Commission* [1998] 5 CMLR 311 at para. 93.

22 *Op. cit.*, No. 19 at para. 44. 'As is apparent both from the case-law and the practice followed by the Commission in adopting decisions, information exchange agreements are not generally prohibited automatically but only if they have certain characteristics relating, in particular, to the sensitive and accurate nature of recent data exchanged at short intervals.'

23 Cases T-25/95 to 87/95 *Cimenteries* v. *Commission* [2000] 5 CMLR 204.

24 'circulation of price lists and other price information reinforced the general agreement on non-transhipment to home markets. Exchanges of information on production capacity, output, sales and prices on home and export markets were an autonomous infringement, because they created a system of solidarity and reciprocal influences designed to achieve co-ordination of economic activities.'

25 *Ibid.*, at p. 485.

26 *Ibid.*, at p. 1320.

27 *Ibid.*, at pp. 1325 and 2622.

28 See Case 169/84 *COFAZ SA* v. *Commission* [1986] ECR 391.

29 [2000] E.C.R. II-3207.

30 [2000] ECR II-4055.

31 Article 3(2)(b), Regulation 17/62.

32 See Regulation 1/03 which will replace Regulation 17/62 on the 1st May 2004. This regulation decentralises the system of European competition law enforcement. National competition authorities and national courts will be the primary enforcers of competition policy within the EU.

33 [1995] ECR II-265.

34 [2002] 4 CMLR 35.

35   [2002] 3 CMLR 1.
36   Cases C 282/85 *DEFI* v. *Commission* [1986] ECR 2469 and C-6/92 *Federmineraria* v. *Commission* [1993] ECR I-6357.
37   Cases C-313/90 *CIRFS* v. *Commission* [1993] ECR I-1125 and T-380/94 *AIUFFASS and AKT* v. *Commission* [1996] ECR II-2169.
38   [2002] 2 CMLR 44.
39   *Ibid.*, at p. 49.
40   *Ibid.*, at p. 50.
41   *Ibid.*, at p. 51.
42   See Case 26/76 *Metro* v. *Commission* [1977] ECR 1875. Note that the standing requirements under Article 3(2)(b) of Regulation will be replaced by Article 7(2) of Regulation 1/03. The substantive terms of the standing requirement will be unaffected by the changes.

Part III

Sectoral Characteristics

7

Primary, Concentrated and Regulated Sectors: Steel

David Rea

Having been a precursor to the European Union (EU), via the 1952 European Coal and Steel Community Treaty, the steel industry has 50 years experience of significant inter-relations between national and supranational authorities, and the development of relevant representative structures. Steel is gradually becoming 'normal', which may be hard to believe when one considers what the United States steel lobby has done in precipitating a trade war with their section 201 actions, but it is true. Steel companies are consolidating across the world; state holdings have drastically reduced; the interventionist measures of the ECSC Treaty are behind us, having expired in 2002; and trade associations are reverting to their normal functions.

In my view, the most important premise here is that an industry producing a key strategic material cannot have a completely 'normal' relationship with government. However much privatisation is achieved, there will always be special features, advantages and disadvantages, that its representational organisations will have to deal with. As national sovereignty migrates to larger blocks such as the EU, so too must the representational sovereignty of trade associations, and along with that, the resources in terms of member company time, and money, needed to make these bodies effective. Similarly, as companies globalise away from single nation status they must adapt their lobbying methods – we in trade associations need to be bold in driving that forward.

Steel has for many years had a comprehensive representation structure covering the global, EU and national levels. What is changing is the balance of resources within this structure. This process of change must be ahead of the curve of European and global integration, if the lobbying capability is to achieve that which is important to the companies. National associations are slimming down, whilst larger

Table 7.1 Global steel consumption of finished steel products

	2000	2001	2002	2003	average % change per annum
CHINA	141	170	182	190	11.5%
CIS	30	32	33	34	4.9%
SOUTH AMERICA	27	28	29	30	3.5%
AFRICA	15	15	15	16	2.8%
MIDDLE EAST	16	17	17	17	1.5%
EUROPE *excl EU*	36	34	36	37	1.1%
EU15	145	142	140	145	0%
ASIA *(excl CHINA)*	204	199	200	203	−0.3%
NAFTA	146	131	132	138	−1.9%
WORLD	760	768	784	811	2.2%
WORLD *excl CHINA*	619	598	602	621	0.1%

Source: IISI, Spring 2002 (Iron and Steel Statistics Bureau)

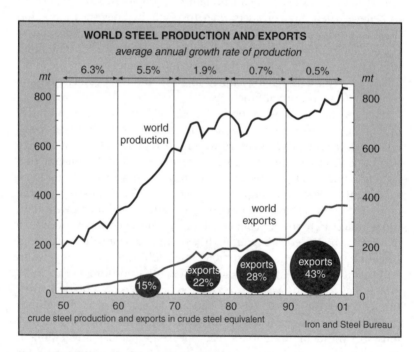

Figure 7.1 Steel production and exports
Source: Iron and Steel Statistics Bureau, with permission

associations spanning continents are coming to the fore, not before time, as world steel consumption (see Table 7.1) and steel trade (see Figure 7.1) increases.

The way the European steel sector is evolving amongst the institutions of the Union and within the global agenda for steel exemplifies the 'undiscovered country' of industry in the globalised world, where the nation state is slowly being eclipsed by nascent regional and global identities. UK Steel is a member of Eurofer, the European Confederation of Iron and Steel Industries, and both in turn are also members of the International Iron and Steel Institute (IISI). Each organisation represents a level at which interests can be pursued, nationally, regionally and globally. Eurofer and the IISI have similar core budgets and staff levels, but relative to the number of companies represented (20 to the IISI's 160, a 1 to 8 ratio not reflected in the staff levels – see Figure 7.2 and Figure 7.3), Eurofer is the organisation with the heavier and more focused work remit. The activities of the EU institutions drive a lot of its work programme.

Global organisation

Although the current trend is towards companies vesting resources in regional trade associations, representation at a global level is increasing in importance. Every October, the plenary conference of the IISI meets to discuss global level issues. Not constituted to take executive decisions applicable outside the affairs of the Institute itself, the Conference

```
                          IISI
            (International Iron and Steel Institute)

    ▪  160 member companies (60% of global output)
    ▪  50 regional and national associations
    ▪  27 staff
    ▪  Core budjet €5.5 m
    ▪  Opt-in programmes €10 m

            – global policy issues
              – trade (WTO)
              – environment
            – market development inc R & D
            – image promotion
            – information
```

Figure 7.2   The International Iron and Steel Institute
Source: Iron and Steel Statistics Bureau, with permission

EUROFER
(European Confederation of Iron and Steel Industries)

- 15 largest steel companies (+ 5 Turkish producers)
- 12 EU national associations + 6 Eastern European associations
- 21 staff
- Core budjet Euro 3.5m
    - formal representational role with EU institutions
    - market intelligence and economic forecasts
    - EU policy issues, particularly trade
    - environment
    - technical and e-business
    - opt-in image promotion

Figure 7.3   The European Confederation of Iron and Steel Industries

nevertheless provides a powerful means for driving image campaigns, technical development projects and global data analysis. Steel has long understood the term globalisation, and in its more refined (and recent) form, 'glocalisation', where local perceptions of global issues interact with global attempts to effect local change. Environmental issues such as climate change and sustainability are the most obvious candidates for transcendence of national or regional borders, jurisdictions or nationalities. As such, the IISI has important working groups and policy forums on the environment, life cycle assessment and climate change.

European organisation

Eurofer's membership reflects the progress of the European experiment and indicates that nineteenth and twentieth century idioms of nation state, government regulation and industrial accountability become less applicable in the context of regional or global economic discourse. Eurofer, for instance, has eighteen national associations on its books, along with large companies such as Corus, who are also direct members of UK Steel and the IISI. For its companies, Eurofer and UK Steel may also provide analysis at different levels of the same category of information, such as market analysis and economic forecasts, or lobbying on the same issues such as the environment, sometimes creating circular relationships, where there may be representatives from a national trade association and a company holding membership of that association sitting together on a committee in Eurofer. The scope for rationalisation is growing rapidly.

UK organisation

At all levels of representation, the steel sector is relatively consolidated as far as trade associations are concerned because it is subject to forces that tend to work against fragmentation of representation. The British sector especially was subject to nationalisation, with the 14 largest steel companies in 1967 being brought under public ownership under the Iron and Steel act of that year. The remaining 147 companies, representing about 15 per cent of the sector's production, came together to form the British Independent Steel Producers Association (BISPA), with many remaining smaller associations putting themselves under its name; BISPA subsequently evolved into UK Steel, receiving back into membership British Steel plc (now Corus) for whom the membership of a thoroughly private sector organisation helped enhance its new, privatised status. The threat of nationalisation, overregulation or some other significant, usually external, threat clearly helps the unity of the organisation.

A single, clear voice for the steel industry also makes for strong participation by companies in trade association work. Some related sectors of the UK economy have a more diverse structure, such as those supplying to the railway industry. Metal forming companies have a choice between a range of specialist product associations *and* the railway industry association, not to mention the CBI, various regional chambers of commerce and other non-sector specific modes of representation. This all dilutes company involvement in trade association work, with a plethora of ways they can deploy a very finite amount of resources, and the competition for them is not always helpful.

Key issues – international trade

The complete dynamics, whereby large, international steel companies can seek solutions to their problems through a variety of routes is evident both in the representative structure outlined above and in events themselves. Furthermore, as a vast steel industry in China evolves, as usual with 'developing' countries, exports are running well below the demand levels of the domestic industry. It will be fascinating to observe its trade practices evolve. Abiding by WTO rules may well run contrary to the ethos of communism, and in such a huge country where the system is so powerfully entrenched the conflict of ideas in the short term would be won by the incumbent, in this case communist, paradigm. Such a victory would make it probable that government intervention in the industry would drive it towards accusations of uncompetitive practices.

The products of the steel industry were 'global' long before their producers and the representatives of those producers even started to approach such a progressive classification. Steel is internationally traded in a big way (see Figure 7.4) and when one looks at how representative bodies can relate to national, regional or transnational authorities, it should never be forgotten, even amongst the excitement about the US steel lobby and section 201, that steel was a key economic element in the Cold War, both in confronting the operations of COMECON and in the subsequent collapse of communism. Having gone beyond the 1990s and the cashing in of the 'peace dividend', the emphasis is now on the war on terrorism and weapons of mass destruction – governments and their agencies remain keenly interested where certain grades of steel are produced and to whom they are delivered. Big companies need relationships with governments that transcend economics, due to the global security implications of the possible nuclear and aerospace applications of their products. Informal checks and balances that apply to companies whose activities are all played out within the borders of a single state do not apply so simply to multi-nationals. Boardrooms that maintain informal links with intelligence

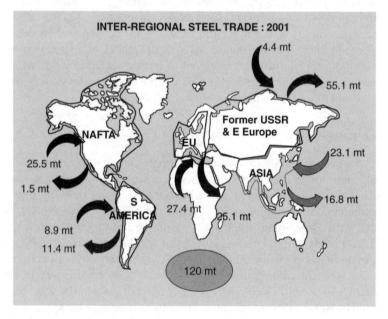

Figure 7.4 Inter-regional steel trade 2001
Source: Iron and Steel Statistics Bureau

services must find different ways of sounding out governments about the security implications of certain products, and their export to certain countries. Inevitably, the role for international trade associations in mediating interests dictated by international agreements and institutions that transcend a national level is not obvious, but the issue remains a live one.

Then we need to look at the changing structure of the industry as it follows, for example, the global automotive and aerospace industries. Flurries of change like the two weeks in April 2002 make us think it's all happening at once (see Figure 7.5). But overall the pace of change is relatively modest. In 1992 about 90 per cent of global vehicle production came from 20 automotive companies whilst the 20 biggest steel producers made 32 per cent of steel output; today it is nine automotive companies that make 90 per cent of vehicles, whilst the top nine steel producers have 26 per cent of world steel output. Nevertheless, fewer and bigger steel producers will lead inexorably to fewer – though not necessarily larger – steel representative bodies.

Two weeks in the Life of the Steel Industry: April 2002

Steel sector structural announcements

– Canada's Selco and Japan's Kawasaki Steel – long term collaboration on automative sheet + large pipes + process technology.
'Improve auto penetration and build KSC in USA'
– Nippon Steel and Thyssen Krupp – electrical steel collaboration 'expand 30 years of cooperation into more comprehensive collaboration'

– Nippon and Arcelor of Europe and Tata Steel of India – automotive steel technology agreemnet 'focus on Indian market'

– Thyssen Krupp and NKK and Kawasaki – technology cooperation on automotive sheet (ahead of Kawasaki & NKK merger in October to produce Japan's largest steelmaker)

Figure 7.5 Two weeks in the life of the steel industry

Key issues – energy

One aspect that is often overlooked in accounts of the steel industry's changing lobbying activities is the energy intensive nature of the steel industry. It is a huge consumer and generator and recycler. So it is a significant player in the environment and CO^2 emissions debate. Hence at every level steel has to play an energetic role in market regulations and lobbying. There is a seriously competitive issue, for example, between the UK and EU energy markets, and in the relative differences in the treatment of climate change levies. So long as national markets and national sovereignty remain in some respects, then steel associations have to provide resources and focus efforts on the specific national regulators and the relevant legislative foundation. But the medium term change is already obvious – EU markets and EU regulation. In the longer term, if we ever get an effective single market for energy in the EU, and a common structure for penalties and incentives for greenhouse gas emissions, will the focus then move on to exerting EU influence on Eastern European markets and producers? Or further afield as changes in technology facilitates geo-political changes?

Areas like energy are such that it is more productive for consumers to lobby on a cross-sectoral basis, which is another challenge as far as trade associations are concerned, particularly in terms of how they relate to companies and decision makers. In the UK the Energy Intensive Users Group (EIUG) is an established example of such a cross-sectoral organisation, representing about a dozen sectors, including glass, steel, cement, paper and ceramics. These kinds of industries tend to have similar concerns as far as energy is concerned; it is a large part of the production cost, and it is possible to influence regulators through unified lobbying. Sometimes interests are divergent on issues like the UK Climate Change Levy or UK/EU emissions trading proposals, but this is not necessarily a bad thing. Core principles, though, remain more or less the same. Trade associations and companies benefit from the economies of scale and the Government prefers unified representation of converging interests because there is only one (better resourced) entity to deal with.

Of course there is also the supra-national level of representation of these interests, which takes the form of the International Federation of Industrial Energy Consumers (IFIEC), of which EIUG is a member. IFIEC has on its books members from the EU15, plus recently, its statutes have been modified to allow membership of energy intensive users' representational bodies from EU accession states, bringing it into line which such bodies as Eurofer. However, only the Hungarian energy intensive users' representative body has joined so far. IFIEC therefore represents companies that account for 70 per cent of industrial energy consumption in Europe. IFIEC also is involved at a world level, having made representations at the Rio earth summit in 1992, putting forward an industrial energy consumer view, and monitoring energy matters at Johannesburg earth summit in 2002.

Key issues – production capacity

One aspect that is never overlooked with steel is overcapacity (see Figure 7.6). Again there is a significant government influence which affects the priorities for change. Mostly, it is because of the social costs or political consequences that, if badly managed, or sudden and unforeseen, the realignment of a high profile industry is sure to have. Look again at the example of the United States. Concerns regarding healthcare legacy costs, housing, pensions and marginal states in the 2002 mid-term elections (where the Bush administration felt itself vulnerable to swings against the Republican constituency) were foremost in the minds of decision makers in Washington. Of course, an interesting indicator of the extent to which the shift in power from the national to the European level has taken place is the unity that Eurofer could present to the United States, during a complicated negotiating procedure, including exemptions from the section 201 import protection measures. Although stressed, the front has remained united. With a significant injection of resources, Eurofer has risen to the challenge to combat the US measures, hiring lawyers in the US, monitoring and challenging the US evidence and deploying the manpower to follow the vast amounts of paper involved.

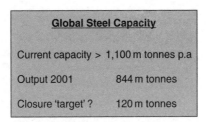

Figure 7.6   Global steel capacity

Major representational changes in UK Steel

In a world where the battles for members' interests are increasingly fought at a higher level, with the available resources migrating to international corporations and international trade associations, UK Steel has adopted a radical strategy aimed at strengthening a manufacturing voice in the UK. The association merged in 2002 with the Engineering Employers Federation, providing a platform from which the steel industry can fight its corner more securely in the medium term. Manufacturing industry as a whole can only benefit from a lobbying group that speaks with one strong voice to the UK government and the institutions of the EU.

So far, the response from UK Steel member companies has been excellent. Pure steel issues continue to be dealt with by a group of highly qualified professional staff operating as a steel division within the EEF. The plan has involved a full merger – liquidation of reserves, integration of staff, relocation to EEF offices. Overlaps, such as general economic lobbying, the maintenance of political contacts and briefings, and the pursuit of cross-sectoral manufacturing issues have been removed. Integrating administration, accounts, pensions, and so on, has dramatically reduced 'back office' expenses, as have accommodation costs. This all means a net reduction in the levies charged to companies in the order of 25 per cent, with much more in some cases. The resulting organisation has the power and the weight to improve steel representational performance whilst we contribute to its breadth of sector coverage.

I could not begin to offer any forecast as to how far other UK trade associations will follow this route, and how far it may also contribute to the changing use of resources though the European and global steel chain. I sincerely hope it does, because the process of change does need to be radically accelerated.

8
Textiles

Michiel Scheffer

Once, when asked to address the annual conference of Euratex, the European Apparel and Textile Association, Sir Leon Brittan stated: 'the textile industry is a normal industry'. This was a shock for the audience; they were not ready to accept this statement, embedded as they were in a special trade regime, the Multifibre Agreement, a system of quantitative limitations being an exception to GATT/WTO rules (Blokker, 1989; Scheffer, 1992).

The statement of Sir Leon now holds true, as from 1994 the industry had to adapt to the gradual phasing out of the international trade in textiles in the general WTO rules (to be completed by 2005). This meant the end of a specific and complex set of regulations. This required a review of the policy agenda of the industry and its representatives both at the regional/national level and the international level. Normality means the departure from a focus on sectoral policies to monitoring and influencing the impact of horizontal policy making.

EURATEX, the European Textile and Apparel Organisation asked us (IFM/Cadmeia, 2000) to examine the impact of the changing context of the industry for the agenda, the methods and the organisation of the European representation. The study entailed an analysis of the dynamics of the industry, a validation of the main trends by key players in the industry and a confrontation with the European main policy projects. This analysis led to the identification of convergence and divergence between the priorities of the industry and the priorities of the European Union.

These changes must be implemented in a complex associative structure. This is partly the reflection of a fragmented industry that is dominated by SMEs. It is also the consequence of a segmentation by fibre, by stage of processing, and by end-use. This industry is also concentrated in certain regions and has at the national level a tradition of strong organisation. Under pressure of industry restructuring, the associative structure is itself in a phase of consolidation and re-examination of its mission, role and means.

In this chapter I reflect on the mission of repositioning an industry that has to face a changing competitive environment where the focus shifts from defensive regulation to fostering competitiveness through innovation. This implies a redesign of structure, organisation and culture, but also involves changing the roles of associations at European and national levels. This may conflict with the demands and expectations of companies. I introduce a portfolio model to analyse the priorities of associations and a helicon model to analyse their roles (Figure 8.2).

The textile/apparel industry and its political context[1]

The textile industry is one of the largest industrial sectors in the European Union (Stengg, 2001). More than 120,000 companies employ altogether around 2 million people. It is an industry that is constantly being restructured, losing year on year between 2 and 4 per cent of companies and employment. The stable level of turnover reflects the growing delocalisation of production, growth in productivity and shift to higher value added products. It is also a fragmented industry with a dominance of SMEs and only a few medium and larger size firms. It is also fragmented in stage of processing, fibre and end-use. It produces goods for mass consumption but also highly fashionable items or very technical products. It combines a somehow dull and traditional image with a glossy and glamorous side with high-tech applications and dedicated craftmanship.

This fragmented industry is also a globalised industry. Since the end of the 1960s the industry has been faced with growing competition from developing countries, fuelled partly by buying and sourcing policies of retailers, traders and, from the 1980s onwards, manufacturers themselves. Global competition has been the reason why the industry in industrialised countries has advocated a specific regime of protection. The European associations have been the protagonists of a system of managed trade known as the Multifibre Arrangement. This system of quotas, over the period of 1972–94, became progressively sophisticated in coverage and management, as well as copied to the trade with preferential countries. Besides this specific trade policy tool, the industry had obtained specific origin rules, maintained a higher tariff protection and benefited from a dedicated sectoral industrial policy.

The second half of the 1980s led to a change of climate. The continuation of the Multifibre Agreement was no longer maintainable in the

Uruguay Round. The opening up of the Eastern Bloc and the policy of fostering stability in the Mediterranean Rim was also not compatible with the prolongation of specific trade barriers in textile products. The 1990s have thus seen a shift to a policy agenda aimed at liberalisation of trade, both in a multilateral and in a preferential framework. At the same time, specific sectoral policies fostering readjustment were brought into line with horizontal policies, both at the European and the national level.

The change in political environment was by no means easy to accept for the industry. Large parts of the industry remained emotionally attached to a protective policy agenda. The industry had organised its lobbying along sectoral lines and was accustomed to specific grant schemes and had little insight in horizontal policies. Last but not least, firms had little inclination, resources or skills to enter into innovation projects. Until the end of the 1990s the industry had a poor track record in getting funding for innovation projects.

Our hypothesis was that there was a major mismatch between the political priorities of the textile industry and the priorities of the public policy makers. This mismatch led textile opinion leaders to state that the 'industry was sacrificed by policy makers'. At the same time, the industry was not optimising support it could get to speed up innovation or getting export market access in third world countries. More innovative forces within the industry were disappointed about the support they could get from Brussels.

A difficult merger between the textile organisation and the clothing association led to a critical assessment of the future of EURATEX. The association seems to be divided along geographical lines 'north versus south' sectoral lines and between more liberal and interventionist forces. In this climate, national associations were less and less inclined to fund an expensive and complex European associative system, as they had to face declining revenues from a downsizing industry.

Matches and mismatches in industry/public policy

The study of matches and mismatches aimed at identifying the major points of consensus and major policy gaps between the industry and the public arena. The identification of these matches and mismatches could then enable the European Association to highlight its core missions and to map areas of dissent. It could also define subjects enabling positive coalitions with policy makers as well as zones of disagreement requiring more robust public relation efforts. Last but not least it could lead to a reconsideration of the internal organisation and the relations with national associations and companies.

In order to study the match or mismatch between the industry's expectations and the political arena, a questionnaire was sent out to some 100 leading companies in the industry. This questionnaire was based on key trends in the industry as identified in studies, trade press and annual reports of trade associations. The identification of key themes in the public arena was based on analysis of policy documents and interviews with key civil servants within the European Commission and Member States.

At the European level, a major shift was identified from negative integration policy areas to positive integration areas. This is also linked to the completion of the internal market and the conclusion of a fairly comprehensive external trade policy. Trade is more and more linked to sustainable development (trade and environment as well as trade and social responsibility). The attention of the European Union goes mainly to the realisation of the Monetary Union, and linked to it, harmonisation of taxation. Sectoral industrial policy is replaced by a more robust innovation policy. Moreover, the European Union tries to play a more visible role in environment, health and safety. Last but not least: enlargement is a major ambition of the European Union.

The companies showed from the interviews a double interest. As far as the European level was concerned, they had a major interest in the basics of the European Union: trade policy and, by some distance, the internal market. In external policy, most companies showed great interest in a defensive trade policy based largely on tariffs and quotas, preferential origin rules and strict application of trade policy instruments, and in particular anti-dumping. Some contrast was visible between textile and clothing and between Northern and Southern Europe, but less than expected. On the internal level, companies were attached to enhancing trading possibilities within the Union while at the same time wishing a stronger anti-trust policy to avoid concentrations at the upstream and downstream end of the pipe-line.

Companies were also interested in fostering creativity and innovation as well as developing human resources, but saw this primarily as a company responsibility or a national task. So the dilemma was that the European association had a natural role to play in a defensive and declining policy area while it was allocated a marginal role in growing policy areas of interest to companies. Enlargement was seen as a remote issue while environment, health and safety were perceived as purely technical matters.

Despite differences, a clear matrix of policy projects could be identified as well as envisaging the possible roles of the European association

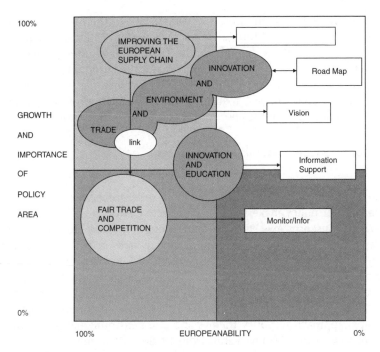

Figure 8.1   Policy mix and Euratex role

(Figure 8.1). In the lower-left corner were the issues of relevance to companies but with limited political interest. However, as the legitimacy and credibility of the European association for companies were based on classic trade policy instruments the associations had a role to play but in a more passive way: monitor, inform and advocate positions. It was advised to invest more heavily in the more pro-active issues such as the opening up of third world markets and linking trade to environment. At the same time, the environment, health and safety cluster could be linked to a more responsive and caring image and linked to innovation. Environment was seen as a broader issue enabling a repositioning of several policy approaches. A more active lobbying approach was recommended and also a positive partnership with the Commission.

It was advised to expand the approach to enlargement from a set of technical questions in the *acquis communautaire* to a more ambitious industrial policy vision based on a Euro–Mediterranean zone of exchange, able to compete with the Far East and the Americas. The concept of enlargement could be linked to the organisation of an effective

European supply chain and also create a link to the internal market, environment, health and safety as well as innovation through the involvement of the structural funds. Thus, innovation was linked to R&D and somehow to human resources and the European Social Fund. The role in these topics as more that of co-ordinator, as the focus was on the development of a road map, the co-ordination of projects and the matchmaking and support of consortia in practical projects.

Reforming work methods and structures

The main conclusion from the matrix was that EURATEX had to develop a more comprehensive policy in order to be seen as a relevant partner for policy makers and as an effective advocate of the industry. Where consensus existed, both dimensions coincided. However, many gaps could be closed by re-labelling policy areas or by linking policy areas. If this exercise could be effected while demonstrating that EURATEX could also play a role as a force of progress and being able to pre-empt needs of firms, a successful repositioning could be possible.

This is by no means a simple task as it requires a more coherent and global approach to policy themes and a less instrumental or technical approach. It may lead to a shift from single issue to multi-issue lobbying as well as from sectoral lobbying to horizontal lobbying. This could also lead to a changing relationship with the textiles unit in DG Enterprise. From sole point of entry this unit should become the agent of the industry within the services of the Commission. Last but not least, the industry had not only to position itself in policy issues but also in project funding. Projects help to strengthen the pro-active position of the industry and enable the creation of coalitions between forces of progress (van Schendelen, 1994).

In the internal organisation, the structure of too many commissions and task forces, often favouring a technical approach to subjects, had to be replaced by a structure assuring a more comprehensive approach to broad subjects. This has to be accompanied by clear mandates and review of work done by subcommissions. These had, in the past, the habit of reconsidering their mandate and developing their own agenda. A mandate and review body were established, made up of the Directors-General of the association or the European affairs spokespersons at the national associative level. The major focus in reviewing the commission structure is to enhance the vision of industrial policy, invest in vision-building on the environment and bring more coherence in research and development.

The burden of horizontal lobbying should not be underestimated. A stakeholder analysis demonstrated no less than 60 units relevant to the textile industry, from several units in the DG Environment to several units in the DG Enlargement or in the DG Information Society. This was a marked departure from the old situation when one unit in DG Enterprise was relevant and a limited number of units in trade policy and innovation/research policy. Moreover, the voice of textiles is only one of many in horizontal lobbying. An approach of creating alliances should then be considered, allowing for increased political weight and the mutual sharing of resources.

Understanding the associative division of labour

The review of the mission of EURATEX had the consequence of reviewing the relations with national and sectoral associations. The repositioning of EURATEX was a starting point for restructuring the sectoral representation of the industry. A stronger European voice led to the downsizing of national contribution to branch industry associations. While in 1995 six branch associations (fibre/process) had a full-time office, by 2002 this was reduced to two associations. However, simultaneously two countries had established their own lobbying bureau in Brussels with two more countries considering such a move and many countries cultivating direct links with the Commission or indirect links through the permanent representations.

EURATEX had to regain the lead in lobbying at the European level. This should be done not by counteracting national lobbying but by promoting synergies between national and European efforts. In another direction, a more robust role of EURATEX in setting up European projects should not conflict with national ambitions. This went even further in another area as privileged access to European information could be used in setting up a direct information service to companies (INFOTEX), bypassing through the internet the national associations.

A helicon model (Figure 8.2) enabled clarification of the roles of associations and distinction between the local/regional, national and European level. The helicon model, initially developed by Ernst & Young but further refined by us, enabled us to examine the basic associative functions and their synergies. We distinguish four functions:

- Strategic positioning of the interest of the industry through lobbying/public relations – the unique selling point of associations. Compared to private service providers (accountants, consultants)

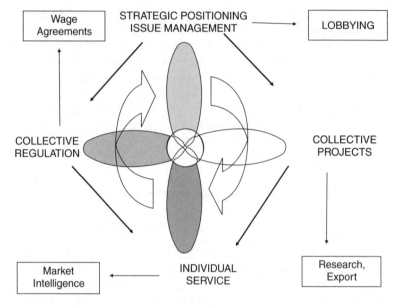

Figure 8.2 The virtuous associative helicon

associations have a quasi-monopoly or natural legitimacy on defending the industry's interest as long as its position is unchallenged.

- Collective regulation is relevant when an association can negotiate agreements with third parties or establish standards with a binding effect for members (such as collective wage agreements). Collective regulation can be a strong driver of membership, rally the members around collective processes and provide a captive access to funding (social levies).

- Collective projects refers to the point at which the critical mass of membership enables associations to set up projects using the synergies or convergence of interest between firms. While this is in research, training or in export promotion, collective projects can enhance the cohesion of the membership and provide sources of revenue.

- Individual service exploits the intellectual capital of the association, especially in regulatory/political insight and helps in maximising the trust of members. In-depth contacts with members also gives a better understanding of the industry to association executives and offers more depth in lobbying. Last but not least, individual service offers the possibility of extra revenue.

The combination of the four elements allows what we call a 'virtuous helicon' as the combination of four functions create synergies. These synergies arise: in the coverage of membership; as members may get a full service; in more depth in strategic positioning as a broad service deepens the contacts between association executives; in offering more opportunities in networking amongst members and thus strengthening the cohesion of the members; and in broadening the financial base of the association as membership fees are complemented by revenues from other levies, projects and commercial services. Reaching these synergies is not simple as it requires a broad range of competencies in several areas of expertise.

Reviewing relations with national / sectoral associations

The fragmentation of the industry has led to a complex associative structure where functions are divided between the national and the regional level. This can sometimes be in a federative structure with strong regions (such as France) or a centralised structure with regional branch offices (such as the United Kingdom). Even more complex is the German structure where the regions are competent in social matters and the sectoral association in economic matters. Each change of role at the European level could lead to different impacts and counterpressure at the national or regional level.

The reaffirmation of EURATEX as the sole speaking partner of the European institutions was a fairly simple task. The downsizing of the sectoral associations led to a more pronounced position of EURATEX. The sectoral association restricted themselves to focused actions and relied more and more on the support of EURATEX. Many national associations were cultivating direct contacts with the Commission. Most often these contacts were focused on projects and funding and less on policy issues and if so it was on very specific cases. The policy was not to go against individual contacts but to have better co-ordination and to use individual contacts for deepening the argumentation. From the Commission a unified position was always preferred over differing national positions, but national input could provide more detailed information.

The positioning of EURATEX in collective regulation has always been difficult. National associations restricted the role of EURATEX in this respect. EURATEX has been involved in a sectoral social dialogue since the beginning of the 1990s but its mandate for negotiation was so limited that it achieved few tangible results. Moreover, many national associations were themselves not competent in all social matters or refused a role for the European level under the argument of subsidiarity. Results like a code of conduct on social responsibility had no binding effect on the membership. EURATEX has only played a limited role in standards other than co-ordinating input in technical norms. As regulation is more and more replaced by voluntary standards, EURATEX underperforms in promoting a level playing field (for example, in safety standards or protection of intellectual property) within the internal market which hampers innovation (such as in the implementation of E-Commerce). The underperformance of EURATEX in the promotion of voluntary standards is detrimental to the industry and limits the possibility to be seen by policy makers as a force of progress and a credible negotiation partner.

EURATEX has tried to strengthen its position in collective projects. However, it is struggling to find a role that does not create conflicts with the national level while at the same time broadening the financial basis of EURATEX. After some experiments in co-ordinating export activities, EURATEX has favoured activities in research and development. EURA-TEX has played a double role, sometimes confusing for the industry and the Commission. A natural role for EURATEX is to develop a vision on research and development and link and co-ordinate the various research institutions. Another natural role is to facilitate access to European funding for research consortia. However, the direct involvement of EURATEX in projects and therefore the participation in consortia is more divisive. This involvement affects the neutrality of EURATEX and may possibly go against the interests of some national associations. The dilemma on the other side is that EURATEX could only work with those national associations or companies competent and skilled enough to participate in EU funded projects.

The provision of individual service to companies was by far the most divisive issue as this might hit the core business of many national and regional associations. Attempts to set up direct information services through the internet were always opposed by the national associations. The direct membership of companies to EURATEX has also been a contentious issue and has been restricted in the statutes. It must be said that EURATEX lacked the capacity to provide direct information and advice to companies and a re-engineering of the service was required for doing so. However, direct contacts between EURATEX and companies could sometimes improve the information level about the industry – and enhance a detailed understanding of specific issues in the lobbying process.

The conclusion of this analysis was that EURATEX could not implement the virtuous helicon model as it was seriously restricted in individual service, limited in collective projects and collective regulation. Its only strong development option is to strengthen its position in lobbying. From a financial perspective EURATEX could not diversify significantly its sources of income. Any broadening of strategic positioning, as advised in the report had to be covered by increasing membership fees. No simple task as national associations were faced with declining revenues. Only the associations that had applied the helicon model and had achieved a broader portfolio of activities and income could afford higher contributions to Brussels. One could even say that the shift to service organisations enabled these national associations to allow EURATEX a stronger lead in public representation.

As far as synergies in advantage of attraction of membership and synergies in information, the only avenue was to deepen the relation with sectoral or national relays. The exercise is to eliminate duplication, improve co-operation between members and speed up the exchange of information. The introduction of the internet proved to be a great help as it simplified the flow of documents and the feedback from both associations and companies. As far as projects were concerned, transparency in procedures and the acceptance of all partners of the principle of 'variable geometry' was of great significance. Considering the diversity in membership, requiring unanimity in project participation meant doing nothing and inhibiting those associations that were able and willing to engage in projects. Variable geometry was necessary in order to avoid a complete fragmentation of the system.

Conclusions

The textile industry is a fragmented industry that had to face a changing policy agenda. The liberalisation of textile trade shifted the focus of specific trade policy lobbying to more horizontal lobbying. For this shift we developed a methodology of identifying companies' needs and expectations in relation to the political arena. This permitted the identification of matches and gaps, and enabled the development of a policy agenda.

The policy agenda focused on innovation and environmental issues. It required a different approach to policy making. The hold of the trade policy thinkers on the organisation had to be broken and the research policy makers had to be brought into the mainstream of policy making. This was done through a suggested mandate and review body.

The policy shift of EURATEX also meant the use of other policy tools. Besides lobbying, this was collective regulation (in those areas where voluntary standards were developing) and collective projects (such as innovation). Even if the provision of individual services to companies had to remain in the realm of national association, the changing role of EURATEX may conflict with local ambitions. A helicon model helped to clarify a vision on the evolution of trade associations. It allowed the identification of key functions and the links between them. The model helped to see actions where the national and the European level may strengthen the effectiveness (lobbying), while in other areas the national associations may benefit from softer actions like monitoring and coordinating.

The study delivered tools to assist associative change in a difficult industry that has had to come to terms with the fact that it is a normal industry. Delivering change requires a daily intervention and a daily monitoring, using tools of understanding and tools to act in the process. This demonstrates that association management is truly a profession requiring its own tools and methods. Making change happen in a fragmented industry is a long-term process best helped by coalitions amongst forces of progress, emulation and competition. A variable geometry is thus a necessary condition for making change happen.

Note

1 Here, the term 'textile industry' is used as a short-cut for the textile and apparel industries. A good overview of the industry is given by Stengg (2001).

9
The Construction Industry

Ulrich Paetzold

I should like to commence with a description of the European Construction Industry Federation (FIEC), its history, and some characteristics of the construction sector. I will then endeavour to explain how these characteristics impact upon FIEC's effectiveness.

FIEC

The first meeting of FIEC took place in 1905 in Belgium, that is, a long time before anyone thought about a European Union. Over all these years, FIEC has always had its registered headquarters in Paris. Consequently, FIEC continues to have French nationality and has, as a 'registered association' according to the French law of 1/7/1901, a legal personality of its own. The installation of our Brussels office was the consequence of the Delors White Paper on the Single Market and the Single Act and goes back to 1989. In the same year I was employed by FIEC to set up the Brussels office.

I have come across numerous statements that European federations are in a process of profound adaptation to recent European developments and similar statements to this effect, and I therefore wondered why I did not have this same impression, as far as FIEC is concerned. Looking back at FIEC's history, I realised that I had joined FIEC at a moment in time when the discussions on FIEC's reaction to the new rhythm of the European developments had already taken place and fundamental decisions had already been taken. In fact, the opening of a dedicated office in Brussels constituted the most visible manifestation of major organisational changes in FIEC's traditional working practices.

Already at a much earlier stage, immediately following the enactment of the Rome Treaties, FIEC had also adapted its working structures by establishing a Standing Committee for European Community matters, which, together with the Standing Committee for International Matters then constituted the working structure of FIEC. Both of these standing committees were managed from outside the FIEC offices and in time developed into organisations legally distinct from FIEC, namely the European Community Contractors (ECC) and the European International Contractors (EIC).

Over the years, the number of EEC member countries increased and, consequently, only a smaller and smaller minority of member federations were not members of the EEC. In this situation, the impetus culminating in '1992' led to fundamental discussions on the task, role and working structure of FIEC, resulting in a major change to the statutes and the standing orders. In this context, the material consequences were the self-dissolution of ECC, the taking back of Community matters by FIEC and the opening of an office 'at the principal seat of the European institutions', which was identified as being Brussels. At the same time, the basic working structure of FIEC, with three standing commissions for economic, legal, social and technical issues, was created and has subsequently been confirmed in further review exercises which have since taken place.

This little excursion into the recent history of FIEC shows that the contractors never ceased to adapt their professional European organisation to the changing political and institutional environment as well as to the growing importance of European issues for their sector. Today, FIEC represents 32 member federations from 25 countries, in the EU, EFTA and candidate countries. Further candidate countries have expressed their interest and are likely to join sooner or later. Through these member federations, FIEC represents the interests of construction firms of all sizes, carrying out all kinds of building and civil engineering activities, as well as all kinds of working methods: separate trades contracting, main contracting or as sub-contractors.

In view of closer collaboration and better coordination, FIEC has the possibility of accepting European specialist contractors' organisations as associate members. This is currently the case with EFFC, the European Federation of Foundation Contractors. Furthermore, FIEC has a co-operation agreement with the Association of Contractors and Builders of Israel and co-operates closely with its sister organisation EIC, the European International Contractors, the former Standing Committee mentioned earlier. This structure is coordinated and assisted by the team at the FIEC office in Brussels, currently composed of eight members of staff and working with a subscription income of roughly €1.4 million a year.

The democratic structure of FIEC is composed of the General Assembly, the Council of Presidents and a Steering Committee of ten members, each of them representing a (large) country or a group of (smaller) countries. For issues with tight deadlines from the EU-institutions, we use a fast-track method ensuring that each member federation has the possibility of expressing its views, rather than the fully fledged detailed procedure also provided for in the statutes and standing orders. In this way, we usually manage to respect both democratic principles and timely effectiveness. FIEC concentrates on sectoral aspects of European policy and leaves horizontal issues to UNICE, or UEAPME respectively.

The FIEC working structure

It is obvious that a staff of nine will not be able, on its own, to deal adequately with all relevant issues. For this reason, and in order not to create another layer of administration, the FIEC working method is based on the combination of, on the one hand, expertise from contractors and federation experts from the national member federations, and, on the other, advice and coordination provided by the team at the Brussels office. This nationally diversified expertise is structured in three commissions and their sub-commissions, dealing with:

- Economic and legal matters such as public procurement, Trans European Networks (TENs) and lower VAT
- Social matters such as free movement, enlargement, health and safety, training and education
- Technical matters such as sustainability issues, environment, CO_2 emissions reduction, waste management, research and development, standardisation

In addition, there is a specific ad-hoc group dealing with central and eastern European countries' matters, such as pre-accession issues, '*acquis communautaire*', sectoral social dialogue, freedom to supply services or free movement of workers.

In principle, issues are being discussed very thoroughly in this working structure, with the aim of reaching consensus. If this is not possible, the statutes provide that both the majority and minority views are presented in position papers. This last principle is based on the conviction that it is neither helpful for our interlocutors, nor fair towards the minority to pretend that unanimity has been reached when such is not the case. We consider that such honesty and transparency provide a better contribution to the political debate, because they ensure the correct information of the real situation.

FIEC and its partners

All of this work is, of course, not being undertaken in isolation. FIEC works together with numerous organisations, mostly on a permanent basis and only very rarely on ad hoc basis for a specific issue.

In this context, the following are significant:

* Based on an in depth study establishing that FIEC is undoubtedly the most representative organisation for employers in the construction industry (Institut des Sciences du Travail, 2001), FIEC is recognised as a 'social partner' in the European sectoral social dialogue, by the European Commission
* By virtue of its representativeness, FIEC has been accepted as first ever associate member of CEN, the European Standardisation Committee
* FIEC is an associate member of the European Commission's Euro-Info-Centre network, a status achieved in a public call for candidature by the European Commission and, for the time being, renewed every year on the basis of an evaluation procedure
* FIEC is a member of ECCREDI, the European Council for Construction Research, Development and Innovation, together with many other construction sector organisations
* FIEC initiated the European Construction Forum, (ECF), an informal platform in which the European federations of architects, cement producers, construction materials producers, asphalt pavement producers/layers, civil engineers, consulting engineers, workers and housebuilders/developers participate together with FIEC, in order to increase the influence of the construction sector as a whole.

Together with EIC, FIEC also participates in work at the world level (World Bank and other International Financing Institutions), as a founding member of the Confederation of International Contractors' Associations (CICA) and as a member of the European Services Forum ESF which briefs the EU-negotiators from the European Commission on the overall positions, views and interests of the European services industries.

Sectoral characteristics of the construction industry

In 2001 the European construction industry had a total construction investment of €873 billion (EU 15) contributing around 10 per cent to Gross Domestic Product (GDP) and accounting for 49.2 per cent of gross fixed capital formation. Cross-border activities amount to approximately 2 per cent of these figures. This percentage seems to be very low but it has to be said that most of the cross-border construction activities take place in a way which is not considered 'cross-border' in the context of statistics of economic activity.

In fact, contractors wishing to work abroad ensure in most cases that they adopt a national/local profile in the country of the construction project itself. This means that they either create a local company, buy a local company or enter into a joint venture with a local company. In these circumstances, there is hardly an exchange of goods or services across borders. It is pertinent to say that construction activities tend to be very local and/or regional activities. The construction industry in Europe is composed of approximately 1.9 million enterprises of which 93 per cent have less than ten operatives and 97 per cent have less than twenty. So, the sector has a clear SME structure. These construction enterprises employ more than eleven million operatives, corresponding to 7.2 per cent of Europe's total employment and making construction the largest industrial employer in Europe, accounting for 28.2 per cent of total industrial employment.

For the political discussion, it is important to take the multiplier effect of construction into consideration, as one person employed in the construction industry gives rise to two further persons working in other industry sectors, resulting in three persons in total. This relationship was established in a major study undertaken some years ago on behalf of the European Commission.

Effectiveness

The expression 'effectiveness' could be interpreted in different ways. On the one hand, there is the perception from the inside, which raises the question of how the members of an organisation evaluate its effectiveness. This question is, of course, closely related to their expectations of their European association. But on the one hand there is also the perception from the outside. How do the interlocutors of a European federation, such as European institutions and other federations, perceive the effectiveness of a European association?

'Effectiveness' is defined in this exercise as the 'ability to come to common positions'. In this context, the wider literature tells us that established, reasonably concentrated industries facing overcapacity problems, invest more in their associations to help them manage the resulting issues than do, say, sectors which are highly fragmented, lacking in definition, and populated by firms of vastly different sizes. It also suggests that sectors where interests are highly contested tend to be more cohesive in political action.

These parameters are supposed to facilitate an evaluation of the investment by a sector in its European association, as well as on its cohesiveness in political action. The question is whether they can be validated in the case of the construction sector. With reference to the characteristics of the sector which I have explained earlier, it seems that it is not possible to come to clear conclusions on FIEC and the construction sector that it represents.

As concerns the first aspect, the construction sector is certainly an established sector: it has a long-standing tradition, it is a visible part of the economy, it is known to every citizen, it is working for the wellbeing of society, and it provides all kinds of job opportunities, both low-tech and high-tech. According to the wider literature, this should be supportive of a higher investment in the association and increased cohesiveness.

Secondly, construction is also a highly fragmented sector with firms of different sizes: from the one person firm to the world player, specialist trades, main contractors, sub-contractors and finishing trades. These parameters may, according to the wider literature, indicate a lower level of investment and reduced cohesiveness.

Thirdly, the construction sector also has some overcapacity, certainly not in all countries or regions but a critical problem wherever it occurs. At the same time, it is regularly reported that shortfalls in the availability of skilled labour are widespread. According to the wider literature, this parameter suggests more investment and cohesiveness.

This brief evaluation indicates that the construction sector corresponds to parameters of both sides of the argument, so that it does not seem possible to clearly identify one of these sides as the more typical. In conclusion, I do not see, in the case of FIEC and the construction industry, that these features mentioned usefully contribute to explaining why associations vary their abilities to come to common positions between their members. This does not mean that I doubt the significance of these findings, but they do not seem to fit the construction sector and FIEC. One of the reasons for this might be that, contrary to the scientific world, I am not comparing FIEC with other European associations, but am only speaking about FIEC in isolation.

Personal experiences: the effectiveness of FIEC

Based on my personal experiences in FIEC, there are, however, a number of other parameters which seem to have a considerable impact on FIEC's effectiveness. Some of them have already been mentioned in the preceding chapters.

One is that FIEC positions benefit tremendously from the fact that our national member federations have already carried out their national coordination, so that we receive well reasoned views from each country. This reduces the number and increases the quality of answers received and at the same time, improves the chances of reaching agreements, that is, increased efficiency.

Another aspect is that an issue perceived as containing dangers tends to increase both the quantity and the quality of the positions, as well as the details of the argumentation and the speed of reaction. Consequently, in this case, we have a more solid basis for drafting a FIEC position.

Also, in cases of short deadlines or other time pressures, it seems to be easier to agree on common positions than in situations where there is no such time constraint.

In a number of cases, the capacity or willingness to compromise in a meeting is very decisive. Sometimes, this depends on the mandate or the brief delegates have received for a particular meeting. On other occasions, it is based on the fundamental importance of a certain point for one or several national federations. In this case, discussions can take a long time and there is no guarantee of reaching a consensus. In this case, both majority and minority views will be presented.

As FIEC is rather broadly representative and works on the basis of a democratic structure, finding a common position can sometimes be relatively cumbersome. But this is the price every representative European association sometimes has to pay. Less representative organisations may find it easier to agree on a common position.

In addition to those general parameters, there are also a number of very practical parameters which have a major impact on the effectiveness of FIEC. One of the biggest problems we have faced over a long period, and which seems to decrease only slowly, is the existence of linguistic differences, often together with underlying cultural differences. They lead to misunderstandings if they cannot be resolved immediately.

With respect to this, all members of the FIEC staff have to be multilingual, and we try to employ staff from several different nationalities. This blending of nationalities enables the FIEC team to serve as a catalyst, improve mutual comprehension amongst the members and prepare common positions acceptable to the members. Budgetary or manpower constraints may also have an impact on effectiveness, in particular if a lack of prioritisation leads to a dispersion of the means.

In conclusion, I think that the most decisive elements for the effectiveness of FIEC as a European trade association, in coming to common positions, do not seem to be particularly closely related to the characteristics of the construction sector. However, it is important never to forget that construction is essentially a 'people business' and FIEC's activities are about people working with people and not robots, so that the entire scale of human relations is of the utmost importance for good co-operation. In addition, it is very helpful if all participants are profoundly convinced about working for a common cause, that is, the interest of the European contractors affiliated to the federations. It is important that all concerned are prepared to accept compromises and acknowledge that differences exist. Otherwise discussions will never lead to a result, or they would leave a bad taste with a minority that does not see its views communicated. So long as these very basic features are of good quality, it will always be possible to be 'efficient', that is, to come to a common position for the benefit of the sector.

10
Operating in Contested Environments: The Experience of the Chlorine Industry

Barrie Gilliatt

What do solar panels and micro-chips have in common with dioxins and PCBs (polychlorinated biphenyls)? The answer is chlorine. Few people have problems with the first two; many of us have concerns with the latter. And herein lies the challenge for the chlorine industry – do the benefits of chlorine chemistry outweigh the disadvantages?

Many environmentalists do not think so. Rachel Carson's *Silent Spring* – whether one agrees with her assertions or not – raised environmental chemical problems into the developed world's social consciousness and placed chlorine, in the guise of DDT (dichlorodiphenyltrichloroethane), dioxins and PCBs, at the head of the queue as public enemy No. 1. The Greenpeace campaign *'Chlorine-free by '93'* in the late 1980s jolted what had been a low-key introspective industry into a drastic re-appraisal of its role.

Because chlorine is inherently dangerous, European manufacturers have a history of collaboration on developing safety standards for its production, storage and distribution. This was started by Euro Chlor's predecessor, an internally-focused organisation called *Bureau International de Technique de Chlore* (BITC), whose existence was virtually unknown outside the chemical industry. Formed in 1954, BITC produced an impressive array of more than 100 technical guidelines. These covered topics such as how to maintain bellows valves or design a chlorine rail tanker or how to conduct a pre-delivery safety audit at a chlorine customer's premises.

The producers found these activities to be of extremely high added-value to themselves. Although BITC started with a small number of members, there was a clamour to join because such safety work was seen to be of mutual benefit to everyone in such a high-density industry. Because there were comparatively few producers with common interests and concerns, they could work together at low cost to deliver a product that they all needed.

Chlorine production is a mature industry. First produced industrially in 1880, chlorine consumption has grown steadily. Until very recently, economists viewed chlorine production as an economic barometer since the development of a country or region could be measured by the state of its chlorine industry. As the world prospered during the period from 1950 to the mid-1970s, the chlorine industry grew as well. It was an essential industry because many of the technological advances taking place required chlorine chemistry. Chlorine was both profitable and innovative. Today, 55 per cent of the chemical industry uses chlorine at some stage of production; thus many chemicals, plastics and medicines depend on chlorine though the end product is often chlorine-free.

During the 1960s, technology in the chlorine industry evolved considerably with the introduction of precious metal catalysts into the process providing a corresponding reduction in energy consumption. The control rooms for the electrolysis cells became computerised and some of the first process control applications in industry were adopted by the chlor-alkali sector. Because measures were required to ensure that the overall process was safe, producers developed the use of quantitative risk assessments to assess and improve the safety of installations. Apart from the nuclear industry, the chlor-alkali industry was the first to use such quantitative risk assessment techniques.

In the late 1980s, a new form of technology for producing chlorine – known as membrane cells – was developed. This solved some of the problems related to previous technologies that had used either mercury or asbestos. So for 30 years, from the 1950s, when the BITC was formed, to the 1980s, the chlorine industry prospered. The world then changed. The post-war boom fuelled by a policy of 'growth at any price' gave way to concerns about the quality of life. In the developed world, society had become richer, enjoyed more leisure time and had become more concerned about the environment and consumption of essential resources. Simultaneously, an industry that had been profitable watched earnings nosedive – primarily because prices for electricity, which can account for up to 70 per cent of the variable production costs, rocketed following the oil crises of the 1970s. The development of natural ash had taken some of the market for caustic soda, a co-product produced simultaneously with chlorine. Furthermore, although the new membrane electrolysis cells enjoyed lower operational costs, they were extremely capital intensive.

To add to the industry's difficulties, an electronic communications explosion occurred: incidents that happened on the other side of the world had an almost instantaneous impact in Europe. Previously, three or four weeks could have elapsed before news reached Europe by which time the effect was softened. But the Bhopal chemical plant explosion, for example, had repercussions that echoed almost immediately around the global chemical industry. This ease of communications helped kick-start the expansion of the 'green' movement with national or regional issues rapidly globalised.

Many of the early environmental attacks on chlorine were stimulated by concerns about damage to wildlife. Several writers had highlighted the fact that bird life was being affected by over-use of the chlorinated compound DDT then widely used to kill malaria-carrying mosquitoes. Even that symbol of the United States of America, the bald eagle, had been affected. Rising prosperity in the US meant that DDT was being used there as a commodity product to kill almost any flying bug. Before barbecues, it was common practice to have the garden sprayed with DDT to prevent insects bothering guests. Due to such practices, environmental concentrations of DDT in the United States were excessive.

In nature, where seals and alligators had suffered, chlorine chemistry in general was blamed because of alleged concerns about persistence and bio-accumulation of organo-chlorines. Opponents described chlorine as the man-made *devil's element*. There was no recognition of the fact that there are several thousand naturally-occurring chlorine compounds. Indeed, chlorine is useful because it reacts very readily with other substances to create a whole range of chemicals and plastics with different properties. It is estimated that there are more than 15,000 chlorinated compounds – not all of them on the market – that have been synthesised by chemists.

In Europe the European Community was beginning to flex its environmental muscles on regulating the production, use and disposal of certain chemicals and many of those – due to environmentalists' clamour – were chlorine-based. Many claims by environmentalists in the 1980s and early 1990s were wildly exaggerated. It was not unusual to read media reports that chlorine was a threat to the entire human race. Endocrine disruption was beginning to emerge as an issue with postulations that if chlorinated chemicals affected wildlife, could they not also be responsible for reductions in human fertility or increased breast cancer or even rising asthma statistics? Left unchallenged, such attacks threatened the very existence of the chlorine industry and survival meant companies and the organisations representing them had to rapidly change from being intro-spective to being more open and transparent.

However, our industry was not starting from scratch. A basic organ-isation in the shape of BITC with a small staff existed along with a network of companies where dialogue was ongoing. On the negative side, however, we lacked comprehensive scientific information about many of our products. Was there an element of truth in the various claims about chlorine? We needed to improve our science so that we could confirm or deny such claims often presented as facts. And we needed to improve our ability to communicate our viewpoints on issues of concern. But to whom should we talk and how? We needed to be more consistent in our messages and to work and act together under strong leadership. We had never really operated in the political arena and with the European institutions beginning to show their regulatory teeth, we did not understand the workings of the EU political process. Which of these should we address? How would we do that? What kind of advocacy messages would be effective? At the same time, it was important that work continued on the original BITC safety mission – the stewardship of our processes and products.

The first priority was to re-engineer our organisation and signal that with a new identity. BITC metamorphosed into Euro Chlor. From just product stewardship, we now had to embrace science, communications and advocacy in a coordinated manner. It was necessary to strengthen both our staff and our professionalism. From two part-time staff in 1990, Euro Chlor has grown to 14 full-time employees in 2002, with 10 professionals and four support staff. The team is drawn from business management, academia, science, manufacturing and the communica-tions profession. Five hold PhDs and almost all are graduates. As we have to address all Member States, staff must be multi-lingual. Between them, our staff can speak nine languages with English as the core work-ing language.

With the establishment of Euro Chlor in 1990, we also took a funda-mental look at the mission of the new organisation. Our *raison-d'être* became

> To develop and promote initiatives that serve the European chlorine producing and consuming industries, the authorities and the public in the fields of safety, health and the environment.

It may be instructive to examine some of the underlying implications of that statement.

Creating an industry presence

Until that time, the sole mission had been to serve the chlorine producers by improving safety standards. We decided to expand membership to encompass the related chlorine consuming sectors downstream: the European Chlorinated Solvent Association and the Chlorinated Paraffins Sector group became part of Euro Chlor, which also opened its doors to both users and suppliers.

From perhaps 15 member companies in the 1950s, membership has increased to almost 100. These include consumer companies using chlorine-based products for such applications as dry cleaning, household bleaches and detergents and suppliers to the industry. 97 per cent of the chlorine production capacity in the EU and EFTA countries and about 70 per cent of the Accession countries' capacity is in membership.

Creating social cohesiveness was one technique that we used to improve collaboration between our members. Because of the specialisation of the industry, many people stayed in the same jobs for long periods and it was possible to build strong relationships by ensuring that they met regularly. In the early days, we had an average of 250 committee and working group meetings per year. We encouraged members to bring their partners to regular industry conferences. This meant that people got to know each other well. The net result was that greater trust and understanding existed, thus permitting more rapid decision-making on issues of mutual concern.

Advocacy with the authorities was a new field for our industry. It became clear that we had to address not only the European institutions but also regional bodies such as the marine conventions that control discharges into the seas and global institutions such as the Organisation for Economic Cooperation and Development (OECD) and UNEP (United Nations Environment Programme).

We were helped by the fact that as chlorine is produced in most European countries a network of local working groups in national associations already existed. Through our member companies' participation in both Euro Chlor and national associations we were quickly able to establish an effective pan-European network. In each country, a lead member company was nominated to liaise with the chlorine group of the national chemical industry association in order to develop an active network of companies co-operating at the national level. In structuring Euro Chlor's management committee we took care to ensure that not only the major players were represented but that also some of the smaller companies were involved. This mix gave us a geographical spread over the whole of Europe. We also ensured that, wherever pos-sible, the management committee member was also the chairman of the relevant national association chlorine group. This collaborative approach ensured that key messages and positions on issues developed within Euro Chlor were rapidly and consistently relayed via member companies and national associations to national authorities, environ-mental agencies and governments. Importantly, we also received rapid feedback that helped us in modifying our communications to take account of any concerns that were raised.

At the European level, two approaches were necessary. Both the European Parliament and the Council are structured along national lines and it was natural that the organisation that had been created to talk to the national authorities should be the one to be used primarily for advocacy with MEPs and Council ministers. For the European Commission, however, it became clear that it would be much more effective to communicate centrally through the Euro Chlor Secretariat, which represented the industry as a whole.

A third focus for advocacy was the regional marine conventions such as OSPARCOM (the Oslo Paris Convention for the protection of the North Sea), HELCOM (the Helsinki Commission for the protection of the Baltic Sea) and BARCON (the Barcelona Convention for the protec-tion of the Mediterranean Sea). Here we preferred to communicate via the Euro Chlor Secretariat and so sought and gained NGO observer status with these organisations. This allowed us to provide significant scientific and environmental contributions through participation in committees and working groups.

Finally, there were global authorities such as the various groups within the UN and OECD. In contacts with them, we have used both the central Euro Chlor Secretariat and our pan-European network, since it is important to work with the individual national delegations. Initially, we formed an alliance in the United States, where our counterpart on the technical standards side, the Chlorine Institute (CI), has existed since 1924. Two years after the new Euro Chlor was formed in 1990, the Chlorine Chemistry Council (CCC) was founded as a separate body to complement the CI and fully represent American manufacturers of chlorine and chlorine-related products for advocacy, science and communications.

But since the chlor-alkali industry was being attacked around the globe, it rapidly became clear that purely regional organisations were not enough and in 1992 industry leaders created the World Chlorine Council (WCC). This now has members from not only Europe and the

USA but also from Canada, Japan, Australia, South America, Korea, Taiwan, India, Russia and, as observers, China. The secretariat of WCC rotates biennially between CCC and Euro Chlor.

Under the WCC umbrella, we set out to develop and exploit the same high-speed electronic response capabilities as the environmentalist networks. In 1998, we launched a private, confidential Extranet on the worldwide web to share news, information and scientific data. Today, more than 1,700 chlorine industry managers in 35 countries can access this Extranet, including 500 members of Euro Chlor and its sister federation, the European Council of Vinyl Manufacturers (ECVM), representing PVC producers – chlorine's largest downstream user.

Through the WCC we achieved UN Non Governmental Organisation (NGO) observer status and hence participation in the working groups of UNEP and UNECE (United Nations Economic Commission for Europe).

Developing and promoting initiatives

We also concluded that it was not enough to produce technical documentation and issue reassuring statements that effectively told people we were doing a good job. The industry had to communicate more effectively and demonstrate that it wanted to be part of the solutions to perceived problems. In short, it had to gain credibility by enhanced transparency and by working effectively with agencies and governments.

We co-funded with the German Government a study on dioxins in Thailand. Although the Thai concerns had no direct connection with the chlor-alkali industry, dioxins are a minor unwanted by-product of certain chlorine reactions and we had expertise that was not available in Thailand. As a result of this capacity-building exercise, Euro Chlor not only provided the Thai authorities with the ability to perform similar assessments unaided in the future but also enhanced its own political credibility.

Another initiative, in co-operation with the World Health Organisation, was the publication and distribution in 17 languages of guidelines to assist public authorities in Eastern European and Arabic countries to improve their water supply infrastructure. This activity not only underscored chlorine's role in water disinfection but made a real contribution to improved public health.

Euro Chlor was also invited by UNEP to speak at regional POPs (Persistent Organic Pollutants) seminars in Iran, Croatia, Slovenia, the Emirates, Zambia, Mali and Russia. Here, we shared information on best practices and the most appropriate environmental processes for minimising POPs emissions – particularly dioxins and furans – from incinerators.

Risk assessments provide an example of Euro Chlor co-operation with the EU. For a particular hazard, the associated risk comes from exposure. If there is no exposure, there is no risk. To assist those carrying out risk assessments, the EU had produced a Technical Guidance Document (TGD). Although successful in producing a methodology for assessing risks in air, soil and fresh water, the EU scientists had struggled with assessing risks in saline waters.

Euro Chlor was able to help because it had developed a technique for risk assessments for chlorinated compounds in seas and coastal waters. In 1995 our industry voluntarily launched an ambitious programme to perform such assessments and 23 have now been completed. Most have already been peer reviewed and published. In the past year, the TGD has been expanded to include a methodology for marine risk assessments and although not identical to the pioneering Euro Chlor techniques, the differences are believed to be insignificant with the exception of pragmatic 'safety factors'.

Euro Chlor has also worked closely with OSPARCOM. Since 1990, OSPARCOM has each year asked national governments with discharges to the North Sea to provide data on mercury emissions to both air and water from chlorine plants. In fact, Euro Chlor has gathered such data from its members since 1977 and, in many cases, it was more complete than that assembled by the national governments. OSPARCOM has now assessed both the Euro Chlor data and methodology and concluded that it is of such quality that since 2000 Euro Chlor has replaced national governments as the official provider of data.

An initiative started in 1995 was Euro Chlor's work on endocrine modulation. It was being suggested that certain chemicals had the ability to modify human and animal endocrine systems. For example, it was said that birds of prey – at the top of the food chain – were at risk if they had consumed fish that had eaten other small marine animals that may have been contaminated with DDT. This was due to bio-accumulation in the food chain so that by the time that the bird of prey consumed its meal, the levels of DDT had become dangerous. One manifestation of the endocrine effect was the thickness of eggshells, which could prevent the birds from hatching and eventually lead to certain species becoming extinct. A frequently-quoted example was the American bald eagle, whose reduced hatching-rates were being linked to high levels of DDT in the environment.

In Scandinavia, where elemental chlorine was being used for pulp bleaching mills, it was shown that dioxins were being discharged into the rivers. These dioxins were alleged to be changing the sex of fish to the extent that male specimens developed female genitalia, with a subsequent decrease in breeding rates.

Several hypotheses were presented to show how the human and animal endocrine systems could be affected. It was alleged that most of the endocrine disrupters were chlorinated substances and this led to even more attacks on the chlor-alkali industry.

Euro Chlor took these allegations seriously and an industrial scientist who was also a professor at the University of Liège joined the Secretariat to investigate this and other scientific issues. The initiative expanded into a chemical-wide endocrine modulation activity within the European Chemical Industry Council (Cefic) and is now part of a global chemical industry long-range research initiative on the effect of chemicals on animal and human life.

Incidentally, technology has changed and chlorine is no longer used for pulp bleaching. Interestingly, it has subsequently emerged that downstream of some pulp mills that had not used chlorine, the fish stocks showed the same degree of hermaphrodism. This suggests that the problem was not dioxin-related, although blamed on chlorine at the time.

Euro Chlor has also been active in initiating product stewardship seminars in India and Brazil. In the latter case, with co-operation from both industry and the government, several programmes were developed that improved the application of best practices in areas such as safe handling of chlorine, reducing mercury emissions and the safe handling of asbestos from the diaphragm electrolysis process.

Enhancing transparency and openness is a key element in winning trust and confidence and Euro Chlor works continuously to provide access to information about its activities and positions on issues of concern. For example, we have had an active website (*http://www.eurochlor.org*) since 1998. This is a key information source and is especially useful for handling contentious issues, such as those relating to dioxins and dioxin-like PCBs. At the time of the 'PCBs in chickens' scare in 1999, the Belgian government needed reliable information about dioxins and their effects. Lacking data of its own, the government chose to create an automatic hyperlink to such information on the Euro Chlor website – a clear indication of our credibility.

Euro Chlor also works closely with national federations. In France, for example, the local chlorine producers co-operated with the consumer associations and two ministries to develop a range of information posters and pamphlets to encourage users of swimming pools to improve their standards of personal hygiene. By so doing, the levels of irritant chloramines in pools could be significantly reduced and lead to a much more pleasant leisure experience. This, together with other education campaigns on domestic uses of bleach and safety in the home, were well received and according to surveys increased the confidence of governments and the French public in the chlor-alkali industry.

Lessons learned

So overall, what have we learned? First of all, *trust must be earned*. Many surveys have shown that the credibility of the chemical industry is at an all-time low – environmentalists, academics and the media are all deemed to be more credible. Euro Chlor believes that the public will judge us by what we do, not by what we say. There is absolutely nothing to be gained by telling the public that 'we know best, don't worry'. Public trust must be earned by deeds.

Secondly, *we must co-operate with those groups who are more trusted*. Euro Chlor has found that alliances with government are easier to foster outside the somewhat bureaucratic and rigid EU structures. In our experience, bodies such as OSPARCOM are more informal, more approachable and more inclusive – even if the government representatives on such bodies are often the same people who attend EU meetings. As Euro Chlor has formal NGO observer status, active participation in such regional bodies can develop close working relationships. This can lead to better acceptance at the EU level, where a basis of mutual trust and confidence may already have been established. The same is true at the UNECE and UNEP, where the ability of Euro Chlor to provide assistance (for example, in the Thailand dioxin project) has enhanced our international reputation, which can then strengthen our credibility within the EU itself.

Another, third, lesson that has been learned is that *we have to engage – we have to listen and learn*. Euro Chlor believes that you cannot preach to people. In the past, industry thought that if you repeated something often enough, people would believe it. In reality, that does not work. Although the chlor-alkali industry's environmental performance has continuously and significantly improved over the past 20 years, we have not fundamentally improved public understanding of our sector because there has been no sustained engagement with the public. It is essential to listen – not only to the articulated concerns but also, if possible, to determine the unspoken anxieties – and anticipate public concerns. It is necessary to talk, at an early stage, with all the stakeholders (regulators, scientists, opinion formers, environmental groups).

Fourthly, *we must not try to defend the indefensible*. Responsibility for past mistakes or errors – and the chemical industry has been wrong in the past – must be accepted and admitted.

Although the EU is now the prime mover in Europe, the national governments and regulators still have important roles. Whilst the EU issues directives, they must be implemented by national governments, which also determine the shape of final national legislation. To quote an oft-used phrase, Euro Chlor has to *think globally, act locally*. We must develop overall strategies at the global and European levels, but work through national associations to influence local regulators and legislators. Like all industry associations, Euro Chlor cannot afford to act exclusively at the EU level in Brussels and Strasbourg. We must work through our pan-European network to communicate consistent but tailor-made messages to all the Member States. A similar approach through the WCC global network is necessary for UN agency issues.

Finally, we have learned that the key to success is leadership. When the Commission or the European Parliament makes a proposal, it is essential to respond quickly. Environmental groups have proved to be extremely effective in this regard. In the past, industry has often been lax, claiming that it takes time to canvass and collect all members' views. Within Euro Chlor, the members have consciously delegated the authority to a strong and powerful secretariat to act rapidly on their behalf. Whilst the secretariat endeavours to fully consult, it is not always possible due to time pressures. However, because of the carefully nourished relationship of trust previously mentioned, the association retains a clear mandate to act on the members' behalf. Our members see the Euro Chlor Secretariat *as leaders and not just as a mouthpiece for policies that they themselves have determined*. Because our sector is almost permanently in the EU front line, members expect the secretariat to set a direction and to take the lead. This has become increasingly important since recent consolidation and manpower reductions within our industry force our members to reduce the amount of executive time that can be made available to support Euro Chlor.

The future

How can the situation be improved in the future? Euro Chlor believes that it must continue to work with a broad cross-section of the chemical industry, which depends so much on chlorine chemistry. We need also to build, or strengthen, alliances with consumer organisations, trade unions and regional or global bodies. The need for such public–industry partnerships was one of the main themes of the 2002 Johannesburg World Summit on Sustainability in which Euro Chlor, through WCC, was a registered NGO.

There is no doubt that the chlorine sector and indeed the broader chemical industry is going to be subject to an increasing level of legislation. Even so, we believe there is parallel scope to propose and enter into voluntary agreements. For example, Euro Chlor has made voluntary commitments to address the environmental and economic concerns related to the conversion of more than 50 per cent of European chlorine capacity over the next 15–20 years to alternative technologies.

In the medium term, if the European chemical industry is to retain its leading position as the EU's largest exporter, there is a need for workable and efficient legislation and that implies working closely with the legislators. We need to understand their needs and to ensure that they are achieved in the most effective way. Industry has the technological know-how and can best evaluate the economic consequences of regulatory changes. Only by dialogue and collaboration can we ensure legislation is efficient, effective and workable.

In the future, Euro Chlor will continue to expand its activities into the EU Accession countries. Already technical assistance, plant inspections and health seminars are offered to the 50 per cent of plants which have been full members of Euro Chlor since 1995. It is the association's ambition to reach the remaining producers and to achieve harmonised environmental, health and safety standards throughout an integrated Europe. Euro Chlor will continue to expand its scientific knowledge on emerging issues, such as endocrine disruption and children's health. While it is true that children are healthier today than they have ever been with child mortality rates at their lowest ever levels, illnesses, such as asthma, are increasing. We need, therefore, to be alert to any potential issues that may arise from the use of our chemicals. Euro Chlor does not believe that any of its products are implicated in these problems, but we have to perform the scientific research and analysis in order to ensure that our knowledge is up to date and based on sound science.

Long-term sustainability for our industry is important both for our members and the economy. We have to demonstrate that our technology can be made sustainable. Sustainability was defined at the 1992 Rio summit as development that meets the needs of the present without compromising the ability of future generations to meet their own needs.

In other words, we must not use resources to the extent that our great-grandchildren and their children will not be able to do the things that we are capable of doing today. We predict that sustainability will be the environmental driving force for the twenty-first century. The environmental provisions of the various European treaties are unique. In no other jurisdiction is so much prominence attached to environmental matters. It is clearly an area in which Europe leads – and wishes to be seen to lead – the community of nations. Taken together with its comparative prosperity and its history of social justice, all the three elements of sustainable development – economic security, social well-being and environmental conservation – are present. It is not surprising that European governments are continually stressing the importance of sustainable development. The same message is heard from Europe wherever international organisations meet. It will be Euro Chlor's principle objective in the future to ensure that our industry also strives towards a sustainable future.

The effective European associations of the future will be those that not only understand and influence European policy but those that contribute to areas where Europe is trying to influence the world. Trade associations that understand Europe's mission to green the world as a whole, and can work on the international scene, will be those that will have the greatest impact.

Part IV

Internal Environment

11

David against Goliath: Are Big Lobbying Organisations More Efficient than Smaller Ones?

Daniel Guéguen

Let us be clear: a number of factors has caused the multiplication of the lobbying structures at European level. Does this fragmentation improve the impact of big associations at the expense of the small ones? Not at all: the size of an association – meaning the number of employees and the perimeter of activities – is irrelevant for its effectiveness.

There is an ever-growing number of lobbying associations in Brussels and this will be described in the first part of the text. The second part outlines the major reasons for the fragmentation of the lobbying structure. After describing this structure, I analyse the effectiveness of lobbying associations in relation to their size. Since size does not seem to be the relevant factor the text presents other more pertinent parameters, which determine the effectiveness.

The multiplication of European lobbying associations

When you come to Brussels and stroll around the district of the European Institutions, everywhere you will notice signs of European Lobbying associations. The picture looked very different more than twenty years ago. What is the history behind this development? What are the characteristics of these European lobbying associations?

An ever-growing number of lobbying organisations

The first lobbying groups in Brussels were agricultural associations. The Common Agricultural Policy was the first integrated policy at European level; highly regulated, it became the largest expenditure of the EC. Farmer organisations therefore opened up offices in Brussels from the

Table 11.1   Number of lobbying associations in Brussels

Type of association	Number
Corporations (business representations)	>500
National and European trade and professional associations	+/−1000
NGOs (development, churches, family, environmental)	>750
Regional offices and cities	+/−250
Consultancies in European Affairs	>150
Law firms specialised in European law	+/−200
Total of lobbying associations	+/−2500

Source: Own estimates[1] based on the European Public Affairs Directory 2002 (Landmarks, 2003)

very beginning of European integration in the sixties. Social partners (trade unions and employers' organisations) also began to establish lobbying associations in Brussels, which became increasingly important during the 1970s. The agricultural lobby was followed by a growing number of associations in the food sector as the Single Market initiative led to deeper integration in this sector, where common legislation was needed to implement a common market.

In the aftermath of the European Single Act, associations based in Paris and other EU capitals moved to Brussels, increasingly the centre for European Institutions. The number of EU lobbying associations has constantly increased during the last 15 years and is still growing.

The predominance of small lobbying associations

What are the characteristics of these various European lobbying associations? Compared with the size of the national associations, lobbying associations are relatively small in Brussels. For instance, while UNICE (Union of Industrial and Employers' Confederations of Europe) has a staff of 50 employees in Brussels, more than 240 employees are working for the MEDEF in Paris (the representation of the French employers). There are only a few big European trade and professional associations in Brussels.

Table 11.2 shows the four largest trade and professional associations with a relatively high number of staff:

Most of the associations in Brussels are small. A typical European federation consists of three to five persons. Organisations of this size monitor legislation, draft position papers, organise regular technical meetings for its members, and networks among European professionals and civil servants. These associations really represent their sectors.

Table 11.2 The largest European lobbying associations

Name of the association	Number of employees
Cefic (European Chemical Industry Council)	140
UNICE (Union of Industrial and employers' confederation of Europe)	50
COPA (Committee of Agricultural Organisations)	47
ETUC (European Trade Union Confederation)	45

Source: personal practice

Approximately one-quarter of the associations are run by one single person. The activities of this kind of organisation are much more limited. Often a manager, close to retirement or already retired, collects some information, without any strict methodology, and takes care of his contacts without any systematic approach. In some cases, one person can represent up to ten different associations!

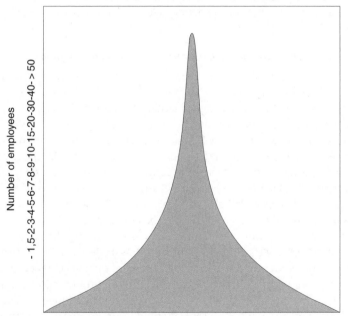

Figure 11.1 Pyramid of lobbying associations in ratio to number of employees

An extreme example of this fragmentation can be found in the chemical, food and agricultural sectors. About 200 associations represent the interest of the chemical and pharmaceutical industry, over 140 associations deal with food issues, and more than 100 organisations are active in the field of agriculture compared to approximately 50 associations that defend the interests of the entire electronics industry.

To summarise, the structure of European lobbying associations is highly fragmented due to a multiplication of organisations and predominantly small associations. The number of European lobbying associations has increased since 1992. This trend without any mergers keeps fragmenting the structure. The enlargement to the Central and Eastern European countries will create another boost of European lobbying associations. Consequently, the European lobbying environment will remain fragmented.

Five reasons for the fragmentation of associations

What are the reasons for the fragmentation? Can nothing change this trend? There is no single explanation, but a multitude of interlinked factors. Some of them are related to the growing importance of the EU, while others are signs of the deficiencies within the institutional system of the EU.

The widening scope and increasing level of European integration

The EU competencies have increased with every treaty reform. The Treaty of Maastricht extended the competencies of the EU in the field of education and culture, consumer protection, public health, research and development, environment and development co-operation. The Treaty of Amsterdam determined new EU-competencies in the field of immigration and equality of opportunities. Nobody doubts anymore that the decision-making power of Europe has become increasingly important. One just has to remember Jacques Delors once saying that 80 per cent of national legislation derives from European legislation. For this reason, companies, trade associations, and NGOs need to be established in Brussels.

The EU is not only deepening, but also enlarging. More and more Member States with different political interests due to their history and geographic situation are becoming members of the EU. Each enlargement has brought a number of national interest groups, companies, and associations into the EU, which want to defend their interests. The next enlargement to include the central and eastern European countries will once more bring new interest groups in Brussels.

The complexity of the issues at stake

Deepening of EU integration goes hand in hand with increasing technical complexity of the EU policies. Since a lot of EC regulations are highly technical, they involve very specific problems that demand a high level of technical expertise. Sectors like the WTO, the Common Agricultural Policy, Transport or Environment contain various rules and norms, which are only known to a limited number of experts and require a high level of technical expertise.

The specificity of the problems applies to a lot of sectors. In the chemical sector, for instance, isocynate producers are ruled by different regulations than producers of ethylenes. The specificity of the issues is also linked to the fact that the main activity of the European Union is still standardisation and norm setting. These norms are highly technical and specialised.

The co-existence of umbrella organisations and specific associations

Often one can find overlapping trade associations and many big companies are represented by more than one association. The complexity of the issues forces firms to be represented in industry associations and in specific producers' associations. The level of detail dictates whether a specific or an umbrella organisation takes position on a given policy.

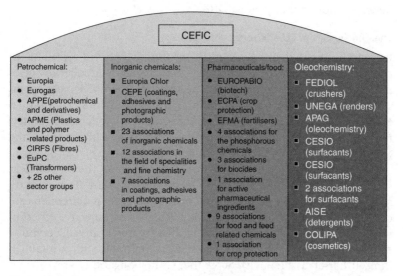

Figure 11.2   Example of the representation of the chemical industry in Brussels

While umbrella organisations can represent the general interests of an industry, their members' associations can face very different problems. The example of the Cefic (European Chemical Industry Council) illustrates this phenomenon. As an umbrella organisation it gathers different chemical associations under its roof. They are organised according to different products and different steps in the chemical production chain ranging from the refining of raw material for chemicals to the production of consumer products. The associations are mainly based in the same building in order to facilitate the exchange of views.

The subsidies at the Community level

Increasing specialisation alone cannot explain the mushrooming of European lobbying associations. The European Commission also contributes deliberately to this trend. It attracts lobbying associations by generously distributing subsidies to various activities. A large number of associations were founded with the unique purpose to attract these European subsidies constituting a large portion of the new European associations. This large distribution of European subsidies constitutes one of the main reasons for the foundation of new European associations. This is particularly true in sectors deeply subsidised by the EU budget and the structural funds, such as agriculture, rural policy and regional policies. In a number of cases these European subsidies are given to de facto associations, which are not registered in Belgium and, hence, do not have any legal status.

The deficiencies of EU advisory committees

Last but not least, deficiencies in the institutional system contribute to this fragmentation. One example is the tremendous number of socio-professional advisory committees. The advisory committees correspond generally to an empty frame. Even though a lot of advisory committees exist, in particular in the field of the Common Agricultural Policy, they do not enjoy sufficient influence. There is no obligation for the Commission to follow their line – in case they have one!

The example of the advisory committees illustrates the lack of clear rules on whose opinion has to be taken into account. There are no rules or any kind of legal framework on lobbying. No requirements are determined to define a lobbying group. There is no objective criterion for defining to what extent an association is representative. Everybody can set up an association that 'represents' certain interests or establish himself/herself as a lobbyist. Since there is no obligation to reveal who funds the organisation it is easy to conceal who issues an opinion.

This lack of rules leads to a system which is often accused of being obscure and cumbersome. Furthermore, it contributes to the multiplication of structures, since everybody attempts to contribute, even though the organisation might lack all necessary conditions to make a valuable contribution.

Setting requirements for lobbying associations and regulating participation in decision-making processes would enhance the efficiency of the system. A legal framework and clear rules are necessary. To summarise, the more effective the advisory procedures are, the more they lead to the concentration of lobbying associations, while the more ineffective the system is (which is the case) the more it contributes to fragmentation.

This section has shown five essential reasons for the high fragmentation of lobbying associations:

1. The deepening and enlarging of the EU
2. The growing complexity of EU policies
3. The necessary co-existence of umbrella and specific lobbying associations
4. The importance of subsidies distributed at Community level
5. The lack of clear rules for lobbying associations

Do small lobbying associations in this context lose out in comparison to larger associations?

Does size matter?

The size of a lobbying association might have an impact on its effectiveness. Efficiency can be understood as the ability to impact on decisions. There are some assumptions which argue for a link between the size and the effectiveness of a lobbying association. However, practical experience does not confirm any causality between the size of a lobbying association and its effectiveness.

The assumed link between size and effectiveness

It is commonly believed that associations representing a large constituency have more difficulties in taking decisions, while highly selective associations can easily agree on common positions. Big associations like the COPA (Committee of Agricultural Organisations in the EU) often face the same difficulties as the Agricultural Council of Ministers itself. Their interests are very fragmented and follow national divergences.

Even though big associations are assumed to have difficulties in reaching a common position, one might think this is outweighed by a higher level of legitimacy. This means that associations representing large constituencies enjoy a higher level of legitimacy, as they are more representative and therefore exert more political weight.

Experiences contradicting the importance of the size

However, examples of trade associations, NGOs, companies' representation, and consultancies show that there is not necessarily a link between the size and the effectiveness of a lobbying association. Small associations can be more effective in lobbying than big organisations, as demonstrated by the European group for animal welfare, a very small lobbying association which has achieved a lot of its objectives.

Big associations representing large constituencies do not always have problems in agreeing on a common position. Since they have to take so many interests on board, their positions remain on a very general level. They sometimes agree more easily on common positions based on the lowest common denominator. Such a position might be easy to reach, but not very effective for achieving precise objectives. Smaller associations define a specific position more easily and thus they are also more credible. However, sometimes small lobbying associations might not succeed in reaching a position, since they do not have any means to solve conflicts about very technical details.

To conclude, size in terms of the number of employees, associated members and the scope of activities is not the essential factor for the effectiveness of a lobbying association. Effectiveness depends on other elements.

The relevant factors that matter for effectiveness

Other factors are much more relevant for lobbying associations in terms of efficiency. The next part describes the most important ones.

Defining priorities with an action plan

In order to be effective an association has to define its priorities: the drafting of a policy platform accompanied by an action plan should be an absolute must for every European association. This platform has to be drafted in very concrete terms: definition of the association's priorities, intervention of the association in the European legislative procedures (tabling of amendments, participation in public hearings, contribution to Green Papers, drafting of position papers, and so on).

This exercise allows the association to focus on its priorities and measure its influence in relation to its objectives, which have been fixed in advance. Of course, in such a complex system with so many different agents, one can hardly spot a direct and monocausal link between a certain organisation and a specific action taken by another organisation. However, only if objectives are set in advance can a lobbying association measure where these objectives have been achieved, even if this is not a result of its own actions.

Drafting credible position papers

The drafting of a position paper is a very tricky undertaking. In many cases, position papers only criticise the European Commission's proposals. When an alternative position is proposed, it often enjoys little credibility. In order to avoid discussing and taking a stance for a more difficult, hence, braver solution, some associations just express their demands and describe claims. Such an approach, however, lacks credibility.

Position papers must contain viable alternative solutions. Only papers voicing a concise technical opinion, or an alternative solution acceptable to the EU Commission, have a chance of influencing the outcome of legislation.

The capacity to vote by qualified majority

In order to be effective, conditions must be set to reach a compromise and to make decisions. The effectiveness of an association relies on its capacity to vote by qualified majority, which means its capacity to discuss, and consequently to reach, a decision. A professional association also has to be operational, meaning ready to take decisions and actions. This implies the need to choose a president, a management board, a secretary-general who are able to negotiate, to discuss and to decide. These conditions are completely independent of the size of the association.

Lobbying – an instrument for providing performance

The European institutions are very open to debates, provided that the discussions are based on credible positions and pro-active strategies. If a European association combines the ability to decide and to adopt credible position papers with a real knowledge of the European decision-making procedures, it will prevail. In this way, being creative certainly is an asset. Based on my experience in this sector I still do not understand why so many European associations remain so timid

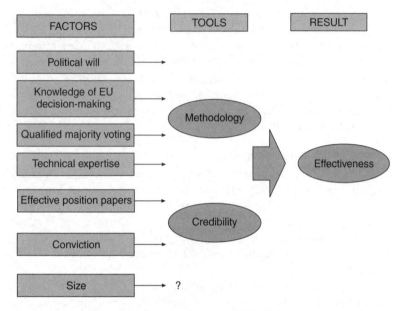

Figure 11.3   Links between factors of effective lobbying

in defining their strategies, and so conformist in taking actions. Nevertheless, credibility is crucial. Today, influence is almost exclusively based on credibility. And there are many good reasons for it.

Conclusion: lobbying – a sophisticated technique

The lobbying structure at EU level in Brussels is highly fragmented. Many small trade associations and other interest groups struggle for influence in an unregulated environment. Under these conditions it is not easy to be efficient. Only the fittest, which dispose of certain assets, will prevail.

In this highly fragmented lobbying environment the size of a lobbying association or the sector it represents does not determine its effectiveness. There are various examples where David has overwhelmed Goliath. Professional methodology and credibility are the crucial factors for granting success. Professional methodology includes:

• Establishing decision-making procedures towards a common position
• Setting objectives

- Defining priorities clearly
- Agreeing an action plan
- Drafting credible positions papers that offer viable alternative solutions

This strict methodology has to be combined with a pro-active approach. If a lobbying association with a professional methodology argues proactively for the common interests it has the winning formula.

Note

1   Some of these figures, particularly for NGOs and companies, are somewhat higher than are the number of entries to be found in sources such as the European Public Affairs Directory (Landmarks, 2003). While I cannot prove these figures, I believe them to be a reasonable indication, in that a large proportion of my clients are not registered in these sources, and many of my professional encounters through talks and training events involve meeting otherwise unlisted organisations.

12

Juggling Resources and Autonomy: Issues and Opportunities for 'Specialised Associations'

Alfons Westgeest and Bruno Alves

Is there space for the independent advisor of associations in today's political and industrial environment? Where and how? Throughout the 1980s, major professional services firms realised the potential to sell new business management concepts to a corporate market thirsty for solutions that would allow them to be more competitive and bring results to an increasingly impatient community of shareholders. Business consultants demonstrated the need for corporate downsizing through the application of new technologies, and explained the business management revolution on the grounds of the famous 'train example' – either you're inside the train, or you're standing on the track, in which case you should get out of the way. As a consequence of these and other such illustrations, the role of middle management was severely reduced and empowerment became the corporate buzzword of the decade.

Today's approach to the management of associations is substantially different to that followed by corporate business consultants in that it does not base its theories on the replacement of man-power by technology and processes. Yet the 'train example' may still apply to some associations, and certainly the empowerment concept is very much a part of today's association vocabulary. The train is moving fast towards the revision of the EU institutions and of the various forms of business representation. In addition, associations are increasingly empowered by the EU authorities on self-regulatory activities and are developing their scope to new areas, for example as a result of the enlargement process. Some argue nevertheless that the degree of empowerment transmitted by national members to the EU association to accomplish these self-regulatory plans is proportionally inverse to that granted by the EU authorities.

Most EU associations are faced with a considerable number of challenges that go beyond the global economic downturn. The challenges resulting from the changing political European landscape should rank among the top priorities of EU associations in the post-Nice Treaty environment. As fundamental discussions take place to clarify the role of Member States and national parliaments in the renewed EU, so too, the role of national associations is changing in relation to its political correspondents at European level, the EU business associations. Another important aspect is the revision of the EU's institutional framework in preparation for enlargement, and the consequences of this process in the business representation processes currently followed by some national associations.

The flexibility to adapt to new economic and political realities has always been a requirement for EU business associations. Specialised EU associations have allegedly the highest flexibility, yet the lowest intrinsic capacity to respond to change due to their limited resources. The degree of dependence on its membership is also an important factor when the political discussion entails the revision of powers between the EU and the national parliaments. Moreover, the nature of the organisation behind specialised EU associations also suggests that the small and very technical structures that usually provide the management of the organisation are less likely to respond adequately to broad political changes that may not appear to directly relate to the activities of the association.

We propose to analyse throughout this chapter the tools available for specialised associations to deal with economic and political change in compliance with their respective missions. Whether part of the Belgium national association, or the international industry group, run by the part-time employee of a member company or managed by the association management company, the specialised associations seem to appear in virtually every corner of every sector of industry.

Specialised associations

European business associations vary in size and competencies almost as much as they vary in management models. Looking into the reality of specialised associations is in itself a challenge considerably different from working with an association of a more horizontal scope of activities.

Smaller narrow-scope associations represent in many cases the totality of a certain industry sector; yet have to cope very often with a low level of resources. They usually have a narrow scope of activities and a very focused representation mission-statement which is concentrated on the vital issues for that industry sector, yet do not always gather enough resources to satisfy the demand for membership value. These aspects would generally resemble a contradiction, if it were not for the concrete client examples that we have gathered at Ernst & Young over the last 15 years. Approximately half of the EU and international associations that we have worked with, or currently work with, at Ernst & Young can be considered specialised or narrow-scope associations.

The services approach that we apply to these groups is substantially different in nature from the management and advisory approach that we apply to large associations and interest groups. The reasons why any organisation initially contacts Ernst & Young are diverse, but two common factors that we find in all the specialised groups that we have worked or work with are:

- the request for an independent advisor, and
- the wish to gain access to technical knowledge and a range of added-value services to members.

These are not easily available when the association is part of a shared-management deal with another national or international association. Our services include audit, tax, accounting, legal compliance, but when offering our association management and advisory services it has been very important to develop research into the reasons that lead these types of associations to be more open to new management concepts. This analysis as well as the case studies featured in the presentations obtained from participants in the EuroConferences 2000 and 2002 (www.eyam.be/euroconference).

Autonomy and resources

Specialised EU associations are considerably more dependent on their members than associations with a more horizontal scope of activity. The fact that these EU associations are mainly political representatives of the industry sector, and rarely engage in other activities, limits the resources allocated by the national associations to the EU association. In this aspect the resources available are in some cases so little that in order to slash operational costs the specialised association is managed either by the part-time employee of the largest firm involved in the association, or alternatively is located within the premises of another national or international association based in Brussels, and shares its management and at times its leadership.

This degree of 'addiction' often (but not always) stifles the effective representation of the association when in dialogue with the European institutions and other related organisations. It is up to the association to find the equilibrium between this dependence of resources and the capacity to position itself as a long-term partner of the EU institutions capable of dialoguing, and one that is not a simple vehicle for promoting sectoral members' interests. If the association does not externally demonstrate a certain degree of independence from its membership it is less likely to be seen as a relevant negotiation partner to the European institutions and its counterparts. Moreover the association will most likely be incapable of leading its membership into a strategic overview of the long-term.

If the organisation is politically or lobbying oriented, and yet the association is not recognised by the institutions as a relevant interlocutor, then the very mission of the organisation is considerably weakened. If the EU association is not able to present a solid and objective position about the future of the sector, then national member associations will be even less likely to support and allow progress towards one common goal for the sector. This structural and financial weakness of specialised associations impacts the perception that members have of the services provided by the association, and often leads to a dormant organisation with inactive members that will only consider to utilise the association when the need arrives to promote their own interests in Brussels. Moreover, it evokes serious concern over the responsiveness to any of the challenges that were mentioned earlier on in this chapter.

The key aspect of this weakness relates to what we could denominate a 'syndrome' of over-dependence on members. We use the term 'syndrome because over-dependence is manifested by a set of aspects (limited membership potential, residual interest of membership, inability to grow, and so on) and because it is a pattern common to many associations. The term may also be used because despite the absence of universal remedies, it can often be cured if an adequate number of tools are set in place. To name a few such tools, the association must

- minimise the consequences of a low level of resources through professional, rational management, and
- increase the autonomy from members through optimal and independent association designs.

These tools should be built into the medium-term strategy of the specialised EU association, as a means to ensure its development.

Professional, rational management

The fact that specialised associations are in general groups with limited resources available underlines the need to further rationalise the management of the association. The need for rationalisation has often been confused with the need to operate at extremely low costs. On this basis, the most frequent operating models to be found for specialised EU associations include:

- integration in an existing international group or association: when specialised associations seek a place within the international industry federations. They are usually driven by access to statistics or executive management together with lower costs. A specialised association without historical presence within the EU political institutions finds it more important to benefit from the information and the influence of the larger industry federation than operating in relative isolation. The geographic proximity coupled with the attractive proposition of lower investment costs than those involved in setting-up an office in Brussels often lead to the agglomeration of specialised associations under the aegis of major industry federations – for example in the chemicals and food sectors.
- management by a national association; when specialised EU associations are run by the office of a national member association in Brussels (this may be the Belgian member association or the European office of another national association). The cost-factor here is the main element if not the only aspect that is considered when opting for this management structure.
- management by the largest company-member seems to be a decreasing model as ad hoc issue driven interest groups of direct corporate membership increase in the EU landscape. Over the years, large corporations have come to realise that there is only very limited interest in hosting international associations, or that it can create significant competition law issues, and thus have moved towards the creation of ad hoc interest groups driven by very short-term issues.

Although this presents a linear perspective on the benefits of each management and representation model, most specialised associations cannot be blamed for making a more or less effective choice in terms of their operational model. In reality, almost the totality of EU specialised associations that fall under one of these three categories have been created or supported at some stage by the hosting organisation on the basis of overall industry interests. This means that some of the specialised associations that currently exist under the hosting of another organisation see it as the only viable alternative to setting up an office, and cannot conceive another way of operating. Nevertheless, a considerable number of specialised EU associations operate with their own office and staff in a similar way to other larger associations but with less operational costs and overheads. The main drawback of this model is the lower level of overall alignment between competence of staff and the number of responsibilities and tasks. It can also lead to lesser competence development opportunities in the staff and could lead to a low retention level of staff due to lower career prospects in small staff structures (natural for specialised EU associations).

The staff structure is a determinant factor in the definition of the operation model of the association. The necessity of engaging specialised staff at low costs assumes an even greater importance in a small structure with a specialised technical field of activities, such as specialised EU associations. Although the Brussels labour market is a highly competitive one, the hiring and retention of staff is increasingly important for EU associations in general. Through the Ernst & Young network and our connections with firms providing human resources services, we have come to realise that there is an increasing demand from European and international associations based in Brussels for compensation studies and benchmarking exercises with other organisations in the Brussels' employment market.

From the early beginnings of EU business associations two variations on the above models have been used:

- a part-time executive managing the association
- the appointment of staff from a hosting organisation

The first variation occurs when a part-time executive manages the specialised EU associations in retirement or pre-retirement phase. Although this is a staff structure that ensures little continuity, it could be a cost-effective one. The association will hold the executive at a relatively low-cost and will have the advantage that it will not have to invest in the learning curve compared to hiring someone who does not know the sector in great depth. The disadvantages of this staff structure relate to the eventual low-involvement of the executive in the organisation, sometimes little ability to understand the details of EU business and political representation (for those with a background in the corporate industry sector) and eventually the connotation to one of the members of the association, risking low effectiveness in view of the lack of neutrality from membership. Sometimes motivation of the executive is a problem – depending on why he or she was 'sent to Brussels'. Finally, the continuity problem extends to the lack of permanent support staff to ensure constant availability and access to the organisation.

A second possible variation for the specialised EU association is the appointment of staff from a hosting organisation (international industry federation, national association or member company). This professional would dedicate part of his/her time to the running of the association. The advantages of this staff structure are the low operational cost for members (probably included in the renting of premises and services to the hosting organisation), and the relatively well developed understanding of the industry sector and the operations of other organisations (through the work pursued in the hosting organisation). The major drawback is the reduced ability to pursue strategies independent from the hosting organisation, generating an over-dependence on the hosting organisation when it comes to representation and content. Again the results (especially in the case of hosting by member association or company) are the lack of independence and absence of neutral strategic assessment by the association staff.

Association management companies, and to a certain extent public affairs firms which are offering association services, have been able to explore the necessity that these associations have for independent advisors and executives. This becomes a clear opportunity when in the associations' life-cycle the need for independence from the hosting organisation appears.

Association management firms have developed to become more competitive service providers than ten or fifteen years ago. In the past, these companies were competitive solutions for associations on the grounds of cost effectiveness and risk control; it was less risky and less expensive than setting up an office with all the legal, fiscal and social obligations that such investment would entail. Nevertheless, these firms have not always been able to respond to the specific technical needs nurtured by specialised EU associations. Although the risk and cost effectiveness factors are still applicable today, association management companies are now able to offer a dedicated team of professionals with credentials and solid technical knowledge of the industry sector or policy area where common action is envisaged. This in itself represents a natural development in the business of representing interests in Brussels, whereby firms recognise the need to develop the services tailored to specialised EU associations. For Ernst & Young, for example, this has lead to the support of new industry coalitions.

The Figure 12.1 illustrates this process of development that has revealed to be a common pattern for many specialised associations.

Independent association designs

In any operational model the association must strive for creating the adequate governance structure. The membership interests should be taken into account because a lack of clear responsibilities and internal communication can jeopardise the existence of the association. The dependence of the membership can be characterised in two different ways: financial dependence and content dependence.

When addressing financial dependence, the most obvious way to tackle it is to look for alternative financing opportunities like those offered by the European Commission in different EU support programmes. These funds are often enough to concentrate the activities of the association in bringing value to the EU institutions in its political, industrial and research activities, which is definitely a positive aspect in the case of specialised EU associations.

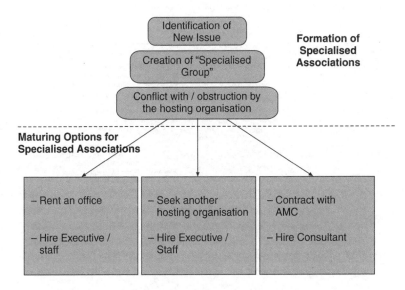

Figure 12.1   Options for specialised associations

Other ways of creating additional revenue streams that can reduce the level of dependence from membership dues are those related to creating new activities or services. Like national associations, some EU associations sell consulting services to their members (individually or to group of members) or seek corporate sponsorship (from members or their suppliers) linked to an activity (conference). Other EU associations have decided to impose an additional levy on the membership dues for the production and publication of statistical information, and make this information available to non-members for a fee. This activity expansion is more difficult to accomplish in a specialised association because start-up investment is usually too high for the association, and the staff resources are too limited to afford investment in the development and materialisation of these services.

The second type of over-dependency relates to the dependency of content owned by one or two members of the association. This usually results from the lack of data and market information available, leading the association into over-dependence from members' to enter dialogue with the EU institutions and present relevant information. This type of dependency is to a certain extent a result from the market and industry structure and can only be reduced by investment in the creation of alternative information and data sources with other associations, think-tanks or with groups of members willing to take part in a certain market research initiative. Another way is to outsource this function

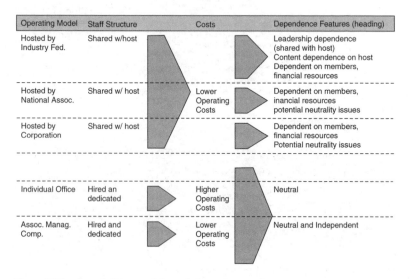

Figure 12.2   Association models and dependence of resources

and have the association only coordinate such services. Among others, Ernst & Young has been asked to provide economic and benchmarking studies to several associations for that very reason of independence and quality approach.

Below is a description of general links between operating models and dependence features of EU specialised associations.

On the operational perspective, the role of the board and the staff of the association must be defined in accordance with the objectives of the function within the group. In many specialised EU associations entrusting the management of the association to a non-industry expert or organisation, supported by members focused in specific project groups, has turned out to be a key success factor. This way, if there is effective coordination with the overall association objectives, the association naturally moves away from a stagnant dependence on members' interests and creates a certain degree of financial and content independence.

This entails a new approach to role definition within the association. The management of the association becomes a coordinating entity, whereas the members focus on the implementation and planning of specific issue-driven project actions. The benefits of this model include:

- more active participation from all members (through project work) yet avoiding a situation where those members with more resources to invest in the association rule its destiny
- higher perception of membership value as members concentrate their resources on the project groups that more closely affect their interests
- more effective use of the resources of the association, as the staff concentrates on the coordination and facilitation of actions, and the members concentrate on technical content

Experience has shown that there are a number of important conditions for this model to work effectively:

- the objectives of the association must be solidly and clearly communicated internally so as to avoid each project-group becoming a self-standing entity potentially damaging the interests of other less present members in the group
- the staff of the association must be able to roll out some concrete project management and planning capacities in order to avoid the project-groups growing into stagnated committees without goals or time frames.

Conclusion

Even though specialised EU associations may suffer from occasional structural deficiencies identified in this chapter, they can be overcome. Even more so, the same could apply to other types of larger associations and interest groups. The pattern that has been described as the 'over-dependency' syndrome is nevertheless a clear case for thinking about solutions for a large number of associations.

The tools to solve these problems are put forward by a focus on the fostering of professional and rational management and independence of resources. These tools result from Ernst & Young's experience in the hands-on management of associations but also the advisory role offered to specialised EU associations.

The acknowledgement that these principles must be at the forefront of any analysis of association structures will, in our view, constitute an important advancement for the association world, independent of which operating model and staff structure they choose.

13

The Role of the Secretary General

Zygmunt Tyszkiewicz

Put very simply, the aim of any EU business association is to be heard, understood and (if possible) supported by the EU lawmakers. As more and more regulations and policies affecting business are defined and decided not at the national but at the EU level, the main tasks of these associations are to:

- promote and defend *vis-à-vis* the EU decision makers, the interests of the companies they represent
- make sure company priorities feature high on the EU agenda
- obtain early warning of EU initiatives affecting companies, inform members, help them define their collective views and ensure the EU lawmakers receive these in good time and take them as fully as possible into account.

This is easy to say, but very difficult to achieve. To make it all happen, each business association needs its own highly competent secretary general.

The ideal secretary general

Picking the right person for this job is fraught with difficulties. Brussels is littered with the remains of failed secretaries general, often because the recruiters made the wrong choice. The ideal candidate should have:

- board level experience in international business and in international associations. The combination of these two is important. To be credible as spokesperson for companies, the secretary general must have first-hand company experience. But in companies, power flows from above, while in EU associations it comes from 'below', that is, from the national members. An EU association cannot be managed in the same way as a company and newly appointed secretaries general who have only company experience often fail to make the necessary mental adjustment

- a deep knowledge of the EU and its methods of working
- skills as a linguist, communicator, leader, diplomat and administrator, equanimity, robust health, boundless energy and stamina
- the will and the courage rapidly to become a well-known personality on the EU scene
- feelings of delight, not exasperation, when faced with European diversity and idiosyncrasies
- the confidence to speak to prime ministers and the humility to lick the stamps and post the letters
- motivation mainly from factors other than pay, such as European integration, the market economy, the politics of business, the challenge of achieving the impossible, and so on.

The first difficulty comes when searching for the ideal candidate. Few people combine top level business and association experience. The average remuneration package is not especially attractive for business people and taxation levels in Belgium are high. No training exists nor are there any manuals to help prepare future secretaries general for their tasks. Handling a multinational organisation where membership is voluntary and over which the secretary general has no hierarchical authority is a daunting challenge. Such organisations have a natural tendency to split into factions and it is the secretary general's constant task to prevent this from happening.

The job can be a lonely one. National members of EU associations have only a limited knowledge of EU affairs and methods of work. Understandably, they usually give first priority to national affairs. The top officials of national associations cannot devote much time to EU matters nor do they feel comfortable acting on the EU scene, where they are not as well known as in their home countries. EU associations are seen by their national members as relatively expensive cost centres, the benefits of which are difficult to measure and not immediately apparent, especially to officials who have only a superficial knowledge and understanding of EU processes. The result is that the national members tend to spend a disproportionate amount of time studying the internal administration and organisation of their EU associations, ('navel-gazing'), instead of concentrating on the regulatory and political issues of concern to companies, which they were created to handle.

The chronic problem of an expanding workload and lack of resources can be frustrating and exhausting for the secretary general. Well funded national associations, while recognising that regulatory and other decisions affecting companies are increasingly taken not nationally but in Brussels, have yet to redeploy a proportionate share of their manpower and financial resources to strengthen their EU associations in Brussels. There is the paradox that the success of an EU association contains the seeds of its failure. That is because the better the association performs the more will be asked of it, but resources will never grow in proportion.

If aspiring secretaries general knew all the above, no doubt they would look elsewhere for employment. It also explains the high failure rate of EU association recruitment to such positions. Yet despite the odds, many secretaries general of EU associations do succeed. It is useful to examine some of the methods they employ and actions they take to overcome the difficulties and to face the challenges of the job.

Internal relationships

Perhaps the number one priority for a new secretary general is to win the support and confidence of the staff in the secretariat. Most are competent and loyal but invariably overworked and sometimes abused by members. It is important that they feel supported by their secretary general.

In recruiting new staff for the secretariat, it pays to take on young people with little or no experience but with a good EU academic background. The College of Europe is an excellent source. It turns out graduates of outstanding ability who quickly learn and become highly productive. They of course do not stay for more than three or four years, but that in itself is an advantage since it avoids the problems arising from long-serving but unproductive staff remaining on the payroll until retirement. Budget constraints must not preclude a competitive remuneration policy accompanied by an annual performance revue and system of merit increases. It is better to have less staff but a good remuneration system than to have more staff, who are not properly rewarded.

Very early on, the new secretary general should find out if the association's statutes (the 'rules of the game') are clear, well known and fully supported by all members. If not, rapid action must be taken to remedy the situation, including, if necessary, renegotiation of the statutes, which are the glue that holds the organisation together. The secretary general must then be seen to act as principal custodian of the statutes, making sure they are respected. Secretaries general need to understand association power structures and learn to handle them expertly. The approach must be 'bottom-up', in other words, they act always according to the collective wishes of member associations. However, the latter do not always have a clear idea of what those wishes are, so secretaries general help by giving the lead. While leading, they constantly glance over their shoulders to see if their members are following. An American once accurately commented that 'secretaries general do not exercise power. They organise the power of others.'

Sound relations between the EU association's president and its secretary general are crucial for success. Presidents can be tricky. Left to themselves they can sometimes act like unguided missiles. Differences may well arise but these must always be discussed and resolved strictly in private. It is up to the secretary general to take the initiative and to create a harmonious partnership with the president, though this may sometimes require hard talk. Secretaries general should make full use of the president's political stature and influence to propagate the association's views. They should organise frequent meetings for the president with top officials, politicians and opinion formers. If offered a prestigious platform, secretaries general should first offer it to their president and never appear to be stealing the president's limelight.

Secretaries general must also earn the trust and respect of the EU association's decision-making bodies and more generally, of all the members. This is achieved partly by treating all members with equal respect, never showing personal favouritism or national preferences and by acting with complete transparency. It is achieved also by taking pains to discover the real reasons why one or other member organisation is finding it impossible to support the majority. This may be because of domestic political pressures or because of misunderstanding of the issues or even mistranslation of documents. The secretary general who takes the trouble to investigate such matters will earn much respect and can usually find ways to solve the problem. UNICE is fortunate in having the Committee of Permanent Delegates, composed of the representatives of the national member organisations resident in Brussels. This committee meets every two weeks with the secretary general. Good relations between the secretary general and the permanent delegates leads inevitably to good relations also with the presidents and directors general of the member associations. The reverse is equally true. Furthermore, because permanent delegates live in Brussels but are in close touch with their national association, they are well placed to explain national positions and to negotiate compromises.

External relationships

Politicians will always attempt to 'divide and rule' the business associations, which unfortunately are often inclined to compete instead of co-operating with each other. This weakens the business voice. Secretaries general must recognise such attempts and make sure they do not succeed.

Secretaries general of all the major EU business associations must work in harmony, keeping each other informed as required, exchanging draft papers where two or more associations are working on the same issue, avoiding contradictions or, when agreement on an issue is not possible, 'agreeing to disagree' while maintaining respect for each other's positions.

With the EU Institutions, secretaries general should work hard to develop genuine partnership, (but without complicity), by gaining a reputation for their association as one that helps the legislators make better legislation. Such organisations will readily be invited for consultation on EU initiatives, because they are seen as constructive and helpful and not simply as negative, and opposed to any regulations whatever.

Coping with insufficient resources

Secretaries general should, prudently and diplomatically, keep reminding their members of the disparity between the work they demand and the resources they are willing to provide. However, national associations also have financial constraints, so secretaries general must be realistic: resources provided by members will always be insufficient. They must learn to live with this constraint.

Secretaries general must show themselves to be prudent administrators. Careful budgeting and expenditure controls, avoiding deficits and erosion of reserves, creates confidence and may incline members to greater generosity. Nevertheless, secretaries general can strengthen their secretariats by finding sources of finance and manpower additional to those provided by member subscriptions.

Companies and national associations often want high potential younger staff to gain experience on the European scene. To secure such training, they are willing to make such staff available on secondment at no cost to EU associations, for periods of two or more years. Alternatively, companies may have competent older managers who become redundant but the company is willing to pay them two or more years' salary on secondment to an EU association, so they can learn new skills and possibly find new employment in EU affairs. For years UNICE has benefited from very many secondments in both categories, and continues to do so.

The creation in 1990 of the UNICE Advisory and Support Group (UASG), composed of companies, was an added source of income which greatly strengthened UNICE's capacity for the defence of company interests. However, UNICE made it a rule never to use finance from such external sources to subsidise member associations. It is used exclusively to pay for additional staff or activities which otherwise would not have been possible.

There is also limited scope for obtaining financial support from the EU Commission for specific projects. However, it is not recommended that EU associations become so reliant on such finance that their independence is compromised.

The work programme

A wise secretary general concentrates members' minds on issues and resists their preference for 'navel-gazing'. Most EU associations are 'confederations of confederations' at some distance from companies. Members therefore need frequent reminding that the organisation exists to defend company interests.

The secretary general can avoid many problems by ensuring early on that all members agree on the basic '*raison d'être*' or mission statement of the EU association. In UNICE, after much discussion, all members finally agreed that its mission was to influence the EU legislators. This simple statement of purpose made it possible to resist member demands for time-consuming, unconnected work.

It is equally important to gain members' agreement on a basic set of broad priorities, on which the organisation's limited resources will be concentrated. A technique for selecting such priorities is to plot the issues on a graph where the vertical axis indicates their importance to companies and the horizontal axis shows the degree to which association action is likely to influence the outcome. Items in the top right hand quarter of the graph will obviously merit the most attention.

In drawing up its own work plans the EU association must necessarily take into account the programmes of the EU Commission and of the Presidency. The technique described above can also be used to rank the business elements of these programmes in order of priority.

The EU association should include in its programme of work a minimum of original research to underpin its statements and positions.

Though resources for this type of work are scarce, it pays high dividends and therefore must be done. It can attract sponsorship from companies or project finance from the Commission (UNICE's reports on competitiveness, state aids, regulatory reform and its benchmarking studies are examples). The work programme must include concrete plans for 'selling' the association's messages at both the EU and the national levels. Well coordinated action at these two levels has the strongest political impact but unfortunately, EU associations have great difficulties in orchestrating their members, whose differing national priorities stand in the way of coordinated EU-wide action.

Quality standards

The secretary general is the ultimate controller of the quality of the association's products (position papers, press statements, speeches, studies, and so on.) since nothing can be made public without the secretary general's approval. The association's credibility will suffer if papers are issued too late, if they contradict other positions published by the association, if they do not convey a clear message or if they are not fully supported by all members, who must be prepared to endorse them nationally. The secretary general's task is to verify all this.

Equally important is the style and quality of published material: the style must be clear and direct. The test is to ask whether it would be understood by an intelligent fifteen-year-old. There must be no typing or translation errors, no jargon, no fudge, no long-windedness. Longer papers must begin with a short summary. If EU proposals are being rejected, well argued alternatives should be offered whenever possible. Failure to pay sufficient attention to such details can severely diminish the impact of the association's statements. EU officials and politicians are swamped with paper which they have little time to read. Verbal communication is therefore of utmost importance.

As much effort must go into selling the association's views as went into their preparation. Successful secretaries general create and exploit media opportunities and set-up meetings with key politicians. Secretaries General must ensure that they, and all others who present the association's views in public, have received proper training in presentation skills, in handling the media and, most importantly, in the correct technique for speaking through interpreters. The latter skill is sorely neglected in Brussels, with the result that even the most eloquent orators fail to get their messages across to people who do not speak their language and have to listen to simultaneous interpretation.

Responding to mindsets and clichés

All secretaries general of EU associations from time to time will hear statements such as 'you are an institution which is too slow and whose views represent the lowest common denominator'. The answers are: Yes, we are an institution that works democratically, consulting its grass roots and presenting a consensus view to the politicians. We are only 'too slow' if our views do not reach the EU decision makers in time to influence their decision, and that is seldom the case. Those who deride consensus views developed in multinational bodies as 'lowest common denominators' would do better to consider them as 'miracles' that so many different nationalities succeeded in agreeing common positions. Progress in the EU depends always on consensus and can be achieved in no other way.

Of course the CEOs of big corporations are more glamourous and express views more rapidly than associations, but their opinions cannot be taken to represent the wishes of the majority. In UNICE, when faced with remarks of this nature, I would refer the speakers to our position papers and challenge them to find a single one which did not clearly convey our position on any particular issue to the EU politicians.

Assessing performance

As already mentioned above, because members see their EU associations as cost centres whose benefits are not easy to discern, secretaries general must find ways to assess and to measure the performance of the organisation. That can be done by looking at actions taken on specific issues and asking, did we make a difference? Did the legislators accept some or all of our main recommendations? Did we prevent or water-down undesirable measures? What desirable measures were adopted because we promoted them?' More generally, the question that must be asked every year is, to what extent do the programmes of the Commission and of the Presidency reflect the business priorities our association is advocating? Have we helped to write the EU agenda ?

Finally, the secretary general should also assess the reasons for failure to influence the decision makers on specific issues. If such failure is due to the organisation's own limitations in terms of manpower or finance or its weakness in coordinating actions at EU and national levels, members should be made fully aware of this and invited to take the necessary remedial steps.

The issue of autonomy

As explained in previous chapters, EU associations are dependent to a very great extent on relatively meagre financing provided by their national members. That naturally limits their autonomy and increases the influence of the national membership. Thus the EU associations are 'bottom-up' organisations where power is retained by national members over whom they exercise no hierarchical control. The question is: is that a good or a bad thing?

Associations must reflect the views of their members and must ensure that their members support those views in public. Failure to achieve this would lead to complete loss of credibility and therefore of political influence. It is also true that members of EU associations need strong and inspiring leadership to help them overcome their differences and rally round a single, well articulated viewpoint. The task of the secretary general and of the permanent staff in the secretariat is the delicate one of 'leading from in front while keeping an eye to the rear to see if the members are following'. That's easily said but takes a lot of hard work and skill to achieve. The secretariat must:

- find out what the members think they want
- understand why some want the exact opposite of what others want
- through bilateral and multilateral discussions begin to narrow these differences, emphasising that an agreement reached by members will always be better for business than one reached by the politicians
- produce the draft policy paper which best articulates the members' common views and then invite, cajole and convince the members to approve it. As a last resort, offer dissident members the possibility of expressing their objections in a footnote.

The skill and leadership of the secretary general and secretariat are essential for successful management of this process. However, if the association and its secretariat became so autonomous that they began 'inventing policy' without reference to the membership, they would rapidly be disowned by the members and ignored by the politicians whom they are trying to influence. The EU association must clearly be seen as the creation and the property of its members and under their control. Yet it draws strength from the fact that without it, its members never could reach the collective viewpoint which gives them political influence at the EU level. Members need their association and the association needs its members. It is not a matter of autonomy but of interdependence.

Conclusion

Secretaries general of EU business associations do a job that is necessary, valuable, difficult and demanding. It can also be tremendously rewarding when, because of their personal efforts and skills, their multinational members march together in the same direction. Secretaries general, their presidents and their secretariats can then say with much justification that they have played a part in the economic strengthening and integration of the European continent.

14

Establishing an EU Business Association under Belgian Law

*Dirk Lontings**

As the importance of Brussels as the *de facto* capital of Europe has grown, an increasing number of associations have emerged with the purpose of defending, promoting and/or representing the interests of their corporate membership and/or a certain industry (hereinafter 'business associations') (Lontings, 1994). Belgian law offers these organisations various options in the legal form they may adopt.

Freedom of association

As is the case in all democratic nations, the Belgian Constitution, in its current Article 27, explicitly guarantees the freedom of association. This right is confirmed and elaborated in the law of 24 May 1921 'guaranteeing the freedom of association' and in a number of international treaties to which Belgium is a party, such as the European Convention on Human Rights.

With reference to these provisions and to certain laws specifically addressing non-profit structures, the international non-profit association, the domestic non-profit association, the so-called 'factual association' and the Belgian presence of a foreign association have become the most common structures for EU business associations.

The international non-profit association ('INPA')

On 25 October 1919 the Belgian legislature adopted a law 'regarding the granting of legal personality to international associations with a scientific

*The author wishes to thank Frédéric Franckx for his assistance in preparing this contribution.

purpose'. The law was the result of twelve years of intensive legislative labour, interrupted only by the Great War, aimed at perpetuating Belgium's pre-eminence as the world's then most important centre of international non-profit activity.

A law of 6 December 1954 expanded the purposes to which INPAs could be dedicated, so as to include humanitarian, religious, artistic and educational purposes. The 1954 amendment, together with the increasing importance of Brussels as the main centre of the European Union, resulted in an unprecedented boom of INPAs. By 1993 no less than 994 INPAs had obtained legal personality under the law (Lontings, 1994). Today there are between 1200 and 1500 INPAs.[1] Although no precise figures exist, it would appear that the vast majority of EU business associations active in Brussels have adopted the INPA form.

On 2 May 2002, the Belgian legislature adopted the law 'regarding the [domestic] non-profit associations, the international non-profit associations and the foundations', which (i) modified the existing law of 27 June 1921 'granting [domestic] non-profit associations and foundations legal personality' (see below), (ii) modified the law of 1919 on INPAs, and (iii) integrated the law of 1919 in the law of 1921 to henceforth constitute one legislative instrument governing the most important Belgian non-profit structures (the 'New Law'). By 16 January 2003 the New Law had already been amended.

The New Law will only enter into force following the publication of one or more Royal Decrees aimed at executing the New Law and existing INPAs will have between one and five years to comply with the New Law (newly created INPAs will have to immediately comply with the New Law). Because it will soon become the status quo position, the comments that follow are comments on and with reference to the New Law as it is currently expected that the New Law will become operational in the course of the year 2003.

Definition

Article 46 of the New Law lists the criteria an association must meet for it to be granted legal personality and be recognised as an INPA:

- the association may not carry out industrial or commercial activities and may not strive to procure to its members a material gain;
- the association must pursue a non-profit-making aim of international utility;
- the association's membership must be open to Belgians and foreigners alike;

- the association's registered office (in the sense of real seat or 'siège réel/werkelijke zetel') must be located in Belgium; and
- the association's purpose or activities may not be contrary to the law or public policy.

If an association meets the aforementioned criteria, the Belgian King (in practice, the Belgian Minister of Justice) can grant legal personality to the association and formally recognize it as an INPA.

The first two criteria in particular are important to understand the nature of an INPA.

Limited economic activities

When the New Law stipulates that an INPA 'may not carry out industrial or commercial activities and may not procure to its members a material gain', it uses exactly the same words as are used to describe the non-profit nature of domestic non-profit associations ('ASBL/VZW') in Article 1 of the New Law.

With regard to ASBL/VZWs – and thus also with regard to INPAs – there has existed since the 1920s a controversy on the scope of the economic activities a non-profit association may engage in and the benefits its members may derive therefrom. The New Law has not resolved this controversy.

Following a 1996 decision of Belgium's highest court ('Cour de Cassation/Hof van Cassatie'), a majority of Belgian legal doctrine and case law currently seems to accept that the rule that non-profit associations 'may not carry our industrial or commercial activities' signifies that ASBL/VZWs and INPAs are allowed to engage in economic activities, provided that (i) the economic activities are incidental to the association's non-profit purpose, (ii) the economic activities promote, directly or indirectly, the non-profit purpose of the association, and (iii) the revenues derived from the economic activities are used to promote the non-profit purpose of the association (Denef, 1997).[2]

In addition, all agree that when a non-profit association 'may not procure to its members a material gain' this means that members of a non-profit association may not receive direct economic benefits from the association (such as dividends), but that they may receive indirect economic benefits (such as a reduction of expenses and access to discounted advice services).

Given the nature of the activities usually carried out by EU business associations, they should easily pass the limited economic activities-test.

Non-profit-making aim of international utility

While previously INPAs had to pursue scientific, humanitarian, religious, artistic or educational purposes, they must now pursue 'a non-profit-making aim of international utility'.

This concept was copied from the European Convention no. 124 on the Recognition of the Legal Personality of International Non-Governmental Organisations of 24 April 1986 (the 'European Convention'), which was concluded in the framework of the Council of Europe to facilitate the cross-border activities of NGOs.[3]

According to a Belgian official who was instrumental in drafting the New Law, it is the explicit intent of the Belgian legislature – through the use of the concept of 'aim of international utility' – to broaden the purposes for which an INPA can be used, including establishing INPAs whose main purpose is to defend and represent the interests of their members (Briet, 2002). Under the law as it previously stood, the Ministry of Justice accepted the defence and representation of the interests of the members only as a secondary purpose of an INPA, subject to a primary scientific, humanitarian, religious, artistic or educational purpose, thereby forcing business associations to carefully craft their purpose clauses. In practice, this meant that a business association incorporated as an INPA would usually have a primary scientific and/or educational purpose (for instance, the study of a certain industry) and a secondary purpose (the defence and representation of the interests of its members).

To acquire a better general understanding of what a 'non-profit-making aim of international utility' means, one must turn to the European Convention. Although the European Convention does not contain a formal definition of this concept, it does stipulate in its preamble that NGOs 'carry out work of value to the international community, particularly in the scientific, cultural, charitable, philanthropic, health and education fields, and that they contribute to the achievement of the aims and principles of the United Nations Charter and the Statute of the Council of Europe'. The aims and principles of the United Nations Charter and the Statute of the Council of Europe explicitly refer to 'solving international problems of an economic . . . character' (United Nations Charter, Article 1.3) and to 'facilitating of their economic . . . progress' (Statute of the Council of Europe, Article 1.a.), concepts which are key to the operation of business associations.

Also, on the occasion of a 1998 seminar on the application of the European Convention organised by the Council of Europe it was concluded that (i) NGOs endowed with consultative status with the

Council of Europe or the United Nations 'may be considered as being in compliance with the criteria of international utility', (ii) national criteria of recognition for public interest may be taken into account at an international level, and (iii) the concept of international utility will not be determined only from a national point of view.[4]

As regards specifically the 'non-profit-making aim' part of the concept, the explanatory report of the European Convention states that

[t]his condition distinguishes NGOs from commercial companies or other bodies which exist to distribute financial benefits among their members. However, an NGO may make a profit, without altering its character, in connection with a given operation (for example, by renting a property, selling a publication, etc.) if that operation is to serve its non-profit-making aim. (Council of Europe, 1986, pp. 7–8)

The meaning of 'non-profit-making aim' is close to the description of the limited economic activities INPAs may engage in (see above).

Given the nature of the activities usually carried out by EU business associations, they should easily pass the international utility test.

Open to Belgians and foreigners alike

INPAs must be open to both foreign and Belgian physical persons and legal entities as members. The actual composition of the membership, however, has no impact on whether or not an association will be recognised as an INPA.

Article 49 of the New Law confirms what the law of 1919 already stipulated, that is, that members are not liable for the debts and obligations of the INPA.

The New Law does not specify how many members an INPA must have. Although in the absence of a more onerous legal requirement, two members suffice to validly create an INPA, the Ministry of Justice does in principle require – *contra legem* – a minimum of three members.

Under the law of 1919 the management of an INPA had to count at least one Belgian national. Following a 1999 decision of the European Court of Justice, which considered this requirement a violation of the non-discrimination principle contained in the then Article 6 of the EC Treaty,[5] the nationality requirement was removed from the law of 1919 through a special law of 30 June 2000 and has also not resurfaced in the New Law.

It is thus perfectly possible to establish an INPA that has no Belgian members and no Belgian managers.

Legal personality

According to Article 50, §1 of the New Law, an INPA obtains legal personality as of the date of the Royal Decree granting such legal personality. This was not entirely clear under the law of 1919, but the New Law has put an end to this uncertainty.[6]

A controversy exists as to whether or not the Ministry of Justice has discretionary powers to issue the Royal Decree, the Ministry assuming that it has.

Management structure

An INPA must have two governing bodies: a General Assembly and a Board of Directors, although they may be called differently in the INPA's by-laws (Article 48 New Law). It is possible, however, to have more governing bodies.[7] This would allow EU business associations to accommodate the often complicated governance structures desired by their membership.

Under the law of 1919 it was legally possible to have only one governing body, but INPAs desiring to implement such a governance structure usually encountered the opposition of the Ministry of Justice and had to modify their intended governance structure to obtain the Royal Decree granting them legal personality and recognising them as an INPA.

Publication and financial reporting requirements

The New Law has fundamentally altered the publication and financial reporting obligations of INPAs.

While under the law of 1919 an INPA could limit itself to publish its by-laws and director data in the Annexes to the Belgian Official Journal ('*Moniteur Belge/Belgisch Staatsblad*'), it must now deposit a host of documents in a file held at the Ministry of Justice from where certain of the data contained in the file will be published in the Annexes to the Belgian Official Journal (Article 51 New Law). A future Royal Decree will determine who will have access to the documents deposited in the file.

The law of 1919 did not contain any financial reporting require-ments. The New Law, however, distinguishes between three types of INPAs: small INPAs, big INPAs and very big INPAs, which are all subject to certain obligations (Article 53 New Law). Small INPAs must produce simplified accounting records and annual accounts. Big INPAs must produce accounting records and annual accounts pursuant to Belgium's accounting law of 1975 if at the end of the accounting period at least two of the following three thresholds are met:

- the association has an annual average of five full-time equivalent employees;
- the association has revenues of €250,000, excluding VAT and exceptional revenues;
- the association has assets of €1,000,000.

Very big INPAs must comply with the accounting and annual accounts rules applicable to big INPAs and, in addition, appoint a statutory auditor if they exceed an annual average of 100 full-time equivalent employees or if at the end of the accounting period at least two of the following three thresholds are exceeded:

- the association has an annual average of 50 full-time equivalent employees;
- the association has revenues of €6,250,000, excluding VAT and exceptional expenses;
- the association has assets of €3,125,000.

Each year the Board of Directors of the INPA must prepare the annual accounts of the past accounting period and the budget for the next accounting period. The General Assembly must approve the annual accounts and the budget at its first meeting following the decision of the Board of Directors.

A Royal Decree which is being prepared by the Belgian Accounting Rules Commission ('*Commission des normes comptables/Commissie voor boekhoudkundige normen*') will specify and elaborate the financial reporting rules applicable to INPAs.

Major advantages and disadvantages of the INPA structure

Incorporating as an INPA has a number of distinct advantages:

- Title III of the New Law dealing with INPAs is relatively short (it counts only 13 Articles), contains a minimum of mandatory provisions and thus offers INPAs a large measure of contractual freedom to organise themselves as they see fit.
- The INPA's legal personality is granted by Royal Decree, thus offering an INPA a quality mark or seal of approval. This is also the major

reason why the approval via Royal Decree was maintained in the New Law.[8]

- As an INPA has legal personality it can as such own assets, enter into contracts and act as plaintiff or defendant in legal proceedings.
- Given the limited liability of its members, an INPA's debts and obligations are not a member's debts and obligations.

However, INPA status also has a number of distinct drawbacks:

- An INPA's legal personality must be granted via Royal Decree. A Royal Decree is also required to approve certain changes to an INPA's by-laws (Article 50 New Law). In practice, this means major government interference from the Ministry of Justice. The Ministry must also approve any changes to an INPA's by-laws that must not be formally approved via Royal Decree. The insistence of the Ministry to force INPA promoters to accept the Ministry's view on how INPAs should be structured and operated has been criticised in the past (Lontings, 1996). Unfortunately, the situation has not improved since and the Ministry continues to impose requirements on INPAs which are manifestly *contra legem*. In a recent example, the Ministry refused a provision in INPA by-laws stating that the INPA's directors could be remunerated, notwithstanding the fact that this is perfectly legal under the INPA legislation and also as a matter of Belgian non-profit law in general. Similarly, the Ministry continues to insist that the General Assembly of an INPA meet at least every two years, while the law does not require or impose this.
- The slow functioning of the Ministry of Justice makes the process to establish an INPA or modify its by-laws a time-consuming one. Delays of up to six months are not exceptional.
- The publication and financial reporting requirements make INPA status less appealing than it used to be.

The domestic non-profit association ('ASBL/VZW')

On 27 June 1921 the Belgian legislature adopted a law 'granting [domestic] non-profit associations and foundations legal personality'. The law made it possible to henceforth incorporate with legal personality ASBL/VZWs in accordance with a standardised process and without government interference.

It is remarkable, and evidence of the internationalist sentiment prevailing at that time, that the law of 1921 was promulgated after it had become possible under Belgian law to establish INPAs (for a detailed discussion of the origins of ASBL/VZWs, see 'T Kint, 1996).

Subsequent to its adoption, the law of 1921 was modified a number of times and for the last time by the New Law, which aims mainly at avoiding future abuses of the ASBL/VZW form and at creating more transparency (financial and otherwise) with regard to ASBL/VZWs.[9]

ASBL/VZWs are by far the most popular form in Belgium to organise non-profit activities. By 1939 there were already 7131 of them; this figure has since risen to more than 107,000 (Briet and Verdonck, 2002). Although no precise figures exist, a number of EU business associations active in Brussels have adopted the ASBL/VZW form, which, however, so far has been less popular amongst such business associations than the INPA form.

Definition

Article 1 of the New Law defines an ASBL/VZW as an association which does not carry out industrial or commercial activities and which does not strive to procure its members a material gain. As already mentioned above, these concepts have the same meaning and must be interpreted in the same fashion as the identical concepts used with regard to INPAs.

Contrary to INPAs, ASBL/VZWs must not pursue a specific purpose. Subject to the limitations mentioned in the preceding paragraph, ASBL/VZWs can pursue any purpose they wish to advance, including the defence, the promotion and/or the representation of their membership and/or a certain industry. Hence, the purpose(s) pursued can be of international utility, but it is not a requirement that it be so. There are thus no objections against EU business associations adopting this legal form.

Nationality requirements

ASBL/VZWs can be established by both foreign and Belgian physical persons and legal entities alike. The law of 1921 required that at least three-fifths of the members were Belgian nationals or persons duly residing and registered in Belgium. This nationality requirement was deemed illegal under EU law by the European Court of Justice in its 1999 decision discussed above and removed from the law of 1921 through the special law of 30 June 2000 also mentioned above.

The members are not liable for the debts and obligations of an ASBL/VZW (Article 2bis New Law). This principle had been accepted before by legal doctrine and case law and had already been incorporated in the law of 1921 through a special law of 25 November 1997.

An ASBL/VZW must have at least three members (Article 2, 3° New Law).

There are no nationality requirements with respect to the directors of an ASBL/VZW. It is thus perfectly possible to establish an ASBL/VZW that has no Belgian members and no Belgian directors.

Legal personality

An ASBL/VZW will acquire legal personality as of the moment its by-laws and certain other data are deposited at the clerk's office of the competent Commercial Court (*'tribunal de commerce/rechtbank van koophandel'*) (Article 3, §1 New Law). This represents a significant improvement over the regime of the law of 1921, pursuant to which an ASBL/ VZW acquired legal personality only upon publication of its by-laws and certain director data in the Annexes to the Belgian Official Journal, a process which was not under the control of the association's founders and could thus lead to substantial delays in the creation of an ASBL/VZW.

The acquisition of legal personality is automatic. Contrary to INPAs, no Royal Decree or other government intervention is required.

Management structure

An ASBL/VZW must have two governing bodies: a General Assembly and a Board of Directors (Articles 2, 4 and 13 New Law). It is possible, however, in the by-laws of an ASBL/VZW to provide for additional bodies so as to accommodate governance desires of EU business associations. It is not possible to have one governing body only.

Publication and financial reporting requirements

As is the case with INPAs, the New Law has fundamentally altered the publication and financial reporting obligations of ASBL/VZWs. While under the law of 1921 an ASBL/VZW could limit itself to publish its by-laws and certain other data in the Annexes to the Belgian Official Journal and deposit a list of members at the clerk's office of the competent Court of First Instance, it must now deposit a host of documents in a file held at the clerk's office of the competent Commercial Court from where certain of the data contained in the file will be published in the Annexes to the Belgian Official Journal (Article 26novies New Law). Any third party can consult these documents free of charge at the clerk's office and obtain a copy thereof.

Pursuant to Article 10 of the New Law, all members have the right of access to and the right to obtain a copy of a series of documents of the ASBL/VZW, including all accounting records. Members of an INPA do not have such a right of access.

The law of 1921 contained only a few references to a minimal set of financial reporting obligations for ASBL/VZWs. The New Law has substantially expanded these obligations, which are virtually identical to the financial reporting obligations for INPAs discussed above and are based on the same distinction between small, big and very big associations (Article 17 New Law). Two differences, however, are worth mentioning:

- An ASBL/VZW's General Assembly must approve the annual accounts and the budget *each year* and not at its first meeting following their adoption by the Board of Directors only.
- Once approved by the General Assembly, the annual accounts of an ASBL/VZW must be filed with the National Bank of Belgium. INPAs must only deposit their annual accounts in the file held at the Ministry of Justice.

With regard to ASBL/VZWs as well, a Royal Decree which is being prepared by the Belgian Accounting Rules Commission will specify and elaborate the financial reporting rules.

Major advantages and disadvantages of the ASBL/VZW structure

Incorporating as an ASBL/VZW has a number of distinct advantages:

- The legal personality of an ASBL/VZW is acquired *ipso iure* upon completion of minimal publication formalities. There is no government interference in the process. There is also no government interference if an ASBL/VZW wants to modify its by-laws.
- As a result, the incorporation process is swift.
- As an ASBL/VZW has legal personality it can as such own assets, enter into contracts and act as plaintiff or defendant in legal proceedings.
- Given the limited liability of its members, an ASBL/VZW's debts and obligations are not a member's debts and obligations.

However, ASBL/VZW status also has certain distinct drawbacks:

- Title I of the New Law dealing with ASBL/VZWs is relatively long (it numbers 41 Articles) and contains a considerable number of mandatory provisions which must be respected by the ASBL/VZW, thereby limiting the contractual freedom of ASBL/VZWs to organize themselves as they see fit.

- The publication and financial reporting requirements make ASBL/ VZW status less appealing than it used to be. In particular the members' right of access has already caused concern in certain circles as it is perceived to threaten the confidentiality of certain association data.

The 'factual association'

As mentioned above, both the INPA and the ASBL/VZW have legal personality and thus offer their promoters a vehicle which exists as an incorporated entity.

It is, however, not mandatory that an association obtain legal personality. Indeed, an association can exist without acquiring such personality. In Belgium, such an association is commonly called a 'factual association' ('*association de fait/feitelijke vereniging*').[10]

The term 'factual association' is misleading as the association without legal personality does have legal substance. The association is a contract between the members of the association, pursuant to which they decide to pursue a common purpose and pool their resources to that effect. The association is governed by the terms of the contract and by the supplementary rules that, according to the law governing the contract, can or must be applied.

Although no precise figures exist on the overall number of factual associations active in Belgium and, more specifically, on the number of EU business associations that have adopted this form, it is known that a considerable number of EU business associations have chosen to function as factual associations.

Notwithstanding the fact that an EU business association will be active in or from Brussels, it is not required that the factual association be governed by Belgian law. Indeed, as the contract will have an international dimension, the parties (that is, members of the association) are free to choose the governing law. The functioning of the association and the rights and liabilities of the members will thus in large measure depend on such choice.

Assuming the governing law is Belgian law, then a factual association will show the following major advantages and disadvantages.

Advantages

- There does not exist a compelling legal framework, such as the New Law, that factual associations must comply with. There is thus ample room for contractual freedom.

- Factual associations can be established without any government interference. There is no need to obtain a Royal Decree or comply with certain formalities to acquire legal personality.
- Factual associations are not subject to any publication or financial reporting requirements.

Disadvantages

- As a factual association does not exist as a separate legal entity, it cannot as such own, or have other rights on, the assets used to pursue the purpose of the association. Although the precise nature of the rights in these assets remains the subject of much debate, it is often said that they are the common or collective property of the members of the association.[11] The association can also not as such enter into contracts or act as plaintiff or defendant in legal proceedings. Any actions of the association must be organised through appropriate agency structures (*'mandat/lastgeving'*). For instance, a number of years ago an internationally-oriented factual association was sued by a dismissed employee through the association's Secretary-General who was held to have the appropriate powers to represent the association as a party in the proceedings.[12]
- Also because the factual association has no legal personality, the members will be liable for the association's debts and obligations. This liability will be in equal parts (*'parts viriles/gelijke delen'*), unless stipulated otherwise.

The Belgian presence of a foreign association

It is not legally required for an EU business association that wishes to be active in Belgium to structure itself according to Belgian law. Such an association may, for instance, incorporate in The Netherlands and establish a presence in Belgium. This presence can go by a variety of names, such as 'representative office', 'branch' or 'secretariat'.

Although no precise figures exist, it would appear that quite a few EU business associations have chosen this *modus operandi*.

Until recently this type of presence used to entail a host of practical problems for the associations concerned. As no formal registration or publicity requirements for the Belgian presences of such associations existed, these presences did somehow not exist in the eyes of their Belgian counterparts. As a result, it was often impossible or difficult to obtain a VAT number, enjoy postal services, open a bank account, lease or buy property, and so forth.

Only a few avenues existed to obtain some form of formal recognition in Belgium, which would allow the association to solve its practical problems (for a detailed discussion of these see Lontings, 1994):

- Obtain a so-called 'Article 8' certificate from the Ministry of Justice under the law of 1919. This certificate renders it possible to publish the by-laws of an association with international vocation in the Annexes to the Belgian Official Journal, thus giving this association some formal recognition in Belgium.
- Obtain the formal recognition of the foreign association under the aforementioned European Convention.
- Obtain formal recognition under bilateral treaties. Such treaty exists, for instance, with the United States.

Each of these procedures was rather cumbersome and time-consuming. The New Law aims to remedy this unsatisfactory situation.

Foreign associations with a non-profit-making aim of international utility can henceforth open a 'centre of activity' ('*siege d'opération/zetel van werkzaamheden*') in Belgium by complying with the publication formalities imposed by the New Law on INPAs (Article 58 New Law). A centre of activity is defined under this Article as 'a stable establishment without separate legal personality, the activities of which are conform to the purpose of the international association pursuing a non-profit-making aim of international utility'.

A similar regime is provided with regard to centres of activities of foreign associations in Title I of the New Law dealing with ASBL/VZWs (Article 26octies New Law).

It is not entirely clear at present how foreign associations will choose which procedure to follow and, indeed, if they will have such choice. For instance, must a foreign association with a non-profit-making aim of international utility comply with the publication formalities applicable to INPAs or may it choose to register under Title I of the New Law dealing with ASBL/VZWs, given that ASBL/VZWs may also be incorporated with a non-profit-making aim of international utility?

Alternative structures

The structures discussed above represent the most common structures adopted by EU business associations.

From time to time, however, alternative structures are considered as well, most frequently the economic interest grouping and the European association.

Economic interest grouping

The best-known economic interest grouping is the European Economic Interest Grouping or EEIG established pursuant to Council Regulation (EEC) 2137/85 of 25 July 1985 (the 'EEIG Regulation').[13]

A Regulation is an EU legal instrument that is binding in its entirety and directly applicable in all Member States (Article 249 EC Treaty). From time to time it is supplemented by implementing Member State legislation. In Belgium, the EEIG Regulation was implemented through a law of 12 July 1989.

The EEIG Regulation allows for the creation of an entity '[t]he purpose of [which] shall be to facilitate or develop the economic activities of its members and to improve or increase the results of those activities; its purpose is not to make profits for itself' (Article 3 EEIG Regulation).

While it is certainly possible to carry out activities that are often pursued by EU business associations through an EEIG (such as performing studies, acting as a certification organisation, lobbying and monitoring) (Simonart, 2002), there are a number of reasons why in practice this rarely seems to happen (see also Van Gerven, 1996). A number of the most compelling of these reasons are set out below.

Firstly, an EEIG must have as its purpose to develop the economic activities of its members and to improve the results of these activities. An EEIG thus presupposes a number of economic operators coming together with the explicit intent to promote their economic performance and, to that effect, create a joint economic undertaking. This is rarely the intent of the members of an EU business association, which often are competitors willing to a certain extent to share the expense of the promotion of their interests and/or the interests of their industry, but not eager to run an undertaking together. With these considerations in mind, an INPA, an ASBL/VZW or a factual association are more appealing vehicles.

Secondly, the members of an EEIG are jointly and severally liable for the debts and other obligations of an EEIG (Article 24.1 EEIG Regulation). This liability is substantially more onerous than the limited liability offered by INPA and ASBL/VZW structures or the liability in equal parts resulting from membership of a factual association.

Thirdly, only entities which have been formed in accordance with the law of an EU Member State and which have their registered or statutory office and their central administration in the EU (and natural persons active in the EU) can become members of an EEIG (Article 4.1 EEIG Regulation). Third country entities are thus excluded form participation in an EEIG, unless they interpose an EU entity. No such restrictions exist with regard to membership of an INPA, an ASBL/VZW or a factual association.

Fourthly, an EEIG is transparent for tax purposes (Article 21 EEIG Regulation). This is also the case for a factual association, but not for an INPA or an ASBL/VZW. Although such transparency may be desired from time to time, it may also be deemed to unnecessarily complicate the tax planning of the members of an EU business association.

A number of EU Member States have adopted legislation under which it is possible to incorporate a national economic interest grouping.

In Belgium, the Company Code contains a Book XIV dealing with the Belgian economic interest grouping ('EIG').

The rules applicable to EIGs are substantially similar to the rules applying to EEIGs, except that to become member in an EIG there are no nationality requirements. It is thus possible for a non-Belgian or non-EU entity to become a direct member of an EIG. However, the other concerns regarding the incorporation of an EU business association in the form of an economic interest grouping remain valid.

European association

It is at present not possible to form a European association ('EA') as the proposals submitted so far have to this date not resulted in a legally binding EU instrument.

The most recent document is the 'Amended proposal for a Council Regulation (EEC) on the statute for a European association', submitted by the European Commission on 6 July 1993 (the 'EA Proposed Regulation').[14] Even if this proposal would at some future date be adopted, it would in its current form not offer an appropriate vehicle for most EU business associations.

Indeed, while an EA can be created specifically 'to promote the trade or professional interests of its members in the most diverse areas' (Article 1.1 EA Proposed Regulation), only non-profit associations, foundations and natural persons can become *ab initio* members of an EA (Article 3.1 combined with Annex EA Proposed Regulation). Commercial companies, which are the most common members of EU business associations, do not qualify for *ab initio* membership. Only through the conversion of an existing national association into an EA in accordance with the terms and conditions of Article 3.2 of the EA Proposed Regulation may an EA open up to commercial companies.

Also, when an EA is created through an *ab initio* incorporation rather than a conversion from an existing national association, its members must be EU residents.

Conclusions

As has been shown in the preceding pages, there exist sufficient and adequate forms under Belgian law to allow for the establishment of an EU business association.

Which form to use will depend on an evaluation of the advantages and disadvantages of each form and, ultimately, on the preferences of the association's membership.

Now that Belgium's new non-profit legislation has been adopted, it will be interesting to observe if the INPA form – which so far was the preferred legal form for EU business associations – will remain as popular as before.

INPAs and ASBL/VZWs will be subject to very similar publication and financial reporting obligations. These obligations should thus not determine the future choice of legal form. Also, many EU business associations (even if they exist as factual associations) already apply strict internal financial reporting standards and should thus not be deterred or fundamentally influenced by these new requirements.

While ASBL/VZWs will henceforth be easy and quick to incorporate, INPAs will continue to require approval via Royal Decree. INPAs will also continue to need the co-operation of the Ministry of Justice to amend their by-laws, be it via Royal Decree or via an administrative decision of the Ministry. Given the Ministry's reluctance to respect the principle of contractual freedom underlying the creation and evolution of INPAs and given the Ministry's reluctance to accommodate the needs of the modern association world, it remains to be seen if INPAs will continue to be popular. It is certainly not inconceivable that henceforth EU business associations will be more attracted to the ASBL/VZW form or – now that a host of practical problems are resolved – to the establishment in Belgium of a 'centre of activity' of a foreign association.

Notes

1 *Parliamentary Documents*, Senate, 2000–2001, no. 2–283/16, 39 (1223); *Parliamentary Documents*, Chamber, 1998–1999, no. 1883/1, 2 (over 1400).
2 Cour de Cassation, 3 October 1996, TRV, 1997, 217.
3 *Parliamentary Documents*, Senate, 2000–2001, no. 2–283/13, 56.

4   *Seminar on the application of the European Convention on the recognition of the legal personality of international non-governmental organizations* (ETS No. 124), 9–10 February 1998. *Conclusions* (CONV 124 (98) (*Concl.*), Strasbourg, Council of Europe, 25 February 1998, 2.

5   ECJ, 29 June 1999, case C-172/98, O.J., 28 August 1999, no. C 246, 6.

6   That the date of the Royal Decree was the date on which the INPA acquired legal personality was most vigorously stated by Lontings (1994). The preparatory works of the New Law refer explicitly to this source as the main inspiration to resolve the controversy: *Parliamentary Documents*, Senate, 1999–2000, no. 2-283/6, 14.

7   *Parliamentary Documents*, Senate, 1999–2000, no. 2-283/5, 12.

8   *Parliamentary Documents*, Senate, 1999–2000, no. 2-283/5, 11; *Parliamentary Documents*, Senate, 2000–2001, no. 2-283/16, 74.

9   These aims are very comparable to the reasons underlying the forthcoming 'biggest shake-up since Elisabeth I' in UK charities law. See Joy (2002).

10   For a brief general discussion of factual associations in English, see Lontings (2000).

11   For a recent review of these concepts, see Van Gerven (2000).

12   Labour Court of Appeals, Brussels, 12 April 1988, *JTT*, 1989, 275.

13   OJ, No L 199, 31 July 1985, 1.

14   OJ, No C 236, 31 August 1993, 1.

Part V

Trust

15

In the End the Only Thing that Matters – Is Trust

Ian Locks

Business associations usually proclaim their added value as intermediaries by highlighting a mixture of big ideas, policy objectives and their ability to influence and steer others towards common agreed goals. The truth is actually much simpler. All these are but ingredients of an altogether more fundamental asset: trust. Put another way, four things matter for business associations: trust, trust, trust.... and trust. With these in good shape, the association is guaranteed a perception among its stakeholders that it is a successful and valued intermediary.

The first of the four 'trusts' is trust between members. Any one who has sat around a table and observed the banter and camaraderie cannot help but be struck by the incongruity that representatives from warring tribes – people who compete minute by minute, week by week in cut-throat competition – are able to come together to discuss anything at all.

For greater insight, just stand in the hall of one of London's great livery companies and reflect on the list of 'masters' of these earlier trade associations dating back four, maybe six, hundred years. The Worshipful Company of Stationers and Newspapermakers was formed in the fifteenth century to protect stationers – the people who had stalls in busy market places and sold paper and writing equipment and who would also read letters and documents to the illiterate and pen responses for them. Through forming a guild, the professionals could maintain their standards, keep out the rogues and scalliwags who might otherwise defraud the illiterate and maintain the *trust* of their customers in the service they provided.

By working together, and agreeing to compete on what they decided was a level playing field, they could protect their market. They could also decide, or fix, their prices. And that, of course, is the double-edged sword of trust between competitors: What the Americans so aptly term anti-trust. But kept in good order and focused on issues which benefit customers rather than distort pricing, such trust is arguably not only extremely beneficial to customers, it is essential.

I would put it even more strongly. Without trust between the players in any given activity, that service, trade or profession cannot operate successfully. Consider children in a playground: what is the first thing they do when playing a game? They agree the rules. And if the game is working because the rules don't work…they stop and argue out a change of rules. And if someone breaks the rules, they are brought into line. And when they grow up what do they do? They join or form trade or business associations – just as our forbears did in medieval London and before them in the civilisations of ancient Rome and Greece, in the Souks – and, for all I know, in Atlantis.

So the first 'trust' is having sufficient trust to be able to sit down with competitors to agree common standards and protocols, promote the benefits of an industry and protect the environment for success.

The second 'trust' is trust by the members in the business association executive. There is abundant evidence that only when the members of an association have trust in the executive can that association operate effectively to achieve the objectives and goals set for it.

When I was asked to contribute to the discussion on business associations by examining the role of trust it was not something which, in over twenty years of trade association experience, I had ever seriously considered. It was something I guess I had always taken for granted. My predecessor at the ninety-year-old Periodical Publishers Association, the organisation of magazine publishers and b2b media in the UK, had not felt he had the authority to issue a press release without Board approval and had kept the level of communication to the outside world at a minimum. Our communications now include a regularly published magazine, a weekly email service to 4000 or so recipients, weekly press releases, many open conferences, platform appearances and press, radio and TV interviews. Put simply, I believe I can claim after thirteen years to have earned the trust of my members. They trust me – or fire me. They have to.

Times for us had changed. Our industry needed to promote its medium to customers – advertisers in particular – and to government. We needed to be proactive, make quick decisions and manage complex communications messages across a variety of platforms. This just cannot be managed by a Board of thirty industry people meeting three times a year – or even successfully by a committee meeting rather more frequently.

A measure of trust is which business association executives can give an answer with confidence – and who are the ones who have to defer to a chairman, board or council? Undoubtedly there is a trend in associations to appoint executives in whom the members are prepared to invest a great deal of authority and trust to exercise their own initiative and to get on and run the business. Arguments as to why this is so include:

- Businesses are leaner and less able to spare executives to spend large amounts of time on trade association activities.
- Senior executives cannot be seen to have the time to spend on what are seen as extra-curricula activities.
- The business of representation is more complex now than it has ever been with the need for developing and maintaining complex alliances.

These are all perfectly reasonable arguments with evidence to support them. The fact remains, however, that some associations trust their executive to get on and run the show. They have just two or three council or board meetings a year and delegate most of their responsibilities to specialist committees. It is the chief executive who acts as manager and referee – advising committees when they may be exceeding their powers, referring upwards, downwards or sideways: advising on direction, bringing proposals to groups on how they can develop their remit, perhaps encouraging a more commercial approach to funding projects they may wish to undertake and thereby extending their autonomy.

Others, for whatever reason, choose not to go this route. Their chief officer is strictly limited, referring matters of any substance to a board or council meeting as often as monthly. Can both models be equally successful in achieving the aims and objectives of the member companies to promote and to protect their interests? My proposition is that it is the associations that trust their executive to get on and run the show within the remit they are given that move the business on and do the best job for their constituency.

The organisation I run has moved from a turnover of £600,000 to almost £7 m. We employ some forty people against the nine I inherited. Subscription revenue accounts for barely 20 per cent of our turnover. We have just presented a membership certificate to our 450th member – up from the 120 my team and I inherited. We have developed extensions to our association in Scotland and Ireland, formed allied associations in new and developing areas of publishing – customer magazines, online publishing and newsletters – and we have developed a range of services which have high buy-in from our industry. Could we have done this without the freedom to operate as a business? Without the trust of our board and our members? I think not. An interesting but hardly a scientific study, this is a topic which deserves more examination.

The third 'trust' is trust between associations through alliances. Clearly there are examples of business associations achieving lobby objectives independently. But the broad body of evidence suggests that increasingly alliances between intermediaries are fundamental to achieving success. In fact it is hard to envisage any business association able to operate entirely in a vacuum. Alliances are fundamental to what trade associations do. They do so, for example, because the probability is that an issue will impact on or affect the interests of allied groups. Working with them is the most effective way of achieving objectives.

Government tends to end up ignoring a confusing plethora of voices from a single sector. A clear, well-thought out and well-presented case can – and frequently does – receive a good hearing. Governments are increasingly insisting that associations get together into single associations or alliances in order that they may have the ear of government while at EU Level there is, rightly, a wish to hear a position which has the input of many countries.

Trust is the key factor affecting how these alliances operate. The members have the choice of whether to neuter their association to the point of ineffectiveness or give it the autonomy to lobby effectively on behalf of members. Associations of associations – which, of course, is what most EU business associations inevitably are – have a much tougher job than associations of companies.

Building alliances is a key part of trade association work. Each year the UK Trade Association Forum surveys UK trade associations. Three years ago a majority anticipated that they would merge with one or more associations in the following five years. The updated survey shows a clear trend towards creating alliances.

The sector I represent turns over just under €10 bn. Two years ago we formed an alliance with national and regional newspapers, books and journals to form a €28 bn UK Publishing Media alliance. We were following similar movements in the Netherlands, Finland and Germany. We have been working for many years to achieve the same kind of common sense at a European level – so far without success.

Make no mistake: alliances are extremely hard work – but absolutely essential whether it be in talking to government or, for example, in the evolution of e-commerce supply chains and industry-wide transaction systems facing many industries where horizontal and vertical alliances of stakeholders are key.

Which takes us to our fourth 'trust', trust between associations – and the alliances in which they operate – and government. The development of trust between intermediaries and government evolves into a markedly different relationship where the intermediary can be a prime mover in promoting – or preventing – legislation. A particularly striking example of industry and government working together is provided by the European Round Table of Industrialists and the European Commission. The ERT has developed a level of trust in its relations with the EU in which it can apparently almost write the book. Such a high level of trust has been established that some have suggested it could almost be seen as the group that determines the EU agenda in framing legislation for industry. Whatever the truth of the position, the ultimate objective of any business association or alliance has to be to achieve a level of trust with and within government where it is invited to participate in setting the agenda and be party to setting the direction.

At a much more basic level in the UK a group of 30 associations was encouraged by the Department of Trade and Industry to come together in a Digital Content Forum. The objective to provide government with the input they required to develop thinking and policies related to the emergence of online information and entertainment businesses. Such alliances can have great mutual benefit. Handled sensibly, and in an atmosphere of trust on both sides, government and business working together can be a powerful alliance indeed.

Trust, like all assets, cannot be ignored. It should not be taken for granted – at any level. And at any level trust which has taken years to establish can be destroyed. Extreme behaviour can make it difficult or impossible for leaders of an industry to sit down together. An executive can lose trust through one foolish or dishonest action. A high level of trust in an executive can lead to members of an association disengaging. Alliances can fall apart through actions perceived as duplicitous or over-competitive between parties. And government or industry can take a view that one party is abusing the trust between them. The resulting lack of trust can bring the house tumbling down.

On the other hand, too high a level of trust between competing companies can have just as severe dangers with anti-trust behaviour ultimately earning its just reward – bringing its own downfall through loss of trust from customers and from government.

With too high a level of trust in an executive, members can leave it all to the executive, which can lead to a feeling of lack of transparency, influence and control by those who pay for the service.

Successful alliances between associations can lead to mergers – for better or worse. And too close a relationship between government and business can lead to cries of 'foul', or compromise the independence of business association representation.

Trust is built on perceptions which are hard won and easily lost. In the end the only thing that matters – is trust.

16

Trust: A Sceptical View

Wyn Grant

This chapter takes a more sceptical view of the utility of the concept of trust in relation to EU business associations than the previous chapter in this section of the book. Since the conference on which this book was based was held, events such as the Enron scandal would seem to have underwritten the importance of trust as a component of a successful market economy. The argument made in this chapter is not that the concept of trust is of no value when an examination is made of the way in which business associations work. There is certainly value in the concept, but there is also a danger of it becoming a 'warm word' which offers a blanket panacea for the challenges that business associations face. The idea of 'trust' has to be weighed against other organising ideas with emphasis given in this chapter to the notion of effectiveness.

It is worth pausing to consider what is meant by trust. Streeck gives a relatively stringent definition when he argues (1997, p. 202) that 'Trust is the belief that another party will continue to adhere to rules of reciprocity or "fairness" even in circumstances in which it might be advantageous to defect.' A more limited but perhaps more appealing way to look at it is to see trust as a characteristic of an exchange relationship in which the other party will behave in accordance with imperfectly articulated but well understood informal 'rules of the game'. For example, in terms of the relationship between an association and its members or an association and an EU institution, there may be informal understandings about when consultation is or is not necessary before a decision is taken.

The utility of the concept of trust

Before looking at the concept critically, in what ways is trust important to the success of a business association, particularly at the EU level? First, members must have confidence in the ability of the staff of the association. One problem in the past in European associations was that, if they were federations of federations, representation in Brussels often came from the office staff of the national association. The senior management of big businesses often regarded them as little more than middle-ranking managers. Indeed, this tension was one of the motivations for the establishment of 'hybrid' associations in a number of sectors with large firms represented alongside associations. If a European federation is largely dealing with technical matters, then management in firms may be happy to leave matters to well qualified but not particularly high level managers.

In the thirty years in which the writer has studied business associations, one of the biggest changes has been the improvement in the calibre of association staff. This is a difficult change to quantify, but there is no doubt that staff are better educated and drawn from more diverse backgrounds. The gender bias that was apparent for so long is rapidly disappearing. No one would contemplate today filling a vacant post of secretary general in a European association with someone nearing the end of their career in a firm or association, but that was not unknown thirty years ago. Trust in association staff is not generally a problem, but retaining them may be more difficult than it was in the past.

Second, members must have confidence in the structures and processes of the association. For example, small and medium-sized firms must be confident that their particular concerns and interests are taken into account. However, the association's structure must not be set up in such a way that particular interests – or particular countries – can exert veto power. The association should be able to make well considered decisions that have broad membership support, but it should also be able to make them quickly when necessary. Modern electronic forms of communication assist decision-making that is both fast and consensual.

Successful associations have to undergo a process of organisational development. This concept rests 'on two focal points – the degree to which the complex organisational arrangements found in a sector are *ordered* and *coordinated* and the degree to which associations are *autonomous* from their several environments and thereby suited to the assumption of an independent policy role'. (Coleman and Grant, 1984, p. 212). An association needs a measure of autonomy from its membership in order to make judgements about how to negotiate effectively. However, the concept of trust helps to remind us that associations should not distance themselves too far from their members. Structures and procedures need to be devised which inform and involve the active membership.

A third aspect of trust concerns the relationship with the Commission or any other actors that an association is trying to influence. An association must be able to demonstrate that it can speak authoritatively for its membership and that it has a coherent and well argued view. Above all, it must not provide Commission officials or other decision makers with misleading or incomplete information. If it does so, its future credibility will be damaged beyond repair.

Most difficult of all, an association must be able to cope with the challenges of a changing political environment by building trust-based relationships with organisations it may not have dealt with in the past. There has been a shift from a politics of production to a politics of collective consumption (Grant, 2000) leading to a new prominence for environmental and consumer movements collectively referred to as 'non-governmental organisations (NGOs)' (although in terms of United Nations definitions, business associations are also NGOs). Such organisations are naturally suspicious of business associations and creating a constructive dialogue with them is a difficult exercise in the building of mutual trust. For example, one of the EU's leading business associations, the European Chemical Industry Council (Cefic) has initiated a stakeholder dialogue through meetings that involves trade unions and NGOs. Its website on the EU's new chemicals policy contains links to groups such as Greenpeace and the European Environmental Bureau.

Finally, it might be argued that building trust is particularly important in business-government relations at the EU level. This is because of what is generally agreed to be the complex, fluid and unpredictable character of the decision-making process at the EU level. There is no one authoritative centre of decision making. Hence, if the decision-making process is going to work at all, there needs to be a basis of trust between the various participants and in particular between business associations and the various decision-making bodies.

It would therefore seem that there is a powerful case for treating trust as a key element of the relations between members and association staff, and between associations and decision makers, especially at the EU level. Associations need to be able to maintain minimal levels of trust with their members. If they fail to do so, members will exit. They also have to retain the trust of decision makers as reliable partners if they are to remain part of the decision-making process. Trust is certainly a relevant and useful concept, but there is always a danger in relying too much on warm, 'hurrah' words as a basis for action. As was emphasised earlier, the concept of trust needs to be balanced against alternative concepts.

Effectiveness as an alternative concept

One alternative concept is that of effectiveness. Trust is a process-oriented concept, whereas effectiveness is more results-oriented. Advocates of the importance of trust would, of course, argue that an effective process produces outcomes that not only work, but are also enduring. This raises issues about alternative forms of market economy that we will return to later in the chapter. Effectiveness is more oriented towards the 'bottom line', trust is concerned with the broad social conditions that permit a market economy to operate.

Association effectiveness is notoriously difficult to demonstrate, but that will not stop members asking questions about whether they are obtaining value for money from their subscriptions. One reason that it is difficult to make a judgement about whether an association is effective or not is that many actors contribute to a particular decision. This is particularly true in a complex environment like the EU where many different actors are involved in the decision-making process include Community institutions, Member States and EU-level associations. These various actors interact in a system of multi-level governance that is segmented both vertically and horizontally.

Even if one could identify cases where an association was able to secure a particular outcome, boasting about what was achieved might reduce the chances of future success. Commission officials might be offended and NGOs might feel that they had to increase their efforts in the particular decision-making arena.

Members may not always realise the complexity and difficulty of the decision-making environment that a business association faces at the EU level. An association cannot usually reverse or remove from the decision-making agenda a policy initiative that the Commission has begun. Admittedly, business was able to achieve a considerable success in defeating proposals for a carbon tax, but that was an exception rather than the rule. More generally, it is realistic to set as a target delaying and modifying the policy proposal. There is a clear educative role for associations in helping their members to understand what is and is not politically feasible. This task is probably easier in more politically sophisticated industries made up of large firms with their own government or public affairs decisions.

Effectiveness is a difficult concept to operationalise, but this does not mean that firms or EU decision makers do not make judgements about whether an EU-level association is an effective player or not. For example, CEFIC is the largest EU business associations and is generally regarded as highly effective. This was not always the case. In its early years, 'there were frequent criticisms of its organisation and effectiveness'. (Grant, Paterson and Whitston, 1988, p. 185). However, its organisation was perceived by companies to improve considerably from the late 1970s onwards.

If an association has the reputation of being well run, this may of itself contribute to its effectiveness and a virtuous cycle can develop. If, however, an association is seen as being internally fragmented, with staff of a low calibre, too reliant on obtaining member consent before it can act or modify its policies, and having too narrow a focus, it may not be well regarded in the Commission or elsewhere. This profile is not a caricature: such associations still exist in some sectors at the EU level. A vicious cycle of a declining reputation and hence declining effectiveness may then develop.

Why members may emphasise effectiveness

The members of business associations are businesses which means that they want to see a connection between association activity and the profitability of their firms. Of course, at EU level, the relationship is often an indirect one, with federations organising other associations, but this brings its own dangers of remoteness from their membership and their concerns. There are other routes for businesses to represent their interests, through their own public or government affairs divisions or contract lobbyists. If firms perceive that their European association is not effective, there are a number of alternatives open to them:

- resigning from the association. This is almost unknown.
- seeking to reform the association from within. This has happened in a number of EU level associations.
- remaining members of the association, but being less active within it and redirecting effort to lobbying by the firm. This is the worst outcome from the perspective of the association as it will reduce the resources available to the association, while uncoordinated lobbying by a firm may confuse the message coming from the sector.

If anything, globalisation and other intensifying competitive pressures are making it more likely that firms will demand that their business associations are effective. Britain's Industry and Parliament Trust has commented (2001, p. 2), 'Continuing company restructuring in many sectors causes all business personnel to focus on immediate business outcomes.' The Trust observes that government and public affairs departments in companies are increasingly called on to 'fire fight'. 'They are the departments often subject to cut backs when there is cost cutting. They, like all our businesses, at a time of economic downturn, are under great pressure to focus on business outcomes' (Industry and Parliament Trust, 2001, p. 3).

These pressures are also likely to be felt by business associations. An optimal political strategy for both firms and associations is, of course, one that focuses on the long-term achievement of goals rather than 'fire fighting'. However, it has to be recognised that the realities of the current business environment are such that effectiveness is likely to be given a higher priority than trust.

Debates about the market economy

Advocates of the central significance of trust are generally associated with a particular position on the market economy. Influenced by the work of Karl Polanyi, this has sometimes been termed the 'comparative political economy' school. In the literature a general contrast is made between neo-liberal, Anglo-Saxon or American forms of the market economy with what are variously termed organised market economies, coordinated market economies, embedded economies or 'Rhineland capitalism':

> In *liberal market economies*, firms coordinate their activities primarily via hierarchies and competitive market arrangements...In *coordinated market economies*, firms depend more heavily on non-market relationships to coordinate their endeavours with other actors and to construct their core competencies. (Hall and Soskice, 2001, p. 8)

This approach sees clear advantages in non-market forms of coordination. In general, business associations are assigned an important coordinating and developmental role in the latter type of economy.

This debate is specifically related to the notion of trust. Trust is seen as something that 'can vastly improve the performance of both markets and hierarchies'. (Streeck, 1997, p. 201). It is argued that 'product and credit markets exist because they are based on trust in the fulfilment of future transactions' (Boyer and Hollingsworth, 1997, p. 451). Trust is not seen as something that is manufactured, but is based on precapitalist logics that 'are an essential ingredient for markets and capitalism to exist' (Boyer and Hollingsworth, 1997, p. 444). Of course, in so far as the logics involved are precapitalist ones, they are particularly susceptible to erosion under conditions of intensified competition brought about by globalisation.

From the perspective of association staffs, an intermediary role based on trust might be seen to be an attractive one. Member firms might, however, have a different perspective. In particular, it depends how far one wants to move from a market economy towards a regulatory state. Continental European firms are, of course, familiar with the notion of a social market economy in which the state has a clear role in the provision of infrastructure, social services, health and education. Even the notion of higher levels of regulation might have its attractions to business, as regulations can provide entry barriers that deter new entrants to a market and hence reduce competition.

Because it lacks conventional fiscal policy instruments, the EU has a particular temptation to develop as a regulatory state. Much of that regulation is both necessary and socially desirable, for example, environmental regulation. There is, however, an issue of the balance to be drawn so that regulation does not become so pervasive that it discourages entrepreneurship and innovation and imposes costs to such an extent as to reduce the international competitiveness of the European economy. Business associations have an important contribution to make to policy debates so as to ensure that a reasonable balance is arrived at between the demands of competitiveness and social protection.

Conclusion

Arguments that trust is a key to successful business association relationships with both their members and with decision makers have some force to them. However, they need to be viewed with a degree of caution and scepticism. Trust may be a key ingredient of enduring and mutually beneficial relationships, but it needs careful handling. It is not a magic ingredient that can transform apparently insoluble problems. If it is treated insufficiently critically, it can become little more than a warm word that is easy and comforting to utter, but difficult to translate into the policy process.

It is has also been emphasised in this chapter that the academic advocates of trust are associated with a particular intellectual perspective. It is a perfectly respectable and in many ways robust perspective that offers insights of considerable value. However, it does perhaps place too much weight on the social compared with the commercial aspects of a market system.

The discussion of trust returns analysts of government–business relations to an old and familiar dilemma, that of the Janus-faced nature of business associations as intermediaries between their own members and government. Their task is not just to articulate their members' views, but to place them in the context of public policy and to inform and educate their members about what is politically feasible. They must do this while retaining the confidence of their members and without becoming little more than advocates for current policies.

There is no simple formula or set of guidelines that can prescribe how such a dual relationship can be managed in a balanced manner. The first step to managing it successfully is to recognise that the problem exists. If trust is found to be a helpful way of thinking about how such relationships should be constructed, it can make a useful contribution to the debate. If too much reliance is placed on the concept, there is a risk that it will be devalued.

Part VI

Geographical Perspectives

17

The Challenge of Geography: Recruiting and Retaining Members from the South in EU Associations

Irini Pari

The subject of this chapter is the representation of southern business organisations in EU associations, whether there is such a thing as a 'southern' dimension in European Business, and if so, how efficiently is it taken into account. The chapter ends by suggesting some proposals for change.

The insights that follow are my own views based on nearly eight years of experience as Permanent Delegate of the Federation of Greek Industries in Brussels. This work has included representing the interests of Greek Business in UNICE (the Union of Industrial and Employers' Confederations of Europe), the European Institutions, and, for the last four years, being a member of the European Economic and Social Committee. It has also been based on interactions I have had with the representatives from the federations of Italy, Portugal and Spain. The purpose is not to just give a favourable picture of ourselves but to see what could be improved, with all due respect to the organisation and the interests I represent.

The Greek paradox

Business society in Greece is convinced, and has always been convinced, of the importance of the European Union and European integration. Business leaders all put Europe high on the agenda in their public statements and in planning their priorities. They are conscious that a lot of decisions affecting them directly are taken at European level. Yet Greek business taken as a whole does not allocate enough resources to promote and defend the interests of Greek enterprises in Europe. Indeed, when looking at their representation at European level you will discover that:

- Only two organisations (the Federation of Greek Industries and the Chambers of Industry and Commerce) and two enterprises have a lobbying office based in Brussels. Resources allocated to those offices have remained the same from their inception when Greece was still an associated country to the EU. For example, my own Federation, in a visionary move, became a member of UNICE and established its offices in Brussels very early, in 1962. Since then, it has continued to operate with only two permanent staff members, despite the enormous expansion of EU powers. It was only last year that we got a secondment from one of our enterprise members. Efforts deployed to convince some of our more important branch member organisations to be represented in Brussels by themselves or under our auspices did not bear fruit.
- Not all European business organisations have a member from Greece.
- The participation of Greek members to EU business organisations in several cases is passive in the sense that it is more oriented to information-seeking rather than to influencing the decisions taken by those organisations. Very often their participation is at the higher level and not in the working groups of the business associations where most of the work is done.
- It is rare that Greeks are office holders in European organisations.

How one can explain this paradox? The reasons that are most often advanced are:

- The geographical situation of Greece: close to the Balkans, in the eastern part of the Mediterranean sea. Furthermore, being at the periphery of Europe, far away from the centre where decisions are taken, gives a feeling of distance.
- The high cost of maintaining an office in Brussels, both because of high labour cost in Belgium but also because travelling costs are higher and more time consuming.

To these reasons I would add four more reasons:

- Greek legislation is not business friendly and is very complicated, requiring a lot of attention and effort at national level. Furthermore, Greece is very late in transposing the directives at national level and has often used exemptions to postpone implementation, which means that the effects of the decisions taken at European level are not immediately felt.

• Greek multinationals are only a very recent phenomenon. Some Greek enterprises started investing in other countries and started creating what we would call a multinational only during the last decade. These are still in an early phase of opening up to Europe and the rest of the world, and still trying to develop their identity and international network.

• Greek entrepreneurs still rely a lot on their government and close relations they have.

• Finally, collective effort is not part of our culture. Rather, education and society values promote the individual effort rather than the collective. This has, of course, its advantages, but also disadvantages.

Is the Greek case common to the other southern countries?

In my view it is not exactly the same. Portugal seems to be in a similar position to Greece. Italian and Spanish industry are well represented in Brussels at horizontal, branch and enterprise level. It is interesting to notice the different ways between southern European countries of how branch organisations are represented. In the Spanish case it is centralised under CEOE (Confederación Española de las Organizaciones de Empresas), where its Brussels team of about ten people takes care of all issues horizontal, sectoral, and even agriculture. In the Italian case, Confindustria (Confederazione Generale dell'Industria Italiana) provides under its auspices, space and personnel for twelve branch organisations, giving them a certain separate identity but still working closely together, and in doing so creating a lot of synergies.

Concerning the participation in the different meetings and structures of the European organisations, I can only observe what I see in the participation in UNICE. And there one notices that southern members tend to participate quite actively at the higher level in the governing bodies but less actively in the working groups, where all the position papers are being prepared. So for example in UNICE there are seventy working groups. If you look at the nationality of their chairpersons, mostly people drawn from enterprises nominated by the member federations, you will find that only seven out of seventy come from the South, while the Netherlands alone has fifteen, and the UK, twelve. There is room for improvement.

As Zygmunt Tyszkiewicz, a former Secretary-General of UNICE and contributor to this volume, once suggested, 'business interests are convergent not divergent'. So in most of the subjects there is a common

view between the north and the south, the east and the west. Yet, enterprises are part of the economy, the society and the culture in which they
operate. That gives them some characteristics according to the country
they come from. In our work at European level we can feel the difference of approach and expression in the way of doing things and the
emphasis given to issues amongst colleagues coming from the south,
the centre, the Anglo-Saxons, the Nordic and now our eastern colleagues.

In terms of business the ones coming from the south obviously operate:

- in economies with common characteristics compared to the rest of
  Europe (lower income, large number of SMEs, less R&D, more sensitive in deficit and inflation, dependence on some branches)
- in a similar social model, very much based on family solidarity,
  rather than on state systems
- similar industrial relations
- and a certain common idiosyncrasy, temperament

Out of all these emerge some subjects we have in common that we,
the representatives of the South, should promote or emphasise in the
European agenda (for example economic and social cohesion, basic
research and innovation, regional development, and so forth).

Southern countries do not co-operate or co-ordinate their views
as northern countries, especially Scandinavian, seem to do. They do
co-ordinate, but in a very spontaneous way with no structures at all. For
example, in UNICE there is a body called the Committee of Permanent
Delegates – something like the COREPER at European Union level –
where twice a month the Secretary General of UNICE comes together
with the permanent delegates of all its member federations with
Brussels offices, and where current issues, internal matters are discussed
and activities are co-ordinated. When I started working with my
Federation, I very soon realised that, apart from the formal meeting,
there existed some other caucases of permanent delegates. One of them
was the 'snow' group, comprising our Scandinavian friends, and I think
the Swiss and the Austrian, meeting before every permanent delegates'
meeting. I immediately thought it would be a splendid idea to create a
'sun' group and proposed it to my colleagues. The sun group never rose.
So the 'amazons' group was created instead with my lady colleagues, but
that is another story. These meetings of our northern friends take also
place at the level of directors general and even presidents, which 'again'

is not the case for their southern colleagues. Participating in such groups, coming together in a systematic way, exchanging opinions and views, does create in the longer term a certain cohesion where some basic ideas and principles are shared.

Nonetheless, this does mean that southern interests are not effectively represented. Indeed, on the broad, horizontal issues and the very specific country interests there is good and effective lobbying. It is on the more technical issues with little political importance that southern interests are not well represented. So, for example, in UNICE in one fifth of the working groups of a more technical nature, there is no participation of interests by the south.

How important is it that southern interests are taken into account by European organisations?

The European Union is a unique, complex, political construction based on respect for the different cultures and characteristics of its Member States. European business associations, in order to be credible and useful to European legislators, should take into account the interests and sensitivities of all their members, including those from the south of Europe. And here is the big responsibility we have as national organisations to make sure that those sensitivities are properly taken care of, especially at this particular point in time when:

- the European Union is discussing its future
- enlargement is going to take place shortly
- the role of 'civil society' is growing at European level

To achieve this I suggest some proposals. Greek business organisations need to strengthen their representation in Europe by:

- reinforcing their permanent presence in Brussels, especially at branch level. That could be achieved under the auspices of the existing offices
- reinforcing their participation in European organisations at all levels and in a more active way
- awareness that, especially at European level (a multilateral level of negotiations), there is a need to work and develop coalition building

Southern business organisations need to acquire a certain conscience of our common characteristics, and try to develop new synergies at all levels – Brussels offices, members participation, meetings at the governing level – in a more structured way. That would be to the benefit not only of Greek business and the South, but also European business as it would strengthen their representativeness, their contribution to the European legislators, their members and the enterprises of Europe. Finally, I will finish by quoting Mr Matutes who said '*Tenemos seguir mirando el Sud, para no perder el Norte*', meaning 'we have to keep looking at the South, in order not to lose the North'.

18

The Organisation of Business Interests in Central and East European Countries for EU Representation

Nieves Pérez-Solórzano Borragán

The Chambers' Accession Programme for Eastern Europe (CAPE)[1] 2001 Survey on corporate readiness for the European Union (EU) Single Market in the ten candidate countries of Central Europe[2] shows that about 40 per cent of the companies surveyed regard EU lobbying as a 'very important' aspect of their representation activities. Within that group, the majority of companies rated lobbying at the domestic level higher than lobbying in Brussels. On the other hand, about 52 per cent of the companies polled believe EU lobbying not to be very important. However, about 30 per cent of that group still rate EU lobbying as being more important than lobbying at the domestic level. More importantly, despite the degree of importance awarded to EU lobbying, for almost 45 per cent of the companies surveyed, lobbying in Brussels makes more sense than lobbying at the domestic level.

With this data in mind, and in the context of the challenge of change facing EU business associations, this chapter addresses the impact of the forthcoming EU's eastward enlargement on the arena for EU interest representation. More specifically, this chapter sets to identify any evidence that illustrates the transfer of the EU model of interest representation to the Central and Eastern European repertoires for interest intermediation.

By focusing on the experience of the Central and Eastern European Offices of Representation (CEORs) in Brussels, this chapter reveals a dynamic scenario where two parallel processes interact: an increasing Europeanisation of Central and Eastern European interest representation and a continuous socialisation between partners. The analysis that follows will addresses these two processes. The chapter concludes with some reflections on the challenges derived from the incorporation of Central and Eastern European actors to the EU arena for interest inter-mediation and potential future transformations that may arise when the enlargement takes place.

Europeanisation

Although the term 'Europeanisation' is widely used in the literature, a generally accepted definition does not seem to exist (see, *inter alia*, Börzel and Risse, 2000; Cole and Drake, 2000; Grabbe, 2001; Héritier, 2001; Knill and Lehmkuhl, 1999; Ladrech, 1994; Lippert, Umbach and Wessels, 2001; Radaelli, 2000; Risse, Green-Cowles and Caporaso, 2001). For the purpose of this analysis, Europeanisation is understood not as synonymous with convergence or imitation but rather as an incremental process of informal integration and emulation (Jacoby, 2001) that flows parallel and beyond EU activity, clearly influencing the pattern of interest group development in East Central Europe. This informal process includes transnational networking of policy makers, political parties, interest groups and NGOs. I argue that the presence of the CEORs in Brussels and their attempt to find their advocacy cluster in an overcrowded European lobbying arena is clear evidence of this Europeanisation process.

Most candidate countries have a bureau in Brussels. Offices of represen-tation already existed in the mid-seventies. Since 1989 many of them have either been closed, mainly due to financial difficulties, or transformed in tune with new economic and political predicaments. Nowadays, there are 27 interest representation offices operating in Brussels (see Figure 18.1). The overall number does not even reach 2 per cent of the Brussels-based lobbying community. Yet the number of offices has more than doubled since 1996 and there are plans for further expansion.

The status and representation arrangements of these offices are varied and undefined at times. Most offices represent business interests, while others perform a wider function as research and development offices, public relations bureaux or cultural ambassadors. This is a reflection of the heterogeneity of their clientele and the recent development of inter-est group activities and legislation in their countries of origin.

The main tasks performed by the CEORs are very similar to those per-formed by their counterparts from the EU Member States: (i) to inform their members at the national level about EU legislation, funding opportunities, and relevant developments in EU member states; (ii) to represent their members in large European associations; (iii) to provide

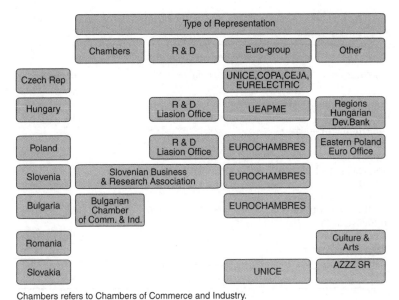

Chambers refers to Chambers of Commerce and Industry.
R & D refers to liaison offices for Research and Development.
Euro-group refers to membership of a sectoral Euro-group.
Other refers to additional categories such as regional offices.
The AZZ SR is the Federation of Employers' Associations of the Slovak Republic.

Figure 18.1   Central and Eastern European Offices of Representation, 2002

members with specific services on request; (iv) to raise their members' profile at the European level; and (v) to design training seminars for their members in order to increase their awareness of the enlargement process. For instance, KIG Euroconsulting, the Brussels office of the Polish Chamber of Commerce, not only offered information and services concerning the EU and business integration to its members but also regularly informed the Polish government on the attitude of Polish entrepreneurs to EU membership (Biznesu, 2000, p. 4).

The lobbying objectives of the business sector in the Central and Eastern European Countries (CEECs) in view of the enlargement are varied. According to the CAPE 2001 Survey on Corporate Readiness for the EU Single Market in the 10 Candidate Countries of Central Europe, these include: (i) derogations; (ii) transitional periods; (iii) concessions for pre-accession; (iv) financial and technical assistance; (v) assistance in dealing with EU institutions; (vi) influencing Member States; (vii) other unspecified issues. Table 18.1 shows the Central and Eastern European business sector's preferences for whether lobbying objectives should be

Table 18.1   Lobbying preferences among the business community in Central European countries

| Objectives | Lobbying objectives (percentage) | | | |
| | Domestic level | | In Brussels | |
	No	Yes	No	Yes
Derogations	78.3	21.7	84.8	15.2
Transitional periods	72.1	27.9	79.7	20.3
Concessions for pre-accession	65.9	34.1	70.9	29.1
Financial & technical assistance	23.4	76.6	37.4	62.6
Assistance in dealing with EU institutions	39.4	60.6	47.1	52.9
Influence in EU institutions	64.4	35.6	63.8	36.2
Influence member states	69.7	30.3	70.7	29.3
Other	80.4	19.6	88.7	11.3

Source: Eurochambres and SBRA, *Corporate Readiness for Enlargement in Central Europe*, 2001

directed at the domestic level or Brussels. The results offer an interesting insight into the short-term planning of business interest in the candidate countries. Their lobbying does not appear to prioritise the immediate application of the *acquis communautaire*, such as derogations, transitional periods and concessions for pre-accession, but is more geared towards learning how to interact with EU institutions while securing technical assistance. Influencing the EU institutions and Member States is only a priority for about 30 per cent of the respondents at the domestic level and at the Brussels level. It is interesting to note that objectives that are not deemed relevant to be acted upon at the domestic level, are not considered relevant to the Brussels level either.

There are a number of incentives which explain the increasing presence of Central and Eastern European interests in Brussels. The first obvious incentive is the possibility of actively participating in the enlargement process by making sure that their concerns are being voiced at the core of the EU decision-making machinery. In fact, the business community in the candidate countries is far from being fully involved in discussion regarding accession to the EU. As the CAPE 2001 Survey on Corporate Readiness for the EU Single Market in the 10 Candidate Countries of Central Europe shows, communication between national governments and the business sector on enlargement related issues is limited (see Table 18.2 below). Only 4.93 per cent of the companies surveyed are regularly consulted, but their national governments are confident that they will fully comply with EU regulations. Conversely, 68.58 per cent only receive general information about the accession process through the media and feel that they do not influence their government's negotiating position at all, while 11.34 per cent of the respondents declared that they receive information about areas that directly affect them.

Secondly, European networking provides candidate countries' interest groups with a source of trust and legitimisation both in the national and supranational arenas (Fink-Hafner, 1997, p. 135). Admission or even close contacts with European interest groups are presented in the domestic arena as proof of their maturity, respectability and Europeanness (Pérez-Solórzano Borragán, 2001a and 2001b). In the words of the Vice-President of the Chamber of Commerce and Industry of Slovenia:

> We believe that [the Slovenian Business and Research Association] is going to be a step forward in acquiring and getting a qualified even more reliable, and what is important, independent source of information for our business community. (Stantič, 2000)

At the same time membership has become overdependent on the provision of selective membership incentives, hence securing an effective

Table 18.2   Assessment of government negotiating positions

	No. of answers	Percentage
Information we obtain are from the media, they are rather general, we had no influence on positions taken	1113	68.5
We have very little information on Negotiations	189	11.6
We are informed on conditions for accession, but they are causing concern for our company	184	11.3
We were consulted on negotiating position, we know the results achieved so far and we shall not have major problems over full compliance with EU regulations	80	4.9
Don't know	57	3.5

Source: Eurochambres and SBRA, *Corporate Readiness for Enlargement in Central Europe*, 2001

access to the European arena constitutes an excellent incentive. The provision of selective membership goods on the supranational arena promotes the emergence of professionals specialised on EU matters. Thus, the establishment of liaison offices in Brussels and membership of Eurogroups serve the twofold purpose of strengthening the position of the groups' entrepreneurs and providing benefits to the clientele membership through the promotion of new economic ventures and immediate access to EU-related information.

Access to the EU *loci* of power in order to influence policy outcomes does not appear to be a priority. As such, the transnational activities of Central and Eastern European interest groups constitute an 'indirect' strategy for the construction of a local 'civil society of interests'. This reflects the asymmetric nature of the relationship between the EU and the candidate countries. The latter are affected by the outcome of Europeanisation but cannot participate in the decision-making process that defines its policy and legislative output. In other words, although the candidate countries need to converge toward the benchmark of the *acquis communautaire* they are not involved in the initial drafting of legislation (Pérez-Solórzano Borragán, 2003).

Thirdly, interest groups in the CEECs lack experience in developing their lobbying activities within the framework of a liberal regime. Therefore, as the next section on socialisation will argue, through membership of Eurogroups, Central and Eastern European interest groups can benefit from the experience of their Western European counterparts. In fact, interest groups from Central and Eastern Europe operating in Brussels expect to make full use of the knowledge that their counterparts have about the EU decision-making process and how to influence it. According to a permanent Slovak delegate to UNICE, her organisation became a member of UNICE in order to become more active at the European level:

With this status, we can participate in a UNICE policy committee, where we have an access to important information what is [happening] at the European level, in the European Commission. (Hudobova, 2000)

Interestingly enough, Central and Eastern European 'lobbyists' working in Brussels regard themselves as 'conveyor belts', transferring the knowledge and experience acquired on consultative politics for the development of a more participative political culture in their countries of origin (Cizelj, 2000; Fink-Hafner, 2000).

The conditions for the fulfilment of their intermediation tasks reflect the extent of the adaptational pressures faced by Central and Eastern European interests. The CEORs lack sufficient human and financial resources. For example, the staff of the Slovenian Business and Research Association (SBRA) comprises only seven employees. Considering that the SBRA aims to encourage co-operation in the domains of business and research between Slovenia, the EU and its Member States, to support members of the Association in their preparation for EU membership and to become the representative and mediator of its members in European associations and informal networks, its human resources are overburdened from the start. The Eastern Poland Euro Office in Brussels has been closed recently due to financial problems. The office was initially set up with PHARE financial support. However, this EU aid had a limited duration of two years. Once the European money ceased the office had to close (Cizelj, 2002).

Central and Eastern European interest groups' access to European institutions, although effective as information-gathering mechanisms are limited by their reliance on Eurogroups. Eastern and Western-specific modes of political exchange interact with EU-level opportunity structures which permit or block access to interest representation. Despite the exiting opportunity structures, to date, there is not any clear evidence of the direct impact of Central and Eastern European interest groups in the enlargement negotiations. Representatives of a number of Central and Eastern European offices acknowledge that they can only play an auxiliary but still important role in the process of accession negotiations by offering an additional interface between the EU and their countries of origin (Cizelj, 2000; Iteto, 2000; Pálmay, 2000).

The CEORs serve a very diverse clientele, hence lobbying in Brussels requires action at numerous and varied flanks. The SBRA is a suitable illustration of this situation: it is a cross-sectoral organisation, whose members comprise the Chamber of Commerce and Industry of Slovenia, the Universities of Ljubljana and Maribor, the Jozef Stefan Institute, and the Co-operative Union of Slovenia as its founding partners. In addition, its associate members include the Port of Koper, pharmaceutical companies such as Krka, Novo Mesto and Lek and the Insurance Union of Slovenia among others. Three different offices, a Liaison office for Research and Development, a regional office of representation and the Duna Holding speak for various Hungarian interests in Brussels. Additionally, national clienteles tend to be very poorly informed about European issues. Consequently, the offices representing the interests of the CEECs in Brussels must perform a wider function not only as lobbyists and advisers but also as agents in the transformation process that takes place in their own countries.

The transnational co-operation between partners from candidate countries has resulted in the creation of the Network of Interest Representation Offices from Candidate Countries (NIROC)[3] in 2000. NIROC's impact has so far been limited to the sharing of know-how. In December 2000, under the aegis of EUROCHAMBRES' CAPE Programme,[4] NIROC members met for a two-day seminar to reassess their strategies while exchanging views of their experience on lobbying in Brussels. This and similar events are being repeated regularly not only in Brussels but also in each of the national capitals in order to bring the EU closer to their domestic members.

Socialisation

In addition to opening offices in Brussels, the supranational route includes membership and close contacts with European interest groups (Fink-Hafner, 1997, p. 135). To improve their European profile, a number of interest groups from the candidate countries have gained some type of associated or affiliated membership of experienced Eurogroups such as the European Consumers' Organisation (BEUC), the Committee of Agricultural Organisations in the European Union (COPA-COGECA), the Association of European Chambers of Commerce and Industry (EUROCHAMBRES), the European Confederation of Iron and Steel Industries (EUROFER), the European Trade Union Confederation (ETUC) and the Union of Industrial and Employers' Confederation of Europe (UNICE), among others. The expanding transnational activity of interest groups from CEECs and their exposure to the EU lobbying environment allows for the socialisation/exchange of norms and ways of doing between partners.

In light of the forthcoming EU membership, Business Interest Associations (BIAs) from the candidate countries have adapted their structures, services and lobbying activities to the needs and opportunities offered by the new climate of relations with the EU and its Member States. As observed by Dr Lajos Tolany, Chairman of the of the Hungarian Chamber of Commerce and Industry (HCCI):

> as the main representative of the business community, the Hungarian Chamber of Commerce and Industry has been actively supporting Hungary's European integration by passing on the views of business people and by representing their interests. The Chamber's policy

reflects the fact that the opportunities open to Hungary on joining the European Union and the Single Market must be realised by members of the country's business community. (Tolnay, 2000, p. 1)

The very structure of the different chambers has been transformed particularly by creating committees specialised in EU matters and by establishing offices of representation in Brussels. For instance, the Polish Chamber of Commerce (PCC) performs the role of an adviser, but it is also an active agent in the Polish transformation process by fostering continuous communication with the government and state administration, while tabling legislative initiatives aimed at ameliorating the state of the Polish business sector (PCC, www.KIG.PL/index_e.htm). Additionally, the internal structure of the PCC has been adapted to the new European environment by creating a Committee for the European Union that focuses its activities on: (i) preparation for negotiations of Poland's accession to the EU, providing information on the functioning of the EU; (ii) representation of the Polish business sector in Brussels; and (iii) co-operation with European business organisations (PCC, www.KIG.PL/index_e.htm).

The Chamber of Commerce and Industry of Slovenia (CCIS) supports the SBRA. It provides strategic advice to its member companies regarding their adaptation to EU legal and socio-economic requirements; and most importantly it enjoys direct representation on the governmental working groups preparing the negotiation process (Stantič, 2000). The effects of the socialisation process were recognised by Dr Cizelj, director of SBRA, who praised the encouragement and strategic support provided by EUROCHAMBRES in establishing SBRA's bureau in Brussels (Cizelj, 2000).

In 1998, the Hungarian Chamber of Commerce and Industry (HCCI) prepared an Action Plan to encourage Hungary's accession to the EU. Among the measures outlined, the HCCI committed itself to strengthening co-operation with the government in defining Hungary's position in view of the enlargement, while it organised a number of training seminars aimed at increasing EU awareness among the staff of the regional chambers and entrepreneurs (Vadász,1998).

The Bulgarian Industrial Association (BIA) has embraced as one of its most important tasks to assist its members in their involvement in the EU accession process, particularly in the implementation of the *acquis communautaire* (Bulgarian Industrial Association, 2002. Similarly, the International Projects and Programs Centre (IPPC) is an essential component of the BIA structure. Its main task is to develop and implement international projects in the framework of externally financed multilateral or bilateral cooperation programs. Thus, the IPPC manages relations with international institutions and organisations such as the International Labour Organisation (ILO) and UNICE, and with counterpart employers and industrialists federations from all over Europe. Most importantly

> the IPPC has become the initiator of building a network between the employers federations of the applicant countries aiming to enhance their capability of full value participation in the accession process and negotiations and to foster cooperation between industries of these countries. (Bulgarian Industrial Association, 2002)

Other positive outcomes of the socialisation process can be observed in the Euro-interest groups' willingness to transfer some of their sectoral information to the newcomers on subjects regarding (i) events concerning individual EU policy areas and EU Member States; (ii) the structure of European institutions and legislative procedures within the EU; (iii) reports elaborated by their policy analysis units; (iv) expert knowledge on the harmonisation of laws; and (v) potential European sources to co-finance projects in the candidate countries (Fink-Hafner, 1994, p. 229: Pérez-Solórzano Borragán, 2003).

For instance, UNICE believes that basic conditions should be observed to encourage Western European companies to develop industrial co-operation with their Central and Eastern European counterparts (UNICE, 1990 and 1992). To further the economic development of the CEECs, UNICE proposes the creation of agencies ready to work as interlocutors in the newly established democracies. These will help ensure the smooth functioning of industrial activity in market economies while offering potential Western investors the necessary information and assistance (UNICE, 1990). Furthermore, for the European companies to be able to develop their commercial relations with the CEECs, it is essential that they are able to deal with partners who are sufficiently autonomous to take decisions allowing for the normal management of production and marketing (UNICE, 1989). UNICE's Central and Eastern European membership features associations that have been granted full membership and associations with observer status (UNICE, http://www.unice.org/unice/Website.nsf/HTML + Pages/UK_index_UK.htm).

EUROCHAMBRES has established its relationship with chambers of commerce and industry from the CEECs at three different levels: institutional, political and operational (Vantyghem, 2000; EUROCHAMBRES, 1994).

1. *At the institutional level,* eleven chambers of commerce and industry from CEECs and the former Soviet Union are affiliated members of EUROCHAMBRES. They are entitled to actively participate in the various decision-making bodies and to express their views and concerns through the committee of affiliated members.
2. *At the political level,* EUROCHAMBRES has been involved in lobbying activities representing the interests of its affiliated members at both European and national levels.
3. *At the operational level,* EUROCHAMBRES has offered expert advice to its affiliated members since 1991, by developing, in collaboration with the European Commission, a number of training and technical assistance programmes aimed at strengthening the position and representativeness of the chambers of commerce and their associated organisations in the CEECs (Pérez-Solórzano Borragán, 1998; http://www.eurochambres.be/ita/ita.htm).

This process of socialisation and exchange presents a number of challenges. It is not easy for Euro-interest groups to identify reliable counterparts in the candidate countries. Moreover, the expansion of membership to such a varied group of newcomers provokes important internal organisational difficulties and policy dilemmas. Euro-interest groups must adapt their operative structures to a larger membership whose demands and interests may conflict with those of existing members (see, *inter alia*, Daugbjerg, 1997, pp. 27–8; Benedictis and Padoan, 1993). As a result, policy dilemmas will need to be solved in order to safeguard the group's cohesion. Eurogroups are not so eager to share their access to the *loci* of power with their Central and Eastern European counterparts. In this sense if any cooperation towards the creation of a policy community between Eurogroups and Central and Eastern European interest groups is to be created it would be based on the former enjoying their access to the 'inner circle' of interest groups contacted by the Commission, while the latter would have to remain in the periphery of the policy-making process, at least until accession takes place. Finally, given the generally acknowledged 'disharmony' in Eurogroups' structure, the eventual incorporation of new members could potentially be disruptive (for discussion on the Eurogroup's weakness see, *inter alia*, Greenwood, Strangward and Stancich, 1999; Greenwood, 2002a and 2002b; McLaughlin, Jordan and Maloney, 1993).

For Central and Eastern European interests, the socialisation with EU counterparts provokes a number of adaptational pressures. They need to rapidly and effectively learn and adapt to the basic rules of the

European game while making sure that their own interests are not diluted in the general interest of the wider organisation. Since they have only been granted associated or affiliated membership their ability to influence the agenda of the European associations is limited, despite the fact that they pay membership fees. Additionally, most European associations would only allow one member per country. This presents problems at the domestic level when there are several associations that represent the same sectoral interest. An exception to this state of affairs is the Informal Group of Research and Development Liaison Offices (IGLO). Initially created as an EU-based group, it adopted new rules in 1999 in order to allow offices from candidates countries to join on an equal footing with their EU counterparts.

Conclusion

The analysis developed above reveals a scenario where Europeanisation occurs as a process of informal integration that flows parallel and beyond EU activity, clearly influencing the pattern of interest group development in the candidate countries. At the same time, the transnational socialisation and supranational activity of interest groups in the CEECs presents interest group politics at the supranational level with new challenges in terms of political culture, the increasing numbers of policy actors and the diversity of their interests.

This chapter has addressed the effect of the enlargement on the structures for interest intermediation in Europe. The evidence presented in this chapter offers an interesting insight into the idiosyncrasy of Central and Eastern European interest representation in Brussels. Despite the lack of resources and the relative inexperience of the lobbying game, interest groups from the CEECs are trying to find an active role in the European lobbying arena. This search for their own space is accompanied by their acknowledged importance as agents in the transformation process that takes place in their countries.

This chapter concludes that Eastern and Western-specific modes of political exchange interact at the supranational level. The challenges to incorporate Central and Eastern European actors to the EU model of interest intermediation evidence the weakness of the CEEC's domestic environment and the own constraints of EU interest representation. There is not sufficient empirical evidence to suggest that the CEORs' activities and their interaction with Euro-interest groups have translated into effective influence on the policy-making process. Rather, it is possible to identify a specific model of interest group politics characterised by the exchange and transfer of information and know-how. It could be argued that this is just an interim situation that will change after accession.

Notes

1 This is a EUROCHAMBRES initiative financially supported by the EU PHARE programme aimed at strengthening Chambers of Commerce and Industry in Central and Eastern Europe and enhancing their participation in the accession process.

2 The empirical data emanates from the CAPE 2001 Survey on corporate readiness for the EU Single Market in the 10 candidate countries of Central Europe, namely Bulgaria, the Czech Republic, Estonia, Hungary, Latvia, Lithuania, Poland, Romania, Slovakia and Slovenia. Through the respective national chambers of commerce and industry, 1658 of the over 3000 companies contacted, participated in the survey.

3 NIROC co-ordinates the activities of the Association of Agricultural Co-operatives and Companies in the Czech Republic (AACC), the AB Consultancy & Investment Services, the Federation of Employers' Associations of the Slovak Republic (AZZZ SR), the Czech Power Company CEZ, the Turkish Progressive Workers Union (DISK), the Eastern Poland Euro-Office, the Representation of the Regions of Hungary, the Economic Development Foundation (IKV), the Hungarian Office for Research and Development (HunOR), the Hungarian Handicraft & Small & Medium Sized Enterprises (IPOSZ), the Representation of Turkish Textile and ready Made Garment Exporters Association (ITKIB), the Malta Business Bureau (MBB), the Hungarian Development Bank Ltd., Brussels Representative Office, the Euro-Polish representation of economic and regional organisations, and the Slovenian Business and Research Association (SBRA), Confederation of Industry of the Czech Republic – Brussels Bureau, Union of Chambers of Turkey, Turkish Small Business Organisation (TSBO), and the Turkish Business, Industry and Employers' Association (TUSIAD-TISK).

4 CAPE is the Chambers' Accession Programme for Eastern Europe.

Part VII

Public Interest Groups

19
The Challenge of Managing Relations with the European Parliament: Insights from a Public Interest Group

Jim Murray

As a consumer organisation we often find ourselves on the other side to business on many issues before the European Parliament and other decision-making bodies. In fact, however, we are not in any sense 'against' business or industry. We often work with allies from business on particular issues. More generally we see our role as offering a balancing and questioning contribution to what business and other interests are saying. (Of course it is essential that we know what others are saying – this is not always the case because there is too much 'private' consultation on the part of decision-makers in the Parliament and elsewhere.)

This month we are working on the following issues (among others) currently before the Parliament:

- Data Protection in e-commerce, including such issues as spamming and the use of cookies.
- Revision of the pharmaceutical directives – raising the possibility of a form of direct advertising of prescribed medicines to patients – which we would oppose.
- Car block exemption – The Parliament is considering a proposal from the Commission to change (or in our view to reform) the current competition rules on car distribution.
- A Commission proposal for a regulation on sales promotion: For various reasons we oppose this proposal and unfortunately it is to be considered by the Legal Affairs Committee which is not known for its 'pro-consumer' attitude.

One of the problems facing general public interest groups such as BEUC is that we have a huge range of issues to work on. For us, any one issue is one amongst many; for our 'adversaries' it is a full-time matter that is often perceived as having a major impact on the relevant industry. There is often therefore a large imbalance in terms of the resources, time, numbers of experts and even political weight brought to the different sides of the same issue. This is an aspect of the wider political problem of ensuring representation of diffuse general interests.

Like any well-managed organisation we try to prioritise and focus our activities, but external demands from MEPs and the Commission often make it difficult to stick to our preferred priorities. Internally different members may also have different priorities and expectations of BEUC.

Looking back over the forty years since the foundation of BEUC in 1962, it seems that the Commission was the main target of our lobbying in the sixties and much of the seventies. The Economic and Social Committee was also a target but the Parliament did not seem to figure very prominently in our campaigning. That situation changed dramatically in 1979 with the first direct elections. From then the Parliament grew in strength and importance, culminating in the acquisition of the powers of co-decision in many areas, including most of the areas of importance to us – with the still outstanding exception of agriculture. From our perspective co-decision was one of the major political events of the last forty years – as was also the Single European Act that ended the unanimity rule in many areas.

Of course business and industry were not blind to these changes and there has been a huge growth in the number of lobbyists in Brussels generally and in those targeting the Parliament. Industry representatives also have increasing links with the Parliament, in terms of access to EP facilities, the organisation of conferences and inter-groups. Taken together these trends carry with them the danger of what would effectively be the privatisation of parliamentary hearings and other consultation processes. Here as in other areas we need much more transparency, much more information about both what is going on and the influences on MEPs.

Any organisation seeking to influence the EU process must bring to that task a pan-EU approach. Coherence is also important, as is solidarity between members. It is very difficult to persuade MEPs who know that your member organisations from their country have a different viewpoint. A high level of expertise, again from a pan-EU perspective, is increasingly essential. In any European association the main experts are likely to be working at national level and may not always find it easy to adopt an EU-wide approach.

Of course national member organisations have an important role to play in influencing their own MEPs. Members of the European Parliament are sensitive to public opinion at home but the degree of sensitivity varies widely. My impression (and it is only an impression) is that MEPs elected on the list system may be somewhat less sensitive than others to public opinion at home. (This is not to suggest that the list system is a bad system as such; there are arguments for and against almost every system.)

Information technology has changed and is changing the role of European associations. The more active national member organisations are no longer grateful to be told what is on the EP or Commission agenda – they can find out on the Internet. At European level, associations will have to focus more on the provision of intelligence and information management. There are still important advantages in having a physical presence in Brussels but there is also better access to information for those who are a long way from Brussels – provided, of course, that they have the necessary means to access and use the information.

Information technology has also, however, brought another problem – the problem of information overload. This affects everybody, including MEPs. I wonder how many MEPs or their assistants now read all of their e-mails?

For the future I assume that the powers of the European Parliament will grow (including co-decision in agriculture also, I hope). Members of the Parliament lay much stress now on their powers of scrutiny; this is a positive development provided it does not degenerate into micro management. The primary role of Parliament is that of legislator.

There is a great deal of discussion currently about possible new forms of decision making or governance in the European Union. I know that members of the European Parliament have some reservations about many of the ideas put forward – fearing that the Parliament may in time be bypassed in certain procedures. In BEUC we are very much interested in the process of developing new forms of regulation but we also insist on the primacy of the public authorities, including Commission, Parliament and Council. Of course we argue for a better involvement of stakeholders and especially consumer organisations in policy making. We do not, however, believe in a Europe run by stakeholders or by European associations, nor even by consumer associations.

Part VIII

Outlook

20
Outlook

Alfons Westgeest and Justin Greenwood

This chapter brings together analysis of the key trends identified in the previous chapters to provide an outlook for the future of the EU Business Associations in the next two to five years. It does not seek to summarise the preceding chapters, an endeavour which is better captured by Chapter 1. Rather, the emphasis here is upon short to medium term 'futurology'.

The Issues

Several authors have analysed the emerging conditions under which EU Business Associations need to operate. For the years ahead, the following issues appear to be significant:

- The 'Governance' agenda will play an increasing role, carrying regulatory opportunities and threats for corporations and not-for-profit organisations alike, though sometimes in different ways. As Jerome Vignon outlines in Chapter 4, in exchange for increased transparency on the part of associations there is the prospect that the EU institutions will commit to increased consultation with them in the context of a formal partnership. This opens up a variety of intriguing role possibilities for, and demands upon, associations in the future.
- There will be an enhanced transparency in everything the EU does, including in its regulatory processes, its committee work, and in its relations with civil society organisations of all types. In turn, civil society organisations will themselves need to display the hallmarks of transparency, both as a reciprocal consequence and in response to the wider public agendas surrounding governance.

- EU agencies will assume greater significance and assume quasi-regulatory roles and beyond.
- The economic downturn and financial constraints will continue to affect business associations in the short to medium term, due to the fact that associations are one or two years behind in the economic cycle.
- Local legislation will impose increasingly stricter laws on the not-for-profit entities and pay more attention to taxation, accounting and valuation of assets (see Chapter 14 and the Appendix).
- Enlargement must be matched by faster internal reform for the public institutions. Business associations will need to review their internal environments to keep pace.
- The historic trend towards hybrid association structures of national associations and direct firm membership organisations shows no sign of abating.
- Information Technology will continue to provide new opportunities for changes in internal association–member relations.

We extend our commentary briefly on each one of the above issues, briefly, in turn.

The Governance agenda, transparency and associations

New forms of control and review of governance for the corporate world will continue to drive change for the next five years. The effect will also impact the association environment. Compared to the US government, the EU institutions have moved rather quickly on corporate governance reforms with emphasis on principles and the legal and independent control function.

On the EU legislative and policy front the governance debate has moved towards more monitoring of credible input from the private sector. It is set to increase, and to balance the interests of larger and SME type corporations, represented by EU business associations.

The key example of the development towards a more balanced input into new legislation is the recently announced Extended Impact Assessments (EIA) (Chapter 4), which cover several new initiatives of the European Commission's Programme for 2003. In following up the White Paper on Governance the Commission has started the EIA process for a number of draft Directives, signalling the commencement of its implementation. From these pilot projects it has already become clear that the EIA will enable:

- More and wider input from all stakeholders, including industry, civil society, and independent parties.
- Increased objective assessment as the EIA will be including input from several Directorate Generals of the Commission.
- More public exposure for at least the other EU Institutions as it is expected that the EP will use it to scrutinise the Commission's rationale for its policy and proposed piece of legislation.

For the other processes in the EU we also anticipate further changes. *First*, for the associations it is important to note that in recent years the EU has also introduced new forms of alternative regulatory models (ARMs). Europe followed the US approach, which has reflected the strong desire of US citizens to limit, if not control, the role of government. In Europe the ARM approach includes co-regulation, self-regulation and the use of codes of conduct. While these trends will continue in years to come, corporate governance issues will continue to feature on the policy agenda and limit the transfer of too much regulatory power and control mechanisms to the private sector. It is to be expected that the US and the EU will pay more attention to the credibility of their private sector interfaces. This will affect in particular the associations that form part of the ARMs.

Second, the Commission-led Regulatory Committees consist of Member State experts and deal with technical adaptation and development of new regulatory approaches. They are better known as comitology and represent the last frontier for reform. The Committees meet behind closed doors and will face increased scrutiny. Expected reforms range from more open access to the checking of speed and accuracy, such as the length of time it takes the EU's bureaucracy to react to disasters like oil spills, food scandals or ethical questions. What will be the future influence of other stakeholders in their debates and how will public pressure groups and media question the outcome of their deliberations?

This brings us to the *third* process: the role of the EU agencies, which now seem set, following the White Paper on Governance, to increasingly support the EU in developing regulatory measures and acting on behalf of the EU institutions. This has laid the foundations for a more independent basis, and when compared to comitology, agencies seem less directly influenced by Member States. The earlier agencies were advisory bodies, such as the European Environmental Agency (EEA), established in 1990 as the main source for EU institutions to develop their policy. Other pan European bodies focus on implementation, such as the European

Patent Office, which grants European patents for the contracting states to the European Patent Convention. However, the newest EU agencies resemble more the US approach of regulatory and policy power. The best examples are the European Agency for the Evaluation of Medicinal Products (EMEA) and the European Food Safety Authority (EFSA). EFSA has been given a wide brief so that it can cover all stages of food production and supply. It gathers not only information for the EU but can also initiate risk assessments on its own behalf and can communicate directly to the public. While the EFSA is the EU's newest agency that concluded its formation during 2003, it is already having significant impact on how the food associations are positioned or organised and is acting as a catalyst for reorganisation, discussed below.

The increased awareness of governance has unexpected consequences. For example, the new directive on Waste from Electrical and Electronic Equipment of January 2003 has led to the immediate realisation of the need for accounting rules about how to state liability and related costs for historic and future waste in annual reports and audit declarations of companies. The Commission proposed new legislation to address the perceived need for clarity and responsibility by corporations.

On the level of the other EU institutions, it is the European Parliament that is anticipated to increase its demands for clear communication and agendas. The new conciliation procedure between the EP and the Council of Ministers, for example, has given the EP much more opportunity to arm wrestle with the Member States. We also note a seeming paradox between research and practice in recording relations between the EP and business related organisations. One is the way in way public affairs consultancies have traditionally developed a specialist niche in managing business relations with the EP. On the other hand, academic research among MEPs tends to have found a higher degree of access for associations than for large firms and consultants (Kohler-Koch, 1998; Wessels, 1999; Beyers, 2003). The basis of this preference appears to be a recognition of the European-wide scope of EU associations (Chapter 5).

From the perspective of associations, transparency is here to stay. The basis upon which decisions are reached in public governance will become clearer, and the information upon which they are based progressively more accessible. This brings both opportunities and challenges for business interest associations. As the institutions develop increasingly transparent practices, so it will bring into public focus the relationship between civil society interests and the political institutions, and by opening up to public gaze may change forever policy relationships with the European Commission, in particular. As governance partners, associations will be increasingly required to develop transparency standards as a condition of participation in public life. The manager of the future, and a future in which trust has to be earned, will need to do everything transparently and operate in an environment in which transparency is the watchword of relationships.

Associations which engage public debate in a spirit of openness and self examination seem best able to position themselves as part of the solution rather than part of the problem. Environmental issues seem set to continue to develop in importance, and associations will need to embrace the public mood for EU environmental leadership, to develop mechanisms to engage with organised public environmental interests in a constructive way, and to display their 'green' credentials. Corporate social responsibility seems a useful vehicle through which to undertake this, as well as the 'social' 'bottom line', although in turn associations will need to develop leadership for their members to bring added value to them rather than leaving it to specialised networks such as Corporate Social Responsibility Europe.

Financing, tax and legislative issues

The economic downturn and cost-cutting of business expenses in 2001–2002 have had considerable impact on the budgets and financial viability of European business interest associations. In times of recession, a larger number of companies than would otherwise be the case have carefully screened the associations that they belong to on both national, EU and global levels. In the decision tree is analysis of whether to continue to fund all those levels, or seek more services for less money by increasing productivity of the association's staff. In some cases, association budget cuts have resulted, particularly where there are no urgent public affairs issues looming. In the EU context, the lead-in time for this phenomenon is longer and more diluted than is evident at the national level given the continued strength of national associations in the composition of EU-level associations.

This behaviour is set to continue for business associations during another few years, due to the fact that associations are usually one or even two years behind in the economic cycle. It will lead to continued consolidation, phasing out, postponement of projects and outsourcing of functions. Corporations will be demanding value for money, but their representatives will also have less time to spend on the association's working groups.

A key, related phenomenon is the cost of participation in EU business associations, and the temptation to reduce voluntary commitments. Associations have responded to this either by introducing a clear strategic planning process in which all members contribute (such as the EU Committee of the American Chamber of Commerce), or by continuing with cross-industry consolidation. An obvious example of the latter is EICTA (Chapter 1), which has made this threat an opportunity and strengthened its power, budget and legitimacy.

Another threat to the financing of associations is taxation. Local authorities may pay more attention to taxation, accounting and valuation of association assets. While taxation will remain the domain of Member States, European business associations will need to monitor the issue. For example, how are reserves classified, what portion is considered a social reserve by law and what portion is considered to be a normal reserve, that is, to allow cash flow during the year?

While each Member State will retain its own way on how to tax not-for-profit bodies, the requirements seem to change. It is not likely to go as far as the US Internal Revenue Service, which has started to tax associations for unrelated non-subscription business income, and considers the portion of dues funding of lobbying as (partially) non-deductible for business expense. However, authorities have put more strict financial control in place. The recent Belgian laws for accounting and audit requirements for the larger international associations (Chapter 14) are an example.

EU institutions and enlargement: the external environment

An editorial in the *Financial Times* of 16 December 2002 commented that

> The EU must also change if it is to remain viable with 25 or more members. The European Convention must find ways of making the Union more transparent and more efficient. There should be more public scrutiny of both the council of ministers and the European Commission and the European Parliament must have a greater role... Without political and economic reform, the EU cannot fulfil its growing continent-wide responsibilities. (*Financial Times*, 2002)

Since the enlargement decisions have taken place, one can no longer speak of Central and Eastern Europe. Europe is Europe, and barring Switzerland and some new Southeast European nations, it is likely that all continental European nations could be joining the EU within this decade. The Copenhagen summit demonstrated again that powerful lessons are learned from smaller EU Member States in brokering deals. Poland played strongly in negotiating with the Danish Presidency in the second half of 2002 obtaining additional funding for Poland. It is fair to say that the future may hold some very interesting leadership from the CEECs that will require a well-balanced governance and political model as the outcome of the Convention.

Indeed the downside of enlargement is the increased risk of fragmentation of the EU political system. It could lead to even more EU architectural fragmentation (see Chapter 3), and slower and watered down decision making. While the tradition of consensus approach and increased use of qualified majority voting will facilitate the process, the domination by one particular association is less likely in a scenario of increased geographical membership.

Fragmentation – presumably an inescapable truth (see Chapter 11) will be challenged by the larger companies with membership in all or most Member States. Will they still accept that the EU of 25 will need as many national associations? Will we see an increase of formal voting rules and percentages, once prevalent in the early European confederations? If the EU stops its rotating Presidency of the Council what will associations do? Will few countries or companies elect the President of the association, and will transparency and governance demand a re-balancing between small and larger countries?

Sectoral characteristics and the internal environment

Some of the answers to the above questions will have to be resolved in the internal structure of the association. The following scenarios could be distinguished:

- The horizontal organisations, and especially the ones which are composed mainly of SMEs (see Chapter 2), will have more opportunities than ever before under an increasingly welcoming EU policy and funding embrace (European Commission, 2002b), which take in a recent White Paper (European Commission, 2002b) and Research Framework Programme VI. Nonetheless, there remains a landscape of high fragmentation in the representation of SMEs, and many dedicated SME associations continue to struggle with insufficient staff and a lack of financial resources. The SME associations must find ways of new revenue stream, including opportunities such as the EU VIth Framework Programme on Research.

- Think-tanks will continue to prosper from a policy and architectural environment built around change. However, the corporate pressures referred to earlier mean that organisations continue to need to reinvent themselves on a regular basis, and unless they do so then their income will decline and others will take over the concept.
- Enforcement of competition law has eliminated (or will soon eliminate if they do not change) historic tendencies to cartel behaviour among associations (Chapter 6). Instead, the new agenda is to focus upon external threats, new EU laws and standards, and new practices for training in their business environment. Some transnational associations, EU and otherwise, and those in the US, have commenced activities such as web based technology training, as well as certification schemes for their members. These have proved popular and demand-based.
- Business interest associations will have to adopt a strategic scanning process. The 'high change oriented' sectors will change towards shorter lifecycles and re-inventing their business. The chances are that those associations that are least bureaucratic and involve members in strategic plans will be apt to survive the new rules and the enlargement process of Europe.
- Generally speaking, annual budgets tend to be lower, reserves will continue to shrink, but the opportunities come from envelopes of funding that the governing bodies will release once the need to spending is presented and validated. Associations will switch from 'standing committees' and develop their issues in project groups and task forces that need addressing during the budget year.
- Although the increase of the number of large firm (or direct membership) associations is levelling off and some may even be losing power, the number of hybrid associations is predicted to increase.
- Confederations will reinvent membership also, as demonstrated already in some sectors, by a new sharing of power of three types of membership: the national federations, European sectoral associations and firms. This process is already evident in umbrella associations, such as the Confederation of Food and Drink Industries of the EU (CIAA), the Liaison Group of the Mechanical, Electrical, Electronic and Metalworking Industries (ORGALIME), and EICTA.
- In some cases the next step will be to increase cooperation of smaller and niche associations with the formation of clusters, with the aim to streamline and increase the overall effectiveness of the sector.
- The process whereby federated sectoral business associations include corporations in their membership is unlikely to change. This will

bring with it more emphasis on business planning rules. The emerging influence of association management firms and outsourcing of some functions is set to increase in order to be flexible and lean. The Association Management sector has grown, and there is evidence of resource sharing and an increasing number of strategic alliances in sectors such as automotive, telecoms, banking and insurance. This process is related to fiscal pressures, and its time lag in the world of associations, referred to earlier in this chapter.

- 'Global' plus 'local' is 'glocal' (ASAE 2002). What can European associations learn from their American or Asian counterparts? How will diversity and the equal opportunity play out? As in the US, comparatively more female staff and executives will make their way to the associations and play an increasing role in leading business associations. Being host to many new cultures and countries the Secretary General will need all his or her talents as described in this book.
- International expansion and global influence of corporations will speed up a restructuring process as corporations reduce their immediate presence in Brussels or give these executives new tasks beyond a representation to the EU, such as the setting up of new pan-European or regional organisations dealing with sustainable development.

Information Technology (IT)

Information technology represents one of the toughest challenges of change for associations worldwide. A number of associations suffered disproportionately through technology based investments when the 'dotcom' bubble burst. The International Association of Business Communicators, for instance, lost nearly all its reserves through technology investments.

The early threat of vertical nets taking over the knowledge domain of associations has evaporated, and many associations have benefited from the innovative technology to get closer to their members (extranet) and using email and website to spread its message and information to the media, EU relations and third parties. For the future the following developments will mature:

- *The challenge of communication and alliance building*
  - Associations which fully realise the power of communication in conjunction with lobbying, with the resulting requirement to invest in technology or risk being an outcast, are likely to reap the benefits.

- Alliance building and strategic public relations will continue to add to the costs, but will enhance the claim of associations to authority in their respective domains.
- Whilst the greater access to information brought by the internet could reduce the dependence by members upon their associations, associations could compensate by cutting a path through the information jungle for their members.
- *EU institutions: power of the web*
  - A vast amount of information broadcasting, such as Europa, will add functionality by including more direct interfaces with the policy making units, including Cabinets of Commissioners, live broadcasting of Council meetings and almost daily reporting of EP sessions and documents. The growth of private portals including EurActiv.com and speciality websites like greenfacts.org, will add to the increasing crowding of the domain but also to choice and diversity.
  - The power of Email communication between EU officials and business associations has already been recognised by the White Paper on Governance. This force can work to mutual benefit for political institutions and civil society organisations. Impact assessments will require smooth knowledge exchange instead of rewriting every piece, every word of input.
- *Internal environment*
  - Automated member registrations for meetings, seminars or working groups will increase, and has become standard practice in the US.
  - Cutting costs by replacing some meetings in person by not just audio calls, but by using 'voice over Internet Protocol'.

In addition to these issues are the related factors identified and debated in Chapter 1. These include:

- the pressures towards membership breadth, including participation of SMEs, led by the White Paper on Governance agenda. These requirements for accountability and representativity are to be traded for a greater partnership role with political institutions. These factors are likely to strengthen EU associations as they assume governance and quasi-regulatory functions, and to reduce the high degree of fragmentation in the associational landscape. This is because associations which have a formalised relationship with EU institutions are attractive organisations to join, and the necessity to seek coherence through high specialisation only will be reduced. A further strengthening factor arising from this new relationship will be the enhanced autonomy which associations will gain from their members. Associations which develop public governance functions as a results of the 'better regulation' and 'White Paper on Governance' agendas are likely to find further autonomy and strength.

- the continuing development of the 'citizen agenda' as the EU continues to need to find ways of legitimising itself to its wider public stakeholder. Together with pressures for a 'level playing field' in EU policy-making and expectations of transparency, such factors will restrict the opportunity for any one type of player to monopolise agenda setting with the European Commission. 'Impact assessments' include not just cost-benefit appraisals upon business, but the impact upon a wider group of stakeholders.
- the related development of the 'Corporate Social Responsibility' agenda, in which associations will need to develop mechanisms to enable their members to respond to wider requirements and expectations that they will be environmentally and socially accountable, as well as financially accountable. At present, this role is being developed by specialised network organisations, such as Corporate Social Responsibility Europe.
- the continued quest among associations to find ways of developing internal coherence through fostering trust between members.
- the likely softening of requirements for direct and individual affect in European law, which is bound to require associations to take a proactive litigant role on behalf of their members, whether defensive or offensive.

These factors signal significant changes ahead for EU associations, and, together, justify our view that the recent past predicts more than just incremental change for them in the short to medium term future. Associations have natural strengths arising from their collective and embracing nature, and those which are not dominated by one particular entity always have the capacity to prosper in an environment which welcomes them into public governance.

Appendix
The International Association: New Belgian Legislation

Luc Stolle and Alfons Westgeest

I   A new perspective

The Law of 2nd May 2002 concerning the not-for-profit association, the international association and the foundation was published in the Belgian official gazette of 18th October 2002. This new law aims to modernise, among others, the legal rules for the International Association, created by the Law of 1919, and to adapt them to new concepts of European and Belgian law.

The rules that are applicable to the International Association have been influenced by the new legislation for the not-for-profit association in Belgium. The legislator, however, has made a number of important differentiating rules. The most important change is the name, which officially is now 'International Not-for Profit Association' (INPA).

The International Association was rather popular in recent decades. We estimate that about 2700 such associations have been founded, of which two-thirds are still active.

The significant increase of this legal instrument was caused in particular by the move of European Union institutions to Brussels. The total revenue of the active International Associations is estimated at €1 bn, 75 per cent of which is spent in Belgium. The importance is further underlined by the contribution to employment (more than 8000 people).

II   What is an INPA about?

Many associations with an international membership have adopted the INPA form. They are mainly based in Brussels. In most cases they are interest groups or lobby associations, which are active in the context of the European and other international institutions. Traditionally they are federations of national associations from various countries, whereby they function as a platform for consultation and exchange of information.

There are several reasons for choosing the INPA. First of all, its name gives it an international flavour. Moreover, as it is a legal entity, it can exercise rights and obligations and has its own assets and liabilities. The members and directors are in principle not personally liable for the association's debt and liabilities. Finally, the INPA has to be formalised by Royal Decree. This means a certain quality label and aura.

246

III Rules for the INPA

Importantly, the legislator stipulates the INPA can only have goals that are in line with its not-for-profit status. The new law no longer refers to a 'charitable, religious, cultural, or education goal'. The new description is certainly less restrictive and it is anticipated that association initiatives will increasingly incorporate in an INPA.

The INPA is not allowed to operate a commercial business or to provide net commercial benefits to its members disproportionate to its status or purpose. Membership incentives are permitted, provided that commercial activity does not become the principle basis of the association. The new law implies that the assets or net revenues, even in the case of dissolution, may not be distributed among members, directors of the Board or third parties.

The INPA has to be open to Belgian and non-Belgian nationals. Contrary to previous legislation, the INPA is no longer obliged to have Belgian members. That provision was ruled incompatible with Article 6 of the Treaty of Rome.

Because the INPA is a Belgian legal entity, its seat has to be in Belgium. However, the association's secretariat or administrative seat may be based abroad. Therefore, INPAs can benefit from the benefits of the legal statute even though they could be mostly active abroad.

IV Formation

Two members can form an INPA. They may be natural persons or legal entities. The statutes have to contain at least seven clauses including the following:

1. Name and address
2. Detailed description of the purpose, goals and activities
3. Rules about members, member categories
4. Rights and obligations of the members
5. Competences and working rules of the General Assembly
6. Governance rules, including at least the competence and working of the Board of Directors. The Board leads the organisation internally and represents the association *vis-à-vis* third parties. These powers can be delegated to one or more Board members acting severally or jointly.
7. Conditions about changing of statutes and rules for dissolution, liquidation and winding down of the association's assets

The above clauses have to be detailed and consistent, and formulated in accordance with legal requirements. In practice the founding members (or their lawyer) write the statutes of the INPA. The statutes can be formalised by the act of a public notary – it is not mandatory.

The statutes have to be submitted to the Belgian Ministry of Justice in order to obtain legal personality. The procedure includes a submission to a special department of the Ministry, which will check the draft statutes for legal compliance. Once reviewed, the founders sign the formation documents. They are again submitted to the Minister for legitimisation, resulting in a Royal Decree and legal personality. An abstract of final documents is published in the Belgian Official

Gazette: including the statutes, the identity of Board members, and the rules about representation of the INPA to third parties.

V   Publication requirements

The law contains new rules about the submission of a file with the Ministry of Justice. This applies to INPAs as well as associations formed under foreign law (abroad) but with a) centre of activity in Belgium. The file has to include:

- Statutes and changes thereof;
- Integral text of the statutes;
- Any acts of the appointment, dismissal and termination of the Board members;
- Decisions about winding down or dissolution;
- Annual accounts

Most decisions have to be published in the Belgian gazette. The above rules are essential in case the INPA would be in Court, as non-compliance would lead to suspension of the proceedings.

VI   Accounts, administration and audit

The law establishes new rules for the administration, the budget and accounts, the audit and publication of the annual report.

As a rule the INPA can adopt simplified accounting systems. A model will be published in 2003.

Large INPA are required to follow the accounting rules of corporations. It applies to INPAs, which at the end of a fiscal year surpass the amounts of two of the following thresholds:

1. An annual average of five employees (Full Time Equivalents)
2. Total revenues of €250,000 excluding VAT (not counting extra-ordinary revenues)
3. Balance sheet total of €1,000,000.

Every year the governing body of the INPA has to approve the annual accounts of the year and the budget of the next year. The larger INPAs (as above) will need to comply with the Belgian Accounting Laws.

A statutory audit was not required up to now. However, several international associations with corporations as members (trade associations) established internal rules requiring the appointment of external auditors, who for the benefit of all members, carried out an audit of the financial state of the association.

As the new law comes into force a new regime starts to apply for the largest INPAs. These are the INPAs that, counted over the fiscal year ended, have an average of 100 employees OR which surpass the amounts of two of the following thresholds:

1. An annual average of 50 employees (Full Time Equivalents)
2. Total revenues of €6,250,000 excluding VAT (not counting extra-ordinary revenues)
3. Balance sheet total of €3,125,000

The General Assembly of these largest INPAs have to appoint one or more auditors to check the financial status, the annual accounts and the regularity of transactions.

VII   Entry into force

The Law of 2 May 2002 will enter into force once the decisions for implementation have been published. They are expected early 2003. Some of those decisions will enter into force immediately. For other rules, such as file of the association, administration, annual accounts and audit, enforcement will start after a certain transition period (less than five years).

Bibliography

Abromeit, H. (1998) *Democracy in Europe: Legitimising Politics in a Non-State Polity* (New York: Oxford University Press).

Almond, G.A. (1958) 'A Comparative Study of Interest Groups and the Political Process', *American Political Science Review* 52, 270–82.

Ansell, C. (2001) 'The Networked Polity: Regional Development in Western Europe', *Governance* 13 (3), 303–33.

ASAE (American Society of Association Executives) (2002) 'Seven Strategic Conversations for Association Executives' (www.asaenet.org/foundation/seven).

Benedictis, L. and Padoan, P.C. (1993): *Europe between East and South* (Dordrecht: Kluwer).

Bennett, R.J. (1997) 'The Impact of European Economic Integration on Business Associations: The UK Case', *West European Politics* 20 (3), 61–90.

BEUC (The European Consumers' Organisation) (2002) BEUC in *Brief*, Issue n. 39 (Brussels: BEUC).

Beyers, J. (2003) 'Voice and Access: Political Practices of Diffuse and Specific Interest Associations in European Policy Making', paper prepared for presentation to the 8th Biennial Conference of the European Union Studies Association, Nashville (Tenn.), March 27–29.

Biznesu, P. (2000) 'KIG Euroconsulting to Help Polish Entrepreneurs Acclimatise to EU Economy', Poland A.M. January 31 (www.wbj.pl/article.asp?id =68215).

Blokker, N. (1989) *International Regulation of World Trade in Textiles* (Dordrecht: Kluwer).

Boleat, M. (2002) 'Trade Association Effectiveness at the European level', report for the CBI Trade Association Forum (London: Trade Association Forum).

Börzel, T.A. and Risse, T. (2000) 'When Europe Hits Home: Europeanization and Domestic Change', EUI (European University Institute) Working Papers, Robert Schuman Centre 2000/56.

Boyer, R.J. and Hollingsworth, R.J. (1997) 'From National Embeddedness to Spatial and Institutional Nestedness', in J.R. Hollingsworth and R.J. Boyer (eds.) *Contemporary Capitalism: the Embeddness of Instiututions* (Cambridge: Cambridge University Press), pp. 433–84.

Briet, H. (2002) 'Les associations internationales sans but lucratif', in Centre d'Etudes Jean Renaud (ed.), *Le nouveau droit des ASBL et des fondations. La loi du 2 mai 2002* (Brussels: Bruylant).

Briet, H. and Verdonck, P. (2002) 'Les associations sans but lucratif', in Centre d'Etudes Jean Renaud (ed.), *op. cit.* (109) 110.

Briquemont, J. (2002) 'The Challenge of Change in EU Business Associations: the media sector', paper prepared for presentation to the conference on 'The Challenge of Change in EU Business Associations', Brussels, May 7–10.

Bulgarian Industrial Association (2002) *About the BIA* (www.bia-bg.com).

Bulmer, S. (1994) 'The Governance of the European Union: A New Institutionalist Approach', *Journal of Public Policy* 13 (4), 351–80.

Cizelj, B. (2000) 'Paper presented to the Conference on Candidate Country Interest Representation in Brussels', in B. Cizelj and G. Vanhaeverbeke (eds), *Candidate Country Interest Representation in Brussels. Conference Proceedings*, (www.sbra.be/proceedings).

Coen, D. (1997) 'The evolution of the large firm as a political actor in the European Union', *Journal of European Public Policy* 4 (1), 91–108.

Coen, D. (1998) 'The European Business Interest and the Nation State: Large-firm Lobbying in the European Union and the Member States', *Journal of Public Policy* 18 (1), pp. 75–100.

Coen, D. and Grant, W. (2001) 'Corporate Political Strategy and Global Policy', *European Business Journal*, 13 (1) pp. 37–44.

Cole, A. and Drake, H. (2000) 'The Europeanization of the French Polity: Continuity, Change and Adaptation', *Journal of European Public Policy* 7:1, pp. 26–43.

Coleman, W. and Grant, W. (1984) 'Business Associations and Public Policy: a Comparison of Organisational Development in Britain and Canada', *Journal of Public Policy*, 4, pp. 209–35.

Coleman, W.D. and Montpetit, É. (2000) 'Multitiered Systems and the Organization of Business Interests' in J. Greenwood and Henry Jacek (eds), *Organized Business and the New Global Order* (Basingstoke: Macmillan), pp. 160–76.

Council of Europe (1986) *Explanatory Report of the European Convention on the Recognition of the Legal Personality of International Non-Governmental Organisations* (Strasbourg: Council of Europe).

Cowles, M.G. (1995) 'Setting the Agenda for a New Europe: the ERT and EC 1992', *Journal of Common Market Studies* 33 (4), pp. 501–26.

Cowles, M.G. (1996) 'The EU Committee of AmCham: the powerful voice of American firms in Brussels', *Journal of European Public Policy* 3 (3), pp. 339–58.

Cowles, M.G. (2002) 'Large Firms and the Transformation of EU Business Associations: a Historical Perspective', in J. Greenwood (ed.), *The Effectiveness of EU Business Associations* (Basingstoke: Palgrave), pp. 64–78.

Cram, L. (1994) 'The European Commission as a multi-organization: social policy and IT policy in the EU', *Journal of European Public Policy* 1, pp. 195–217.

Cram, L. (1995) 'Business Alliances in the Information Technology Sector', in J. Greenwood (ed.), *European Casebook on Business Alliances* (Hemel Hempstead: Prentice-Hall), pp. 23–37.

Daugbjerg, C. (1997) 'Farmers' Influence on East–West Integration in Europe: Policy Networks and Power' (South Jutland University Press: Working Papers on European Integration and Regime Formation No. 9).

de Bronett, G.-K. (2002) 'EU Competition Policy and Associations', paper prepared for presentation to the conference on 'The Challenge of Change in EU Business Associations', Brussels, May 7 to 10 (www.ey.be/euroconference).

Dehousse, R. (1998) *The European Court of Justice* (New York: St. Martin's).

Denef, M. (1997) 'Over V.Z.W.'s, volkstoerisme en handelsactiviteiten met of zonder winstoogmerk', *Tijdschrift voor Rechtspersoon en Vennootschap* (TRV), 4, p. 219.

Edelman/Strategy One (2002) 'Non-Governmental Organizations: the Fifth Estate in Global Governance' (Brussels: Edelman).

EU Committee of the American Chamber of Commerce (2000) 'Position Paper on Alternative Regulatory Models', November 21 (Brussels: AMCHAM-EU).

EUROCHAMBRES (1994) 'Eurochambres' Action Programme in Central and Eastern Europe: Progress Report' (Brussels: Eurochambres).

EUROCHAMBRES and SBRA (2001) 'Corporate Readiness for Enlargement in Central Europe. A Company Survey on the State of Preparations for the Single Market' (Brussels: Eurochambres).

EUROCHAMBRES (http://www.eurochambres.be/ita/ita.htm).

European Commission (2000) *Evaluation of the Bangemann Textile Action Plan* (see: http://www.europa.eu.int/comm/enterprise/textile/competitiveness. htm#action_plan).

European Commission (2001) *European Governance: A White Paper*, COM(2001) 428 final (http://www.europa.eu.int/comm/governance/white_ paper/index_en.htm).

European Commission (2002a) *Single Market: Towards Better Regulation* (http://europa.eu.int/comm/enterprise/library/enterprise-europe/issue9/ articles/en/enterprise09_en.htm).

European Commission (2002b) *Report from the Commission to the Council and the European Parliament: Report on the Implementation of the European Charter for Small Enterprises*, COM (2002) 68 final.

Euroconfidentiel (2002) *Directory of 12,500 Trade and Professional Associations in the European Union* (Genval: Euroconfidentiel).

Financial Times (2002) 'The Challenge of Regaining Europe', *Financial Times*, 16 December, p. 14.

Fink-Hafner, D. (1994) 'Promotion of Slovenian Interest in the European Interest Group Arena', *Journal of International Relations* 1, 2:4, pp. 217–33.

Fink-Hafner, D. (1997) 'The Role of Interest Organisation in the Europeanization of Slovenian Policy-Making', *Journal of International Relations* 4:1–4, pp. 130–47.

Fink-Hafner, D. (2000) 'Paper presented to the Conference on Candidate Country Interest Representation in Brussels', in B. Cizelj and G. Vanhaeverbeke (eds), *Candidate Country Interest Representation in Brussels. Conference Proceedings*, (www.sbra.be/proceedings).

Gorges, M.J. (1996) *Euro-Corporatism? Interest Intermediation in the European Community* (Lanham, MD: University Press of America).

Grabbe, H. (2001) 'How Does Europeanisation Affect CEE Governance? Conditionality, Diffusion and Diversity', *Journal of European Public Policy* 8: 6, pp. 1013–31.

Grande, E. (1996) 'The state and interest groups in a framework of multi-level decision-making: the case of the European Union', *Journal of European Public Policy*, 3 (3), pp. 318–38.

Grande, E. (2000a) 'Multi-Level Governance: Institutionelle Besonderheiten und Funktionsbedingungen des europäischen Mehrebenensystems', in E. Grande and M. Jachtenfuchs (eds) *Wie problemlösungsfähig ist die EU? Regieren im europäischen Mehrebenensystem* (Baden-Baden: Nomos), pp. 11–31.

Grande, E. (2000b) 'Post-National Democracy in Europe', in M. Greven and L.W. Pauly (eds), *Democracy Beyond the State? The European Dilemma and the Emerging Global Order* (Boulder, Co.: Rowman & Littlefield).

Grande, E. and Jachtenfuchs, M. (eds) (2000) *Wie problemlösungsfähig ist die EU? Regieren im europäischen Mehrebenensystem* (Baden-Baden: Nomos).

Grant, W. (2000) *Pressure Groups and British Politics* (Basingstoke: Macmillan).

Grant, W., Paterson, W. and Whitston, C. (1988) *Government and the Chemical Industry* (Oxford: Clarendon Press).

Greenwood, J. (1997) *Representing Interests in the European Union* (Basingstoke: Macmillan).

Greenwood, J. (ed.) (2002a) *The Effectiveness of EU Business Associations* (Basingstoke: Palgrave).

Greenwood, J. (2002b) *Inside the EU Business Associations* (Basingstoke: Palgrave).

Greenwood, J. and Aspinwall, M. (eds) (1998) *Collective Action in the European Union* (London: Routledge).

Greenwood, J., Grote, J. and Ronit, K. (eds) (1992) *Organized Interests and the European Community* (London: Sage).

Greenwood, J., Strangward, L. and Stancich, L. (1999) 'The Capacities of Euro Groups in the Integration Process', *Political Studies* XLVII, pp. 127–38.

Greven, M. and Pauly, L.W. (eds) (2000) *Democracy Beyond the State? The European Dilemma and the Emerging Global Order* (Boulder, Co: Rowman & Littlefield).

Haas, Ernst B. (1958) *The Uniting of Europe. Political, Social and Economic Forces 1950–1957* (London: Stevens & Sons).

Hall, P. and Taylor, R. (1996) 'Political Science and the Three New Institutionalisms,' *Political Studies* 44, pp. 936–57.

Hall, P.A. and Soskice, D. (2001) 'An Introduction to Varieties of Capitalism', in P.A. Hall and D. Soskice (eds), *Varieties of Capitalism: the Institutional Foundations of Comparative Advantage* (Oxford: Oxford University Press), pp. 1–68.

Hartenberger, U. (2000) *Europäischer Sozialer Dialog nach Maastricht – EU–Sozialpartnerverhandlungen auf dem Prüfstand* (Baden-Baden: Nomos).

Héritier, A. (1999) *Policy-Making and Diversity in Europe: Escaping Deadlock* (Cambridge: Cambridge University Press).

Héritier, A. (2001) *Differential Europe. The European Union Impact on National Policymaking* (Lanham: Rowman & Littlefield).

Hooghe, L. (1996) (ed.) *Cohesion Policy and European Integration: Building Multi-Level Governance* (Oxford: Oxford University Press).

Hooghe, L. and Marks, G. (2001) *Multi-Level Governance and European Integration* (Lanham: Rowman & Littlefield).

Hudobova, L. (2000) 'Paper presented to the Conference on Candidate Country Interest Representation in Brussels', in B. Cizelj and G. Vanhaeverbeke (eds), *Candidate Country Interest Representation in Brussels. Conference Proceedings* (www. sbra.be/proceedings).

IFM/Cadmeia (2000) *Vision 2005: from vision to action*, Report for EURATEX.

Industry and Parliament Trust (2001) *Annual Report and Accounts 2000–01* (London: Industry and Parliament Trust).

Institut des Sciences du Travail (IST) (2001) *Report on the Representativeness of the European Social Partner Organisations, part 2* (Louvain: IST).

Iteto, A. (2000) Interview with the author, Budapest, April 13.

Jacoby, W. (2001) 'Tutors and Pupils: International Organizations, Central European Elites, and Western Models', *Governance* 14:2, pp. 169–200.

Joy, P. (2002) 'An Act of Charity', *Commercial Lawyer*, November, pp. 40–9.

Kerremans, B. (1996) 'Do Institutions Make a Difference? Non-Institutionalism, Neo-Institutionalism and the Logic of Common Decision-Making in the European Union', *Governance* 9 (2), pp. 217–40.

Knill, C. and Lehmkuhl, D. (1999) 'How Europe Matters: Different Mechanisms of Europeanization', *European Integration Online Papers (EioP)* 3:7.

Kohler-Koch, B. (1998) 'Organised Interests in the EU and the European Parliament', in P.H. Claeys, C. Gobin, I. Smets and P. Winand (eds) *Lobbying, Pluralism and European Integration* (Brussels: European Interuniversity Press), pp. 126–58.

Kohler-Koch, B. and Eising, R. (1999) (eds) *The Transformation of Governance in the European Union* (London: Routledge).

Kohler-Koch, B. (1999) 'The Evolution and Transformation of European Governance', in B. Kohler-Koch and R. Eising (eds), *The Transformation of Governance in the European Union* (London: Routledge), pp. 20–59.

Kohler-Koch, B. (2000) 'Unternehmensverbände im Spannungsfeld von Europäisierung und Globalisierung', in W. Bührer and E. Grande (eds), *Unternehmerverbände und Staat in Deutschland* (Baden-Baden: Nomos), pp. 132–48.

Ladrech, R. (1994) 'Europeanization of Domestic Politics and Institutions: the Case of France', *Journal of Common Market Studies* 32:1, pp. 69–88.

Lahusen, Christian (2002) 'Professional Consultancies in the European Union: findings of a survey on commercial interest intermediation', *Bamberger Beiträge zur Europaforschung und zur internationalen Politik*, 6 (Bamberg: Universität Bamberg).

Landmarks (2003) *European Public Affairs Directory 2003* (Brussels: Landmarks).

Leibfried, S. and Pierson, P. (eds) (1995) *European Social Policy* (Washington DC: The Brookings Institute).

Lippert B., Umbach G. and Wessels W. (2001) 'Europeanisation of the CEE Executives: EU Membership Negotiations as a Shaping Power', *Journal of European Public Policy* 8:6, pp. 980–1012.

Lontings, D. (1994) 'The international non-profit association: A Belgian vehicle for transnational collaboration between commercial companies', *International Business Law Journal*, 5, pp. 585–90.

Lontings, D. (1996) 'The practice of the Ministry of Justice regarding international non-profit associations', in Byttebier, K., Coeckelbergh, D., De Schutter, A., Lontings, D., Peeters, H., Thys, J.-R., Van der Borght, K. and Van Gerven, D. (eds), *Driekwart eeuw internationale vereniging in België en haar alternatieven* (Ghent: Mys & Breesch), pp. 11–27.

Lontings, D. (2000) 'Factual associations/Associations de fait/Feitelijke verenigingen. Legal rules, facts and anecdotes', *FAIB News*, no. 4, pp. 7–8.

Lontings, D. and Neven, W. (2002) 'Establishing an EU Association under Belgian Law and the Brussels property estate,' paper prepared for presentation to the conference on 'The Challenge of Change in EU Business Associations', Brussels, May 7–10.

McLaughlin, A.M., Jordan, A.G. and Maloney, W. (1993) 'Corporate Lobbying in the European Community', *Journal of Common Market Studies*, 31, pp. 191–212.

Mandell, M.P. (1988) 'Intergovernmental Management in Interorganizational Networks: A Revised Perspective', *International Journal of Public Administration* 11, pp. 393–416.

March, J.G. and Olsen, J.P. (1989) *Rediscovering Institutions* (New York: Free Press).

Mazey, S. and Richardson, J.J. (eds) (1993) *Lobbying in the European Community* (Oxford: Oxford University Press).

Mazey, S. and Richardson, J. (1997) 'Policy Framing: Interest Groups and the lead up to 1996 Inter-Governmental Conference', *West European Politics* 20 (3), pp. 111–33.

Michels, R. (1958) *Political Parties* (Glencoe, Il: Free Press).

Nicolaidis, K. (2001) 'Conclusion: The Federal Vision Beyond the Federal State', in K. Nicolaidis and R. Howse (eds), *The Federal Vision. Legitimacy and Levels of Governance in the United States and the European Union* (Oxford: Oxford University Press), pp. 439–81.

NIROC (2000) Presentation Brochure (Brussels: NIROC).

Olson, M. (1965) *The Logic of Collective Action* (Cambridge, Mass: Harvard University Press).

O'Neill, N. (2002) 'Transparency', BBC Reith Lectures 202 (http://www.bbc.co.uk/radio4/reith2002/).

Palmay, F. (2000) Interview with the author, Budapest, April 13.

Pedler, R. (2001) *European Union Lobbying* (Basingstoke: Palgrave).

Pedler, R. and van Schendelen M.P.C.M. (eds) (1994) *Lobbying the European Union: Companies, Trade Associations and Issue Groups* (Aldershot: Dartmouth).

Pérez-Solórzano Borragán, N. (1998) 'Assessment of Central and Eastern European Interests' Representation at the European Union Level', Working Paper Series No. 36 (Brussels: College of Europe and European Interuniversity Press).

Pérez-Solórzano Borragán, N. (2001a) 'Organised Interests in Central and Eastern Europe. Towards Gradual Europeanisation?', *Politique Européenne* 3: January, pp. 61–85.

Pérez-Solórzano Borragán, N. (2001b) 'Interest Politics in the Light of the EU's Eastward Enlargement. Rethinking Europeanisation and Network Building in the Business Sector' (University of Exeter: PhD Thesis, unpublished).

Pérez-Solórzano Borragán, N. (2003) 'Coming to Terms with EU Lobbying. The Central and Eastern European Experience', in A. Warleigh and J. Fairbrass (eds), (2003) *Integrating Interests in the European Union: The New Politics of Persuasion, Advocacy and Influence* (London: Europa).

Peschke, A. (2001) 'Transnationale Kooperation und Interessenvermittlung in der Europäischen Forschungs- und Technologiepolitik: die Rolle europäischer Wissenschaftsvereinigungen', Dissertation, Technical University München.

Pierson, P. (1996) 'The Path to European Integration: A Historical Institutionalist Analysis', *Comparative Political Studies* 29 (2), pp. 123–63.

Pijnenburg, B. (1998) 'EU lobbying by ad hoc coalitions: An exploratory case study', *Journal of European Public Policy* 5 (2), pp. 303–21.

Polish Chamber of Commerce and Industry, PCC (www.KIG.PL/index_e.htm).

Pollack, M. (1996) 'The New Institutionalism and EU Governance: The Promise and Limits of Institutional Analysis', *Governance* 9 (4), pp. 492–528.

Putnam, R. (1993) *Making Democracy Work: Civic Traditions in Modern Italy* (New Jersey: Princeton University Press).

Radaelli, C. (2000) 'Whither Europeanisation? Concept Stretching and Substantive Change', *European Integration on line Papers* (EioP) 4:8.

Richardson, J. (1996) 'Policy-Making in the EU: Interests, Ideas and Garbage Can of Primeval Soup', in J. Richardson (ed.), *European Union: Power and Policy-Making* (London: Routledge), pp. 3–23.

Risse-Kappen, T. (1995) 'Structures of Governance and Transnational Relations: What Have we learned?' is T. Risse-Kappen (eds), *Bringing Transnational Relations Back is: Non-state actors, Domestic Structures and International Institutions* (Cambridge: Cambridge University Press), pp. 3–36.

Risse T., Green-Cowles M. and Caporaso J. (eds) (2001) *Transforming Europe. Europeanization and Domestic Change* (Ithaca: Cornell University Press).

Sabatier, P. (1998) 'The advocacy coalition framework: revisions and relevance for Europe', *Journal of European Public Policy* 5, pp. 98–130.

Scharpf, F. (1978) 'Organisatorische Voraussetzungen der Funktionsfähigkeit der Gewerkschaften in der Bundesrepublik', in *Gewerkschaftliche Monatshefte*, No. 10, pp. 578–88.

Scharpf, F. (1988) 'The joint decision trap: lessons from German federalism and European integration', *Public Administration* 66, pp. 237–78.

Scharpf, F. (1999) *Governing in Europe: Effective and Democractic?* (Oxford: Oxford University Press).

Scharpf, F., Reissert, B. and Schnabel, F. (1976) *Politikverflechtung: Theorie und Empirie des Kooperativen Föderalismus* (Kronberg: Scriptor).

Scheffer, M. (1992) 'Trading Places: Fashion; Retailers and the changing Geography of Clothing Production' (Utrecht: KNAG).

Schelling, T. (1960) *The Strategy of Conflict* (Cambridge, MA: Harvard University Press).

Schmitter, Philippe (2000) *How to Democratize the European Union and... Why Bother?* (Boulder, CO: Rowman & Littlefield).

Schmitter, P. and Streeck, W. (1999) 'The Organization of Business Interests. Studying the Associative Action of Business in the Advanced Societies', MPIFG Discussion Paper 99/1 (Köln: Max-Planck-Institut für Gesellschafts forschung).

Schneiberg, M. and Hollingsworth, J.R. (1991) 'Can Transaction Cost Economics Explain Trade Associations?', in Czada R.M., and Windhoff-Heritier, A. (eds), *Political Choice: Institutions, Rules and the Limits of Rationality* (Campus: Frankfurt), pp. 199–231.

Simonart, V. (2002) 'Les groupements d'intérêt économique/G.I.E. et G.E.I.E.', *Répertoire Notarial*, Brussels, Larcier, 30–1, p. 85

Stantič, C. (2000) 'Paper presented to the Conference on Candidate Country Interest Representation in Brussels', in B. Cizelj and G. Vanhaeverbeke (eds), *Candidate Country Interest Representation in Brussels. Conference Proceedings* (Brussels: SBRA) (www.sbra.be/proceedings).

Stengg, W. (2001) 'The textile and clothing industry in the EU: A survey' (Brussels: European Commission Enterprise Papers No 2) (http://www.europa.eu.int/comm/enterprise/library/enterprise-papers/paper2.htm).

Streeck, W. (1997) 'Beneficial Constraints: on the Economic Limits of Rational Voluntarism', in J.R. Hollingsworth and R. Boyer (eds), *Contemporary Capitalism: the Embeddness of Institutions* (Cambridge: Cambridge University Press), pp. 197–219.

'T Kint, P. (1996) 'La loi du 27 juin 1921, sa genèse, ses modifications et l'évolution de son environnement', in Coipel, M., Defourney, J. and Hindriks, J. (eds), *ASBL et société à finalité sociale. Quelques aspects juridiques et économiques* (Ghent: Mys & Breesch), pp. 3–29.

Tolnay, L. (2000) 'Introduction', Hungarian Chamber of Commerce and Industry, Introductory Leaflet (Budapest: HCCI).

Traxler, F. (2001) 'Wirtschaftliche Internationalisierung und Sozialdialog in Europa – Herausforderungen und Chancen für KMU', in Wirtschaftskammer Österreich, *Wirtschaftspolitische Blätter*, Vol. 6 (Vienna: WKÖ).

UNICE (1989) Memorandum on Negotiations by the Community with the East Bloc Countries, April 3 (Brussels: UNICE).

UNICE (1990) Preliminary Comments on the Development of Industrial Cooperation with Central and Eastern European Countries, December 6 (Brussels: UNICE).

UNICE (1992) 'Enlargement of the Community as Seen by Business', UNICE Position Paper, December 7 (Brussels: UNICE).

UNICE, http://www.unice.org/unice/Website.nsf/HTML+Pages/UK_index_UK.htm.

Vadász, P. (1998) 'Action Plan and Strategy for the Accession to the European Union', 19 May (Budapest: Hungarian Chamber of Commerce and Industry/HCCI).

van Apeldoorn, B. (2002) 'The European Round Table of Industrialists: Still a Unique Player?', in J. Greenwood (ed.), *The Effectiveness of EU Business Associations* (Basingstoke: Palgrave), pp. 194–205.

Van Gerven, D. (1996) 'Economische samenwerkingsverbanden', in Byttebier, K., Coeckelbergh, D., De Schutter, A., Lontings, D., Peeters, H., Thys, J.-R., Van der Borght, K. and Van Gerven, D. (eds), *Driekwart eeuw internationale vereniging in Belgie en haar alternatieven* (Ghent Mys & Breesch), pp. 116–18.

Van Gerven, D. (2000) 'De golfclub als doelgebonden vermogen', in Cousy, H., Dirix, E., Stijns, S., Stuyck., J. and Van Gerven, D. *Liber amicorum Walter Van Gerven* (Deurne: Kluwer), pp. 449–67.

van Houte, F. (2002) 'Glass', paper prepared for presentation to the conference on *The Challenge of Change in EU Business Associations*, Brussels, May 7 to 10.

van Schendelen, M.P.C.M. (1993) (ed.) *National Public and Private EC Lobbying* (Aldershot: Dartmouth).

van Schendelen, M. (1994) *Politiek en bedrijfsleven; een actuele confrontatie* (Amsterdam: Amsterdam University Press).

Vantyghem, D. (2000) 'Paper presented to the Conference on Candidate Country Interest Representation in Brussels', in B. Cizelj and G. Vanhaeverbeke (eds), *Candidate Country Interest Representation in Brussels. Conference Proceedings* (Brussels: SBRA), (www.sbra.be/proceedings).

van Waarden, F. (1994) 'Is European Law a Threat to Associational Governance?', in V. Eichener and H. Voelzkow (eds), *Europäische Integration und Verbandliche Interessenvermittlung* (Marburg: Metropolis).

Wallace, H. and Young, A.R. (1997) (eds), *Participation and Policy-Making in the European Union* (Oxford: Clarendon Press).

Warleigh, A. (2001) 'Europeanizing Civil Society: NGOs as Agents of Political Socialization', *Journal of Common Market Studies*, November, 39, 4, pp. 619–39.

Wassenberg, A. (1982) 'Neo-Corporatism and the Quest for Control: The Cuckoo Game', in G. Lehmbruch and P.C. Schmitter (eds), *Patterns of Corporatist Intermediation* (Sage: London), pp. 83–108.

Wessels, B. (1999) 'European Parliament and Interest Groups', in S. Katz and B. Wessels (eds), *The European Parliament, the National Parliaments, and European Integration* (Oxford: Oxford University Press), pp. 105–28.

White, A. (1997) 'Dealing with trade associations: a two way process', in Bennett, R. (ed.), *Trade Associations in Britain and Germany: responding to internationalisation and the EU*, London, Anglo German Foundation, pp. 74–7.

Williamson, O. (1975) *Markets and Hierarchies* (New York: Free Press).

Williamson, O. (1985) *The Economic Institutions of Capitalism* (New York, Free Press).

Wright, D. (2002) 'What I need from Business Associations – Personal Views from David Wright', paper prepared for presentation to the conference on 'The Challenge of Change in EU Business Associations', Brussels, 7–10 May 2002 (www.ey.be/euroconference).

Index

Acquis communautaire 107, 117, 216, 218, 221
advisory committees 144
AEA 82
Agricultural Council of Ministers 145
alliances (also trust between associations) 193–5, 243–4
American and European Societies of Association Executives 3
Amnesty International 16
Amsterdam Treaty 66, 142
Anglo-Saxon tradition 21, 40, 202, 210
Antib 77
anti-competitive 74, 77–81, 83–4, 87–8
pro-competitive 88
anti-dumping 106
anti-trust (*see also* competition law; monopoly; quasi-monopoly; trust) 106, 192, 195
APEC 21, 45
ASEAN 22

Belgian accounting law of 1975 177, 248
Belgian legislation on the establishment of International Associations 28
of 1919 28, 171–2, 175–6, 184, 246
of 1921 28, 171–2, 178–81
of 1954 172
of 1997 179
of 2000 175
of 2002 28, 172–82, 184, 188, 246–9
highest court decision of 1996 *TRV* 173
'Better regulation' package 11, 31, 63, 245
BEUC 29–30

BISPA (*see also* Corus) 97
Britain's Industry and Parliament Trust 201–2
b2b media 192

car block exemption 229
carbon tax proposal 200
cartels 7, 18, 74, 76, 242
cartel-like behaviour 18
collusive activity 88
collusive agreements 83
CBI 97
CEA 14
Cefic 21, 131, 141, 143–4, 199–200
Central and Eastern European Offices of Representation 213–14, 219, 224
tasks of 214–15
Chambers' Accession Programme for Eastern Europe 213
'Citizen's Europe' 4, 12
Civil Dialogue 30
CO_2 emissions debate 100
co-decision procedure 66, 230–1
collective agreements 34, 39
collective regulation 110–11, 113–14
College of Europe 163
COMECON 98
comitology 237
Committees of the European Commission 46, 64
Committees of the European Parliament 10–11, 46, 66–8, 71
lead committee 69
rapporteur 69–70
secretariat of 70
Common Agricultural Policy 139, 143–4
common market (*see also* single market) 76, 140

Communication and Consumer
    Electronics Technology Industry
    Association   4
competition law (*see also* anti-trust;
    judgments of the ECJ: Court of
    First Instance; monopoly;
    quasi-monopoly; trust)   7, 40,
    74–5, 84–5, 87–8, 154, 242
    Action for Annulment procedure
        85, 87–8
    fines for breach of   18–19, 83
    general principles   74–5
    locus standi of association
        19, 85–6
    Regulation 1638/98   85
    Regulation 17/62   84–5, 88
    principle of direct and individual
        concern   19, 88
    Treaty regulation of   75–6
competition policy   6, 18–19
conciliation procedure   238
Convention on the Future of Europe
    5, 31, 60, 240–1
co-operative agreement   77, 110
co-operation procedure   66
COPA   141, 145, 215
COPA–COGECA   220
Copenhagen summit   241
co-regulation   14, 18, 63, 237
COREPER   210
corporate social responsibility   4,
    16, 239, 245
Corporate Social Responsibility
    Europe   239, 245
corporatism   18, 21, 31, 58
Corus (*see also* BISPA)   96–7
Council of Europe   174–5
    Statute of Council of Europe   174
cross-sectoral   100, 102
'cuckoo game'   49
cumulative effect   80

data protection   229
Directive on Waste from
    Electrical and Electronic
    Equipment   238
Directorates General   46, 56–7
    DG Competition   7
    DG Enlargement   109

DG Enterprise   108–9
DG Environment   109
DG Information Society   109
DG Internal Market   8
domestic non-profit association   28,
    171–3, 178

EACEM   5
    merger with EICTA   5
e-commerce   12, 112, 194, 229
EC Treaty   75, 85, 88, 175
ECVM   129
Economic and Social Committee   63
economic interest grouping (*see also*
    European Economic Interest
    Grouping)   185–6
EFPIA   21, 27
    Priority Action Teams   27
EICTA   5, 242
    merger with EACEM   5
enlargement   5, 7, 40, 48, 61, 106,
    117, 142, 145, 150–1, 211,
    213–17, 219, 221, 236, 240–2
    Central and Eastern European
        countries impact upon   219
Enron scandal   16, 197
environmental issues (also groups;
    protection and provisions)   23,
    96, 100, 106–8, 113, 117, 123–6,
    128–30, 132–5, 142, 203, 239
Ernst & Young   3, 109, 152, 155,
    157, 159–60
ETUC   52, 141, 220
EU Committee of the American
    Chamber of Commerce   4,
    11–12, 15, 53
EU VIth Framework Programme on
    Research   214
EUDIM   79
EurActiv.com   4, 11, 244
EURATEX   22, 103, 105, 107–9,
    111–14
    role of   111–12
EUROCHAMBRES   29–30, 34–5,
    215–16, 220–3, 225
    CAPE Programme   220
    European National Chambers of
        Trade and Industry   34
    niche of   30

EuroChlor (*see also* WCC)   13, 17,
        23–4, 123, 126–35
    BITC   123–5
    Extranet   23, 129, 243
    history   123–5
    industry conferences   127
    members   127
    reorganisation   125–6
    trust   127
    working groups   17
Euroconference   3, 152
Euroconfidentiel   4
Eurofer   22, 95
Europa web site   244
European Broadcasting Union   22,
        34, 79–80
European business association
    advantages in relations with the
        European Parliament   67
    autonomy (also lack of
        independence)   6, 18, 31, 33,
        37, 41, 51, 71–2, 150, 152–3,
        156–7, 159, 169, 193–4, 198,
        245; independence of finances
        6, 33, 51, 153, 157–60
    chief executive officers of   15, 18,
        27, 168, 193, 195
    cohesiveness of (also coherence of)
        7, 17, 19, 23–4, 61, 108,
        110–11, 120, 127, 199, 223,
        230, 244–5
    common external threat (also
        enemy)   22–3
    dependency of content   158–9
    effectiveness   3, 6–7, 19–21, 24,
        67, 114–15, 120–2, 127, 129,
        135, 145–8, 153, 156, 157, 159,
        192, 194, 197–8, 200–2, 211,
        242; concept of   21, 119–20,
        145; and size   139–49
    functions of   6
    General Secretaries of   6–7, 19,
        24–6, 147, 161–70, 183,
        198, 243
    internal structure of (also internal
        environment of)   5, 7, 21–4,
        50–1, 106, 108, 236, 241, 244
    legal structure of (also legal
        framework of)   7, 24

'lowest common denominator'
        problem   4, 15, 26, 67,
        146, 168
'model business association'   7
number of   5
over-dependence syndrome   153,
        160; concept of   153
type of membership   14–15, 36,
        50–1, 236, 242
European Coal and Steel Community
        (also treaty)   22, 93
European Commission's
        Euro-Info-Centre Network   118
European Construction Forum
        24, 118
European Convention on Human
        Rights   171
European Convention on the
        recognition of the legal
        personality of international
        NGOs   28, 174–5, 184, 188
European Economic and Social
        Committee   207, 230
European Economic Community   37
European Economic Interest
        Grouping (EEIG) (*see also*
        economic interest grouping)
        28, 185–6
    Council Regulation of EEIG   185–6
    Proposed Regulation   186
European Environmental
        Agency   237
European Environmental
        Bureau   199
European Group of Animal
        Welfare   146
European Information Service   4
European integration   26, 45, 48,
        51, 57, 75, 93, 134, 142–3,
        162, 170, 207
European Monetary Union   37
European Round Table of
        Industrialists   15, 53, 195
European Patent Convention   238
European Patent Office   237–8
European Services Forum   118
European Social Fund   108
European Standardisation
        Committee   118

European Voice 4–5
Europeanisation 213–14,
    217–18, 224
Extended Impact Assessments 236–7
    aims of 236–7

factual association 171, 182–3, 185
    advantages of 181–2
    concept of 181
    disadvantages 182
FIEC 24, 115–22
    effectiveness of 121–2
    history of 115–16
    members of 116
    structure of 116–17
    working methods of 117–18
fragmented architecture of the
    EU 20, 241
French law of 1/7/1901 on
    associations 115
funding crisis of 1998 30
'Future of Europe' debate 60

GATT 103
gentlemen's agreements 79
geographical issues
    Central and Eastern Europe
        29–30, 34, 117, 142, 210,
        213–20, 222–5, 240–1
    Eastern Europe 7, 96, 100, 105,
        129, 210, 219
    Northern Europe 106, 210, 212
    Southern Europe 7, 29, 106, 207,
        209, 210–12
Germanic traditions 21, 40
global security 98
globalisation 93, 95–6, 99, 101,
    108, 151, 201, 203, 239, 243
'glocalisation' 96, 243
governance 4, 6–7, 11–15, 20–1,
    31, 36, 40, 45–6, 48, 54, 58,
    61–2, 71–2, 157, 176, 180,
    231, 235–9, 247
    corporate governance 60, 236–7
Governance Team in the European
    Commission 7
greenfacts.org 244
Green paper 146
Greenpeace 16, 23, 123

harmonisation of taxation 106
helicon model 104, 109–11, 113–14
    virtuous helicon 111, 113
horizontal organisations 33,
    35–41, 241
    characteristics 33

IFIEC 100–1
IISI 95
    plenary conference of 95
Information Group of Research
    and Development Liaison
    Offices 224
INFOTEX 109
innovation policy 106
input legitimacy 61
inter-groups 230
internal market 8, 75, 88, 106,
    108, 112
International Association of Business
    Communications 243
International Labour
    Organisation 222
International Monetary Fund
    60, 103
international non-profit associations
    171–82, 184–8, 246–9
    types of 176–7
IRIS b2b technologies 4
issue advertising 71

Johannesburg earth summit of 2002
    101, 134
Judgments of the ECJ and the Court
    of First Instance
    ANTIB v. Commission 77
    Belgium v. Commssion 175, 179
    Cascades v. *Commission* 85
    Cembureau case 83–4
    *Confederacia Espanola de
        Transporte de Mercancias*
        v. *Commission* 84
    Dansk Pelsdyravlerforening v.
        Commission 78
    EUDIM case 79
    Fenex decision 77
    *Fitagi UK, New Holland Ford and John
        Deere* v. *Commission* 82
    FRUBO case 81

Judgments of the ECJ and the Court
of First Instance – *Continued*
IAZ International Belgium NV v.
Commission 78
Jego Quere et CIA SA v. *Commission*
19, 86–7
Metropole TV SA v. *Commission* 79
Roofing Felt case 77
Satellimages TV5 SA v.
Commission 85
*Scottish Salmon Farmers' Marketing
Board* case 79
SPO v. *Commission* 79
*Stichting Certificatie Kraanhuurbedrif
SCK* v. *Commission* 80
Union de Pequenos Agricultores (UPA)
v. *Council* 85–7
Union Française de l'Express (UFL)
v. *Commission* 84
*Wirtschaftsvereiningung Stahl and
Others* v. *Commission* 81

law firms 54, 140
Legal Affairs Committee of the
Commission 229
legitimacy 46, 49, 57
output 61
legislative initiative 36, 68–70
logic of influence 21, 50, 55, 57
logic of interest group formation
52, 58
logic of membership 21, 50, 57
logic of self-commitment 56
'paradox of weakness' 56

Maastricht Treaty 52, 66, 142
Macroeconomic Dialogue 35
marine conventions 127–8
BARCON 128
HELCOM 128
OSPARCOM 128, 130, 132
MEPs 10–11, 66–73, 128,
230–1, 238
MERCOSUR 21–2
mergers 5, 102, 105, 142, 196
Monetary Union 106
monopoly (*see also* anti-trust;
competition law;
quasi-monopoly; trust) 13, 75

Multifibre agreement 22, 103–4
quota system of 104
multi-level system of EU 20, 47–50,
52, 55–60
types of 47–8
multi-level system of governance
45–6, 200
horizontal aspect of 46
vertical aspect of 46

NAFTA 21–2, 45, 94, 98
National Bank of Belgium 181
nationalisation 97
neo-functionalism 50
neo-liberalism 202
Network of Interest Representation
Offices from Candidate
Countries 220, 225
NGOs (*see also* public interest groups)
28, 30, 64, 71, 128–9, 132,
134, 140, 142, 146, 149, 174,
199–200, 214
non-profit aim of 175, 179
Nice Treaty (also Nice summit) 60,
63, 66, 151

OECD 127–8
oligopol 18, 76, 79, 82–3
output legitimacy 61
overcapacity 19, 22, 79, 101, 120

partnership agreements 72
Periodical Publishers
Association 192
Persistent Organic Pollutants 129–30
PHARE 29, 219
pharmaceutical directives 229
pluralism 21, 54
policy input 8–10
political groups of European
Parliament 10–11, 65, 70
background briefs 11, 70
shadow rapporteur 70
procedures of European
Parliament 69–70
public interest groups (also
public interest; *see also* NGOs)
4, 7, 11–13, 21, 34, 134, 229,
231, 239

quality control arrangements   40
quasi-monopoly (*see also* anti-trust;
    competition law; monopoly;
    trust)   110

Report on the Implementation of
    the European Charter for Small
    Enterprises   241
Research Framework V of the EU
    3, 241
Rio Earth summit   101, 134
Rome Treaties   115, 247

sectors (also sectoral interests and
    sectoral associations)   5–7, 9, 18,
    21–2, 37, 67–8, 74, 76, 88, 97,
    99–100, 103–5, 111, 113, 117,
    120–1, 140–3, 151–4, 201, 209,
    219, 222, 236–7, 242
    sectoral definition   5
self-regulation   151, 237
service economy   5
Single European Act   54, 64, 66,
    140, 230
single market (*see also* common
    market)   12, 37, 54, 75, 100,
    140, 213, 215–16, 221, 225
SMEs (*see also* UEAPME)   12, 23–4,
    29, 34–5, 103–4, 119, 198, 210,
    225, 236, 241, 244
Social Dialogue   30, 35–6, 40–1, 52
    sectoral Social Dialogue
    111, 117–18
Social Partner   34–7, 118
sovereignty   93, 100
state aid   84
structural funds   108, 144
subsidiarity principle   36, 40, 112
subsidies   6, 36, 84, 144–5
sustainability   96, 117, 134–5
    definition of   134
sustainable development   23, 106,
    135, 243

target groups of consultation   62
Technical Guidance Document of
    the EU   130
terrorism   98
Thailand dioxin project   129, 132

think-tanks   64, 158, 242
transactions (also transaction costs)
    16, 22, 194, 202, 249
Trans European Networks   117
transparency   5, 9–11, 13–17, 19,
    23, 31, 49, 62, 72, 82–3, 113,
    117, 126, 129, 131, 164, 186,
    230, 235–6, 238–41, 245
Treaty on European Union   12
trust (*see also* anti-trust; competition
    law; monopoly; quasi-monopoly)
    4, 7–8, 10, 16–19, 23–4, 31, 68,
    110, 127, 132–3, 191–204,
    217, 245
    concept of   16, 197
    importance of chief executives
        for   18
    levels of   16, 18
    types of   17–18; between
        associations (also alliances)
        17, 194–5, 243–4; between
        members   17, 191–2; in
        executive   18, 192–4; in staff
        of the association   18, 197–8;
        in structure   198

UEAPME (*see also* SMEs)   34–5,
    117, 215
UK Steel   95–7, 102
UK Trade Association Forum
    17, 194
umbrella organisation   21, 33–4, 36,
    39, 52–3, 76, 80, 143–5, 242
UNICE   12, 25, 27, 35–6, 52–3,
    117, 140, 164, 166–8, 207–11,
    215, 218, 220, 222
    Committee of Permanent
        Delegates of   164, 210
    Secretary-General of   209–10
    UASG   166
United Nations   128, 133,
    174–5, 199
    Charter   174
United Nations Economic
    Commission for Europe
    129, 132
United Nations Environment
    Programme   127, 129, 132
Uruguay Round   105

variable geometry   113–14
vertical associations   33, 35, 37–40
virtual associations   5
voluntary agreements   23, 72, 134
voluntary standards   112, 114
voting systems
    majority voting   47–8, 66
    qualified majority voting
        48, 147–8
    unanimity voting   66

WCC (*see also* Eurochlor)
    128–9, 134
weapons of mass destruction   98

White Paper on Governance   14, 31,
    60–1, 63, 72, 236–7, 244–5
    objectives of   60
White Paper on Modernisation
    of the Rules Implementing
    Article 85 and 86 of the
    EC Treaty   89
White Paper on the Single Market and
    the Single Act   115
WKÖ   4, 37, 39
World Bank   60, 118
World Health Organisation   129
World Wild Fund for Nature   16
WTO   97, 103, 142